A Reader's Guide To
Marcel Proust

A Reader's Guide to
Marcel Proust

MILTON HINDUS

SYRACUSE UNIVERSITY PRESS

First Syracuse University Press Edition 2001

04   05   6   5   4   3   2

Originally published in 1962 by the Noonday Press. Reprinted by arrangement with Farrar, Straus & Giroux.

The paper used in this publication meets the minimum requirements of American National Standard for Information Sciences—Permanence of Paper for Printed Library Materials, ANSI Z39.48-1984.∞™

Library of Congress Cataloging-in-Publication Data

Hindus, Milton.
    A reader's guide to Marcel Proust / Milton Hindus.
      p. cm.
    Includes bibliographical references and index.
   ISBN 0-8156-0695-8 (pbk. : alk. paper)
   1. Proust, Marcel, 1871–1922—Criticism and interpretation—Handbooks, manuals, etc.
I. Title.
   PQ2631.R63 Z626 2001
   843'.914—dc21   00-053171

Manufactured in the United States of America

For my uncle, Maurice Hindus

Contents

Prefatory Note

THE REFERENCES ARE TO ENGLISH AND AMERICAN EDITIONS OF PROUST
WHENEVER THESE HAVE BEEN AVAILABLE. THERE IS NOW LITTLE OF
Proust's work that is not available in English, though some of the
miscellaneous pieces that are discussed still have to be read in
French. The translation *Remembrance of Things Past* is by Scott
Moncrieff and Frederick Blossom and was published by Random
House in New York in 1934. The seven titles of the parts of this
magnum opus (*Swann's Way, Within A Budding Grove, Guermantes Way, Cities of the Plain, The Captive, Sweet Cheat Gone,*
and *The Past Recaptured*) are each analyzed in a separate chapter in the following book. The numbers in the parentheses with
which the text is sprinkled refer to the page numbers of the volumes being discussed in each particular chapter.

The minor works of Proust can be broken down into two
categories: those which he published in his own lifetime and those
which have been published posthumously, exhumed by the patience of scholars from abandoned manuscripts. Three titles belong to the first group—*Les Plaisirs et les Jours, Pastiches et
Mélanges,* and *Chroniques* (this last volume was actually published
after Proust's death by his brother, but it contained only such
pieces as had actually appeared in print in periodicals during
Proust's lifetime). The posthumous works are *Jean Santeuil* and
Contre Sainte-Beuve. Of these various works, I have referred to
the following translations: *Pleasures and Days* (Garden City,
New York, 1957), *Jean Santeuil* (translated by Gerard Hopkins
and published by Simon and Schuster in 1956), and *Marcel Proust
on Art and Literature, 1896–1919* (translated by Sylvia Townsend Warner and published by Meridian in New York in 1958.)
The edition of *Pastiches et Mélanges* which I used was published
in Paris by Gallimard in 1949; the edition of *Chroniques* was published in Paris in 1927. The edition of *Les Plaisirs et les Jours*
(which contains verses not translated in *Pleasures and Days*) ap-

peared first in Paris in 1896; the particular edition I used was the one published by Gallimard in Paris in 1924. I wish to record my gratitude to Random House for its generous permission to quote the Moncrieff-Blossom translation, *Remembrance of Things Past*, and to Simon and Schuster for permission to quote the Hopkins translation of *Jean Santeuil*.

1. Proust's Life and Work

MARCEL PROUST WAS BORN IN AUTEUIL, A SUBURB OF PARIS, ON
JULY 10, 1871; THE TIMES WERE THE MOST TURBULENT HIS COUN-
try had experienced in almost a century. The Second Empire
had crashed in the wake of the Franco-Prussian War, and that
preview of twentieth century Bolshevism which we call the Paris
Commune had been followed by a sanguinary counter-revolu-
tion which produced the Third French Republic. Some biographers have been inclined to speculate on a possible connection
between Madame Proust's anxieties during her pregnancy and her
son's nervous disorders. The subject of pre-natal influences, however, is shrouded in too much obscurity to make such specula-
tions fruitful. It is a fact that his brother Robert, born two years
later, followed his father's profession of medicine, married, had
a child, and conformed to his family's conventional expectations
much more successfully than Marcel. Second children, it may
be observed, are sometimes the ones who profit from their parents' earlier mistakes.

His father, Dr. Adrien Proust, later Professor of Public Health
at the University of Paris and Inspector General of Public Health
in France, was the author of several books in his field dealing
with the prevention of the spread of cholera from Asia into
Europe. His mother, Mlle. Jeanne Weil, sprang from a wealthy
Alsatian Jewish family which had later settled in Paris. In marrying the Catholic Dr. Proust, she did not convert from her own
religion ("out of respect to her parents," as her son was to write
later) though she consented to permit her children to be raised
in the faith of their father. Here, if one is seeking for the cause
of Marcel's neuroses is one much more obvious and potent than
his mother's experiences before his birth. Though baptized in the
Church at his birth and interred by it at his death more than a
half century later, there is little evidence that Proust was profoundly influenced by Catholicism. His great interest (through

his study and translation of books by John Ruskin) in the Gothic architecture of the churches of France, with which he fancifully compared his own work, was aesthetic rather than religious in motivation.

There is a good deal of evidence that Proust found his mother —a beautiful, dark-haired, soft-featured woman—much more intelligent, sensitive and sympathetic than his father. These feelings seem to have carried over to her family as well. André Maurois tells us that he remained in close contact with his mother's family all his life and that each year, as long as his health permitted, he visited the graves of his Jewish ancestors. He wrote regretfully: "No longer does anyone, not even I, since I cannot leave my bed, make a pilgrimage along the Rue du Repos that leads to the Jewish cemetery where my grandfather, in fulfillment of a rite which he never understood, used each year to lay a pebble on his own parents' grave . . ."

At the time of the Dreyfus Case, which was the *cause célèbre* of Proust's twenties, the chasm in his family background became painfully evident to him as he and his mother and his brother took the side of the convicted man (Proust later called himself "the first Dreyfusard" and circulated a petition in January 1898 for a revision of the sentence) while his father, who was a public figure and a personal friend of many ministers in the government, was so far from sharing their opinions that he refused to speak to his sons for a week and indignantly ushered out a colleague who had asked for his signature to a petition similar to the one they were circulating. The famous Case lent fuel both to Jewish nationalism and to anti-Semitism. The Austrian journalist Theodore Herzl was sufficiently aroused by it to start the Zionist Movement, while in fashionable French society where so many of Proust's ambitions were centered anti-Semitism was particularly rife. On one occasion, he felt constrained to remind his aristocratic friend Robert de Montesquiou that while he himself was, by upbringing, Catholic like his father, his mother was Jewish—a fact, we may be sure, which had not escaped the attention of this eccentric literary nobleman who did not mind abusing the Jews in Proust's presence. In these trying times, Proust, while defending the innocent, tried to play the role of peacemaker, and Léon Daudet describes in his *Memoirs* a strange dinner party given by Proust at the height of the conflict in

1901 for sixty guests of various shades of opinion: "Every piece of china was liable to be smashed. I sat next to a charming young person, looking like a portrait by Nattier or Largillière, who, I afterwards learned, was the daughter of a prominent Jewish banker. Anatole France presided at the next table. The bitterest of enemies ate their *chaud-froid* within two yards of each other, for the currents of understanding and benevolence which originated in Marcel flowed about the guests and enveloped them in coils. For the space of two hours the greatest imaginable goodwill reigned among the warriors. I doubt if anyone except Proust could have accomplished that feat."

All of his life, Proust seems to have felt as he did when at thirteen he had replied to a question about his favorite virtue: "All virtues that are not limited to a sect: the universal virtues." André Gide believed that mixture of hereditary strains was a fortunate circumstance for the writer and said, according to Maurois, that "the best critics and the best artists are usually to be found among those who have inherited a mixed strain. In them, opposing stresses coexist, grow to maturity, and neutralize one another." I do not know whether this observation is just or merely perverse, but it seems clear that much unhappiness in Proust's life is traceable to the radically different backgrounds of his father and mother.

According to Schopenhauer, who was a favorite philosopher of Proust in his youth, intelligence is inherited mainly from the mother and character from the father. But along with whatever portion of his genius Proust owes to his mother, his letters to her indicate that she was the focal point of his neuroses (though to blame her, as his biographer George Painter does, for his homosexuality is unwarranted conjecture). These letters are incomparable documents of an invalid's psychology. His asthma, the first severe attack of which he suffered in 1880 at the age of nine, is the subject of most of them. He never tires of torturing her with the most vivid descriptions of his sufferings. He never spares her the smallest details, and he seems completely self-centered, as only a sick man can dare to be. Even the shock of his father's death in 1903 does not appreciably lessen his everlasting concerns with constipation, glycerine enemas, worms, burning sensations when passing water, etc. He keeps his mother mercilessly posted on precisely the amount of amyl, trional, or other drugs he is taking to relieve his pain. The dominant themes of his missives to her are three in number: 1. "Send me money . . .", 2. Constipation. 3. Asthma and other allergies. It is painful to us now to read them; what it must have been to his mother we can only imagine. We see in them the basis in fact of the generalizations he makes concerning the relations of parents and children in his remarkable article "Filial Sentiments of a Parricide" (which I discuss elsewhere in this book among his minor works and which, curiously enough, in spite of its title, deals with a case of matricide!).

When he is not busy asking her for money, he accuses her in fantastic lurid passages in which we can recognize material later to be used in the pages of *Remembrance*. He writes her from his room while they are both living under the same roof: "As I'm unable to speak to you, I'm writing to tell you that I simply can't understand your behavior. You know, or must guess, that I've spent every night since I came back in weeping, and not without good cause; and all day long you say things to me like: 'I couldn't sleep last night because the servants didn't go to bed till eleven o'clock.' I only wish it was nothing worse than that that keeps *me* from sleeping! Today, when I had a choking fit and needed the things for a fumigation, I was so misguided as to ring for Marie who'd just told me she'd finished her lunch, and you immediately punished me for it, as soon as I'd taken my trional, by seeing to it that there was a noise of hammering and shouting all day. Thanks to you I was in such a state of nerves that when poor Fénelon came with Lauris, just for a few words he said (very disagreeable ones, I must say) I went for him with my fists (Fénelon, not Lauris) and without knowing what I was doing I took the new hat he'd just bought, stamped on it, tore it to pieces and ripped out the lining. As you might think I'm exaggerating I enclose a piece of the lining so that you can see it's true. But please don't throw it away, as I shall be asking you to let me have it back in case it's of any use to him. Of course, if you saw him you mustn't breathe a word of this. All the same, I'm glad I worked it off on a friend."

Later in the same letter, he writes: "The truth is that the moment I'm well, as the way of life that makes me well exasperates you, you demolish everything until I'm ill again. It isn't the first time this has happened. I took cold this morning; if it turns to asthma, which is certain to come on again before long in the present condition of affairs, I don't doubt you'll be nice to me again, when I'm in the state I was in last year at a similar period. But it's sad not to be able to have affection and health both at once."

It sounds like a morbid invention by Thomas Mann, but it may be that the most interesting thing about these letters is what they do not say. We are in a position to know that his most pressing emotional problems were just the ones he could never have shared with his mother. He is so free and unrepressed with regard to certain intimate physical details when he writes to her only because he was condemned to be forever reticent with regard to others. It is this aspect of their relationship that he may have had in mind when he speaks pathetically in *Cities of the Plain* of homosexuals as "sons without a mother, to whom they are obliged to lie all her life long and even in the hour when they close her dying eyes." The emotional accents in which he speaks of the "race (of homosexuals) upon whom a curse weighs" undoubtedly were inspired by the fact that he felt himself to be one of these unfortunate sons. Madame Proust died in 1905, and he thereupon carried out a long-standing resolution to enter a sanatorium which might help to cure him of his various allergies and complaints. In December of that year he entered the nursing-home of Dr. Sollier at Boulogne-Billancourt. The treatment, according to Proust's biographer Barker, "was a form of pre-Freudian psychoanalysis. The patient was isolated, kept in bed, and encouraged to eat as much as possible. Meanwhile, in daily conversations with his doctor, he talked about his problems and received advice. In Proust's case the advice does not seem to have been very helpful, perhaps in part because he lacked faith in his doctor." His asthma grew worse instead of better, and by January 1906 he had decided to return home.

Proust's homosexuality is not subject to the doubts and detective-work that have long surrounded Whitman's (though the exact details of his relationships have occupied scholars like Robert Vigneron), since he was considerate enough to take the world into his confidence in the person of André Gide on May 13, 1921 and again a few days later. The confessions were duly recorded in Gide's Journals and can be read there. The truth may have been safely inferred from the amount of space given this form of sexual deviation in Proust's books, but such indirect, circumstantial evidence has never been sufficient to convince sceptical readers no matter how overwhelming it may appear to others more objective. This is notably the case with Proust's work because it is so easy to confuse the narrator of *Remembrance*, who is at one time referred to as Marcel though never as Proust, with the author himself, whose alter ego he is. Marcel in the novel is not homosexual but heterosexual, and this is only one of a number of respects in which he differs from his creator. He appears to be, for instance, completely non-Jewish; the closest he comes to the Jews in the novel is that some of his friends and acquaintances are Jewish. No hint is given that the narrator's mother is Jewish, as Proust's was. And, as a final change, the narrator, so far as we can tell, is an only child; Proust's younger brother Robert nowhere appears in the story of *Remembrance*.

The net effect of these various changes is to integrate Marcel the narrator, to "normalize" him as Marcel Proust the writer was unhappily never to become. The writer emerges from his own letters and the reminiscences of his friends as the victim of physical disintegration and abnormality. But his book provided him with an access to "a life beyond life." The alterations of reality, which enabled him to escape his own conflicts and confusions, were also necessary if the story was to be told from an angle which should not be too removed from the experience of the average reader, for it must be noted that though the subject matter of much of *Remembrance* is in some respects as strange as that of the *Arabian Nights* and was occasionally repulsive even to Gide, the point of view which the narrator adopts toward this material is not at all eccentric so that the most gregarious reader can identify himself with it.

The distinction between a man and his work is something on which Proust insisted all of his life and of which he speaks in an illuminating passage on the novelist Bergotte in *Within A Budding Grove:* "Perhaps it is only in really vicious lives that the moral problem can arise in all its disquieting strength. And of this problem, the artist finds a solution in the terms not of his personal life but of what is for him the true life, a general, literary solution. . . . Great artists, while being thoroughly wicked, make use of their vices in order to arrive at a conception of the moral law which is binding upon us all." (Part 1, pp. 66-67)

In the same vein, there is a passage quoted from one of Proust's notebooks by Maurois: "Maybe it is typical of the age that its artists should be more conscious of the anguish of sin, yet more hopelessly enslaved to sin, than were those of an earlier time, denying their lives to the world at large, clinging to the old standards of honor, to the moral landmarks of a period now dead, from reasons of self-love and because they honestly regard their own conduct as scandalous." It was passages like these that prompted my observation in *The Proustian Vision* that "Proust was a moral rentier as well as a financial one. He lived on the accumulated ethical capital of both his Jewish and Christian ancestors." And I might have added, to continue the same metaphor, that he deposited his income in the consciousness of the narrator of *Remembrance* who is, in many respects, all that his creator was not.

Proust's literary career was foreshadowed in his schooldays at the Lycée Condorcet, which he attended between his eleventh and his eighteenth year and where he was a good student and won some honors. The career actually began in his twenty-first year with the publication of his first pieces in a small magazine, *Le Banquet* (inspired by the title of Plato's dialogue, *The Symposium*), which Proust and his friends decided to found in 1892. From July to December 1893, he published some pieces in *La revue blanche*. These prepared the way for the publication of his first book in 1896—a collection of slight though sensitive sketches, stories, satires, and verses which he called *Les plaisirs et les jours* (an ironic echo of Hesiod's title *Works and Days*). Immediately thereafter he undertook a long, ambitious novel at which he worked for about four years before abandoning it. With all its imperfections, *Jean Santeuil* has been called justly a rehearsal for his later masterpiece. His next large projects were inspired by the English writer John Ruskin, on whose death in 1900 he wrote an obituary notice in *La Chronique des arts et de la curiosité* and articles in the newspaper *Le Figaro,* and in the magazines *Le Mercure de France* and *La Gazette des beaux-arts.* For the next several years he was to occupy himself with two major translations of Ruskin. In 1903 excerpts from his translation of *The Bible of Amiens* appeared in *La Renaissance latine,* and the translation of the whole book was published in February, 1904. This was followed by the publication of his translation of Ruskin's *Sesame and Lilies* in May 1906. These voluminous translations were preceded by extensive introductions which are intended in part to be objective guides to the works translated and in part subjective accounts of the sensibility of the translator. Whatever other importance these translations and introductions may have had, they showed that Proust was capable of sustained hard work at a chosen task. Later, he was to treat them as somewhat trivial literary exercises, but in truth they were far more than that and the distinction of his writing was an earnest of what he would achieve at the height of his powers.

Literary exercises of another kind occupied his attention when in February and March of 1908 he published in *Le Figaro* a series of parodies of well-known French writers, (Renan, Flaubert, Michelet, Saint-Simon, Sainte-Beuve, etc.) upon a theme supplied by the scandalous Lemoine diamond-fabrication case. These parodies were collected in the volume *Pastiches et Mélanges,* published in 1919. In 1908, too, he was concerned with his *Contre Sainte-Beuve,* a curious combination of criticism and creative fiction which was not published until more than thirty years after his death. By 1909, he appears to be well launched upon an ambitious new work, for in August of that year he informed his friend Madame Straus that he had just begun and finished a long book—a statement which his biographers have found difficulty in interpreting. It is certain, however, that what we know as *Swann's Way* began to appear in excerpts in *Le Figaro* in March 1912. In November and December of that year the novel was rejected by the *Nouvelle Revue Française* (where Gide, who was the initial reader, made a decision that he could never forgive himself for) and the firm of Fasquelle. In February, 1913, it was rejected by the publisher Ollendorff where the editor Humblot, in turning it down, made the classic criticism of Proust in a letter to his brother Robert: "My dear friend, perhaps I am dense but I just don't understand why a man should take thirty pages to describe how he rolls about in bed before he goes to sleep. It made my head swim!"

In desperation, Proust offered the new firm of Grasset guarantees to cover the costs of publication, and under these circumstances (as if it were mere vanity on the part of the author to believe in the book's excellence) it was accepted by a publisher who apparently did not even bother to read it. On November 12, an interview with Proust, designed for publicity, was published in the newspaper *Le Temps* and two days later *Du Côté de chez Swann* made its unwanted appearance. Once in print, the book itself began to make influential converts—Gide, Rilke, Mauriac—and in June and July of 1914, excerpts from *Le Côté de Guermantes* began to appear in the fashionable *Nouvelle Revue Française*, which had turned down the previous book. The war intervened to alter everything. Grasset shut down for the duration and in August 1916 Proust, after sharp negotiations, shifted officially from Grasset to the *Nouvelle Revue Française*. Due to the great war and the revision by Proust of his manuscript, another volume of *Remembrance* did not appear until June 1919 when the section which we know in English as *Within a Budding Grove* was published and *Swann's Way* was reprinted. This was the *annus mirabilis* of Proust's life, for on December 10, 1919, his book, after a fierce contention within the Goncourt Academy, received the Goncourt Prize. This has long been a prominent literary award in France and possibly attracted even more attention to its recipient at that time, before the modern multiplication of prizes, than it does now. It was only by the slimmest of margins, six to four, that Proust's book won out with the Goncourt Academicians against a novel about the late war. There was objection in many quarters that the author at the age of forty-eight was much too old for a prize which had been intended by its donors for the encouragement of younger men of talent. The effect of these multiple conflicts and considerations was to heighten public interest in the prize-winning book; Proust received more than 800 letters and telegrams of congratulation (which in the days when mass media of communication and the mass audience were only in their beginnings was really a remarkable phenomenon), and he felt that at last he had succeeded in breaking through the boundaries of a cult or coterie and had reached the large public composed of the people Samuel Johnson had had in mind once when he spoke of "the common reader."

The man who was primarily responsible for engineering this triumph of publicity was Léon Daudet, a friend of Proust's who

was the son of the famous novelist Alphonse Daudet and himself a well-known writer, political publicist, and member of the
Goncourt Academy. Proust's gratitude to him for the role he
played can be read in the fulsome dedication of the next section of
Remembrance to him, *Guermantes Way*. Proust calls him "incomparable friend" and "the author of so many masterpieces"
which he enumerates for the benefit of the public. Daudet had
known Proust for a long time, and in his amusing *Memoirs* had
early proclaimed his recognition of his friend's wit and literary
talents, though nothing in the passages devoted to Proust indicated any real awareness of the glorious destiny in store for him.
So completely unknown was Proust's name to the general public
before his winning of the Goncourt Prize that Daudet felt it
necessary to identify him to his readers as "the author of an
original, rather mad book, full of promise, called *Du Côté de
Chez Swann. . . .*" Daudet went on to utter the following prophecy: "His reminiscences of his own childhood . . . are almost
unbelievably vivid. I feel that Proust is haunted by memories of
himself, that he hears constantly the sound of a thousand tiny
streams flowing through his veins which have their sources in
the hearts of his ancestors and his own youth. If he can manage
to guide his steps, to control himself, to establish firmly his
literary point of view, he will one of these days write on the
margin of life itself something quite extraordinary. All the material is within his reach."

In retrospect, this seems somewhat patronizing and is certainly
far from limitless enthusiasm. But we must remember that at the
time it was written, the overarching plan, the structure, the
"architecture" (as Proust called it) of *Remembrance* as a whole
was not evident, and many other readers beside Daudet must
have considered it something of a rudderless improvisation, a
free-flowing stream of autobiographical associations. Nowadays,
it seems to me that *Swann's Way* has more possibilities of becoming a popular book than does *Within A Budding Grove*. Behind
Swann's Way in 1913, however, there seemed little except the
faith of its author, and it was possible to confuse it with a mere
vanity publication. Whereas behind his second large installment
of *Remembrance*, there stood powerful literary forces: a fashionable publishing house, the prize awarded by a famous academy,
and the critical suffrage of the great André Gide. These things

made the difference. Perhaps the great war had also helped in distinguishing the genuine wheat from the chaff and had encouraged people to look more thoughtfully to books that attempted to make sense out of the pre-war experience (and to recapture its quality nostalgically). The same feelings may have accounted some years later for the international success, both with the general public and the most fastidious of critical cognoscenti, of Thomas Mann's monumental *Magic Mountain*.

Proust was to enjoy his belated fame less than three years. In September, 1920, he was awarded the Legion of Honor, and in October of that year the first part of *Guermantes Way* was published. In May, 1921, the *Nouvelle Revue Française* published an article by Gide, which was the most sensitive and authoritative criticism Proust's work had been subjected to up to that time, and which remains one of the best ever done about him. Also that very month the remainder of *Guermantes Way* and the opening section of *Cities of the Plain* made their appearance. In May of the next year, another installment of *Cities of the Plain* was published. The day afterwards he suffered a serious accident with an injection of undiluted adrenalin, which according to his biographer Barker left him "completely shattered." This was not the final stroke, but it helped to hasten the end, which came a little over six months later when he succumbed to a pulmonary infection for which his lifelong suffering with asthma, an assortment of allergies, and other less tangible if not less torturing ailments had no doubt paved the way. On November 18, 1922, in spite of heroic efforts on the part of his brother Robert and another doctor to save him, he died. His funeral was the occasion for an astonishing show of unity by the French literary world. François Mauriac, in his book on Proust, tells of the reaction of the writer Barrès to this phenomenon: "I saw Barrès for the last time at Marcel Proust's funeral. He was standing in front of the Church of Saint-Pierre de Chaillot, with his bowler on his head and his umbrella hanging from his arm. He was astonished at the clamor of fame all about the deceased whom he had known quite well and rather liked, I believe, without suspecting his greatness. 'Well, what's it all about? . . . he was our young man . . .'" he kept repeating to me, meaning that he had always located Marcel Proust on the other side of the chancel with the worshipers and disciples, he the most intelligent and discerning of all, to be sure, and the one who knew how to burn the most flattering incense under the nose of every master; but that he would some day be able to bestride the Lord's Table and take his place alongside of him, that was something neither Barrès nor any other pontiff of his generation would ever have foreseen."

Mauriac is, of course, justifiably proud that he was not one of the latecomers to the shrine but, as he says, that Proust's "existence and genius were revealed to me through the translation of *Sesame and Lilies* by Ruskin, for which Proust had written the preface. From the first lines of that preface, I felt myself on the frontier of an unknown country. How Gide could have had the manuscript of *Swann's Way* between his hands and not been immediately dazzled by it, is something I have never been able to understand, I whom the simple preface threw into a sort of stupor. . . . If I own a copy of the first printing of *Swann's Way*, it is because I had scarcely deciphered the name of Proust in the bookstore windows when I hastened to obtain the book."

At the time of his death, more than half of *Remembrance* had appeared in print. But the substantial closing sections, which in English bear the three titles of *The Captive, Sweet Cheat Gone,* and *The Past Recaptured*, were still to appear. They were published, in more or less unrevised form, in the five years following Proust's death. Proust died at a moment when his fame had not yet reached its zenith, and if one may speak of a man as being fortunate in the moment of his death he was fortunate in that respect. It is pathetic when, as A. E. Housman puts it, the name dies before the man. Proust's reputation, on the other hand, was still rising when he left the scene, not only in France but in other countries of the world where translations of his work were becoming ever more widely available. He succeeded in winning the great admiration of the scholar Ernst Robert Curtius in Germany, of the poet Paul Valéry in France, of the philosopher Ortega in Spain, of the novelists Joseph Conrad and E. M. Forster in England and of Edith Wharton and F. Scott Fitzgerald in America. With these qualitative conversions he reached quantities of other readers as well. By the 1930's, a decade after his death, he had become something more than a name to most literate people on both sides of the Atlantic; he was a living presence.

Proust's literary work bears the indelible imprint, I think, of being the product of that interim of forty-three years of international peace, so far as France was concerned, between 1871 and 1914. Internally, France in this period was rocked by the Panama Scandal, the Boulangist Movement, the Dreyfus Case and the subsequent anti-clerical reaction, and Proust bore the deep scars of some of these conflicts, particularly, as I have noted, of the Dreyfus Case. New mechanical inventions like the telephone, the airplane, and the automobile also affected radically existing means of communication and travel and left profound impressions on the sensibility of the writer (if, as Baudelaire said, the introduction of gaslight had resulted in an entirely fresh color sensibility in the art of painting, the more sensational and startling inventions of the last part of the nineteenth and early part of the twentieth centuries must have produced even more striking and novel impressions). Yet relatively speaking, especially when compared to the forty years that have passed since his death, Proust's was an age of calm and social stability in which the slightest disturbances were registered by the public mind with the sensitivity of a seismograph. It is not unfair to say that the fate of one man like Dreyfus aroused more general concern and compassion than the annihilation of millions under Hitler or the Soviets. The world has supped on horrors and wonders of such magnitude in the twentieth century that the average man's stomach has become as hard and desensitized as cast iron. Proust saw only the beginnings of all this in 1914 and the years which followed, and in the last volume of *Remembrance* called *The Past Recaptured*, he gave us a remarkably prescient and incisive forecast of much that was in store for the old-fashioned sensibilities in the new century (as I have indicated in my chapter on that volume where I compare some of the wilder soliloquies of the Baron de Charlus with the cynicism of Louis-Ferdinand Céline's *Journey to the End of the Night*).

But the greatest portion of *Remembrance* is concerned with an idyllic, tranquil existence either in the country town, by the seashore, or in the city of Paris. The greatest perturbations are those introduced by the frustrated impulse to snobbery and the frustrated passion of love. The delights of reading in the country, walks in fields and by the river, concerts, pictures, the theater, animated dinner parties in the houses of the aristocracy and of the wealthy, comfortable middle class predominate in the pages of *Remembrance*. It is the ripe (some have thought it overripe) product of an age of international peace. Its interest in the finer, subtler, more delicate shadings of life make it appeal to those who have managed to create an inner life for themselves, a haven of calm in the midst of a terribly stormy, obscure and tragic age. Some may care to recall that the novels of such a writer as Jane Austen, created by a sensibility of similar refinement, were written in a corner of the world in which the great facts were the French Revolution and the ensuing Napoleonic campaigns for the subjugation of Europe. Yet Jane Austen was able to carve out for herself a quiet refuge of the spirit in which she steadily observed English domestic life in its finest detail and has ever since delighted audiences the world over with what she discovered there. Proust aimed to build a similar sanctuary for like-minded spirits, but he was uncertain of the results of his labors. In *The Past Recaptured*, he writes plaintively: "I knew not whether it would be a church in which the true believers would be able little by little to learn some new truths and discover some harmonies, the great, comprehensive plan, or would stand, forever unvisited, on the summit of an island, like a druid monument. But I had decided to devote to it all my strength. . . ." (393) What Proust meant by devoting to the making of a book all of his strength is indicated in a passage in which he speaks of the job a man faces who would "extract the real essence of life in a book." The hypothetical author "would need to prepare it with minute care, constantly regrouping his forces as if for an attack, endure it like an exhausting task, accept it like a rule of conduct, build it like a church, follow it like a regimen, overcome it like an obstacle, win it like a friendship, feed it intensively like a child, create it like a world, without overlooking those mysteries whose explanation is to be found only in other worlds and the presentiment of which is the quality in life and art which moves us most deeply. And in those great books there are certain portions which there has been time only to sketch in and which no doubt will never be completed because of the very magnitude of the architect's plan. How many great cathedrals remain unfinished! Such a book one nourishes over a long period of time, builds up its weaker parts, keeps it safe from harm; but later it is the book itself that grows up, selects our Tomb, protects it against false rumors and somewhat against oblivion. . . ." (384)

Proust, like his revered Ruskin, making a religion of art (though he expressed the hope that it was no idolatry), was ready to lay down his life for it on the altar of his work. His devotion to it in the solitudes of his corklined bedroom (which, like some other wealthy asthmatics of Paris—Henry Bernstein, the dramatist, for example—he had built for himself to combat the sufferings caused him by his illness) has become as mythical to many modern readers and aesthetes as the severed ear which Vincent Van Gogh sent as a present to a prostitute and which has also somehow seemed to them the very symbol of the sufferings of the artist and of his alienation from our world.

2. Swann's Way

THE OPENING SECTION OF FIFTY-EIGHT PAGES OF SWANN'S WAY, WHICH IN ENGLISH IS CALLED THE OVERTURE THOUGH IT HAS NO special title in the French text, has been liberally praised for the way in which the author manages in it to introduce all the principal characters and themes which he intends to develop in the 4,000 pages of *Remembrance of Things Past*. But this was the section, too, which the French publisher to whom Proust originally submitted his manuscript had in mind when he wryly complained that he could not understand why a writer should spend so many pages describing how a gentleman turns over in bed from one side to the other. The extreme slowness of narrative movement in the first half of the volume *Swann's Way* has probably had a similar effect upon many other potential readers of Proust over the years. All that can be said to such readers is that if they will suspend their scepticism long enough, Proust will repay the trouble one has to take at first in reading him.

It is this introduction and the concluding section of *Remembrance* (probably the last half of the volume *The Past Recaptured*) which Proust said he had composed first of all, leaving all the intervening parts of the huge work to be added afterwards. In spite of early objections to his improvisatory formlessness, made by critics before the whole work had appeared in print, no writer has ever had his end in mind more firmly from the beginning than Proust. Edmund Wilson, in his essay on Proust in *Axel's Castle*, makes a point of the very first word in the narrative—in French the word is *longtemps*, translated into English as "For a long time . . ."—which sounds the theme of *time*. The word *Time*, which is present in the title of the work and which dominates the whole coda of *The Past Recaptured* (being in fact the very last word in that concluding volume) is, Wilson points out, *the* principal subject to which Proust addresses himself in his masterpiece.

We should note that the present tense of the opening of *Remembrance* refers to the narrator's later years. The main episode in this introductory section is an incident from the narrator Marcel's childhood (it is clear that, as in other modern authors such as James and Conrad, Proust intended to keep some distance between himself and his alter ego, though not perhaps the same fixed distance which those writers require). What is actually described on the opening page of Proust's *Remembrance* is sleep with all of its wondrous capacity for transformations of reality, sleep *as the element of unreason* in which physical laws and logic which provide a framework for our waking lives are effortlessly suspended and contradicted. A man in his sleep may be changed not only into another person but into a thing and even into an abstraction: a church, a string quartet, or a historical rivalry between monarchs whom the dreamer has been reading about at the moment of dropping off to sleep (as Coleridge was reading Purchas at the moment of dreaming the fragments of *Kubla Khan*).

Dreams dominate the opening pages. Dreams of a distant past —the time when Marcel's uncle had teased and terrified him as a child by pulling at his curls. (3) Dreams of women created by some strain in his physical posture as he is lying in bed. (3) These subjective phantasms (like all the "objects" of love in the pages of *Remembrance*, which clearly shows the influence of Kantian idealism) are brought into being by appetites craving fulfillment. At the moment of awakening (4), facts about space, time, and duration are all mixed up in his mind; his armchair, like a magic carpet in *The Arabian Nights*, traverses the most extensive realms in an instant. Not only does he not know *where* he is at the moment of awakening, he does not know *who* he is (4). His notion of existence seems that of an animal; he is *denuded* of identity. But here memory intervenes and, leaning down, rescues him from the abyss. He passes through millennia of civilization in order to reconstitute his ego. He wrestles with the difficulty of locating himself in relation to things, countries, time (5); memory suggests alternatively many of the rooms he had slept in over the years. With incredible rapidity he makes various hypotheses to account to himself for his present position. (6) After these actual dreams,

Marcel often spends the night in long reveries, waking dreams in which he consciously attempts to restore the vanished past.

On page 7, we are introduced to the subject of habit with its power to anesthetize the pain of life, the powerful ally (as Aristotle knew and the narrator's parents know) of the moral life and the enemy (as the narrator himself feels) of the aesthetic life because it dulls those keen perceptions of reality upon which all art is ultimately based. On the next page (8), all the principal settings of *Remembrance* are named in the order in which they are to take their places in the structure of the story: Combray, Balbec, Paris, Doncières, and Venice. This page ends the first part of the introductory section.

On page 9, we have the beginning of an account of the nightly drama which accompanied Marcel's going to bed as a child in Combray, the place of residence of his eccentric aunt Léonie and his own immediate family's vacationing place for the Easter holidays each year. How difficult it was for him at that time to achieve the peace of mind, the calm and confidence that it is necessary to have before going to sleep. Only his mother's goodnight kiss was capable of restoring the necessary tranquility to him. After dinner, and especially when guests were expected, he would be compelled to leave her to her social duties and to go to sleep without complaint. (11) Later on, she would come up for a few moments to kiss him goodnight (14), but it was quickly apparent that his excessive and nervous demands for her attention were more than she could cope with. The difficulties attendant upon his mother's kiss (and his father's outspoken annoyance at the absurdity of the "rites" surrounding it) were magnified on those evenings when company was expected. "Company" in those days generally meant their neighbor, Charles Swann, whose unfortunate marriage is first brought to our attention in an ingenious parenthesis (14). Swann, who is introduced to us with an anecdote about his strange father (16), is at once enveloped by an atmosphere of magic and romance when we learn that though ostensibly belonging to the same wealthy, conservative middle class as the narrator's family, he leads another unsuspected, adventurous life in French high society and the international smart set. A member of the exclusive Jockey Club in Paris, an intimate friend of the claimant to the French throne, the Count of Paris, of the English heir-apparent, the Prince of Wales, and the President of the Third Republic, Swann (whose name seems clearly symbolic of his rarity and excellence) is one of the most fashionable men in that aristocratic segment of Parisian society known as the Faubourg Saint Germain. He is, in other words, in his own person a refutation of the narrow-minded "Hindu caste-conception" of the world taken by Marcel's very proper, bourgeois family. (17)

We listen to Swann's sophisticated conversation which accounts, in part at least, for his social success—his habitual avoidance of every appearance of pedantry or even of "seriousness," his detailed and rather dry, factual precision when asked for an opinion about the paintings which he collects and on which he is a recognized authority. (18) He delights in telling amusing stories about the Combray pharmacist, about his own cook, about the narrator's family's coachman. (19) These homely narratives seem to correspond to his great interest in Flemish painting of domestic interiors—the art of Vermeer, for example, to whom he has, as we are to learn much later on, devoted years of his life in writing a critical monograph.

Marcel's grandmother accidentally stumbles on the clue to the existence of Swann's brilliant, worldly life. (22) She does so during one of her visits to her old school friend, the Marquise de Villeparisis (with whom she has not cultivated her acquaintance because of her own inflexible conception of the social proprieties) who tells her that Swann is a great friend of her nephew and his wife, the Prince and Princesse des Laumes. The grandmother thus stumbles unwittingly upon a hidden point of intersection between Swann's Way (the name of an actual walk that Proust makes symbolic of the way of life of the wealthy middle class) and Guermantes' Way (another actual country walk which, to him, symbolizes the way of life of the aristocracy). While visiting the Marquise, Marcel's grandmother also makes the acquaintance of a tailor who owns a little shop in her courtyard and is charmed by his good manners (on second reading, we recognize the reference here to Jupien, who has so important a role to play later on in the revelation of the homosexuality of the Baron de Charlus).

But to return to the main line of the narrative from this digression, the only one in the house for whom Swann's visit in the evening was fraught with alarming dangers was Marcel himself.

(26) He had good reason to fear that this guest's coming might interfere with the ritual of his mother's goodnight to him. And indeed, on one unforgettable occasion, when the boy was abruptly sent to bed by his whimsical, quite arbitrary, and unsentimental father without his mother's customary kiss, he had not been able to go to sleep at all and, after exhausting various stratagems to get the servant Françoise to fetch his mother to him, he had ambushed his parents ascending the staircase to their room after the departure of their guest and thrown himself in a fit of hysterical weeping upon his mother. It had been a truly desperate action prompted by an unhappiness approaching a state of hysterical anxiety, and he had fully expected to be "banished" from the house (as had been threatened) for so willful a transgression of all its rules. But instead of banishment, his father, who seemed more obtuse and generally insensitive than his mother, suddenly realized with a shock his son's state of mind and suggested that Marcel's mother stay in her son's room for the night to comfort him. And so the bitterest, blackest night in his life had suddenly been changed into the happiest. Never, never should he forget that traumatic experience from which he was later on to date "the decline of his will," for he had learned the dangerous lesson that he could get his way with his parents even more successfully by self-indulgence than by obedience and self-discipline. (32ff)

The story of this particular evening forms the second part of the Introduction or "Overture" to the work; the third part (53–58) is concerned with the madeleine-and-tea episode which is perhaps the single best-known passage in Proust's work (the only other episodes which rival it are those describing the death of Bergotte in the volume *The Captive* and the description of the party in the house of the Marquise de Saint-Euverte, which are also sometimes anthologized). We should note that this episode takes place many years after the incident at Combray, which because of its glaring, sensational quality had for long usurped completely the conscious memory of Marcel and displaced all of the less garish, more delicately shaded experiences which had formed the substance of his boyhood vacations in the country. Only the chance tasting of a bit of particular pastry dipped into a cup of lime-flower tea reminds him quite involuntarily of the cake which his Aunt Léonie used to offer him long ago and thus reanimates the whole sensitively woven texture of impressions of Combray, with its infinite nuances and subtle gradations of color. He discovers (without being able as yet to interpret fully the meaning or value of his discovery to his vocation as an artist) that a sensory perception, common to two widely separated periods of time, is capable of resurrecting the otherwise dead past.

Many things have been said by different people, including Proust himself, which are relevant to this episode. To the talented though very dry biographer of Proust, Richard Barker (whose book I should recommend in preference to the better-known and more ambitious biographies by André Maurois and George Painter), Proust's description of the thaumaturgic effects of sensory perceptions upon his memory is little more than a formal device by which he managed to order his narrative. According to Barker, it has only a negligible importance in any theoretical, philosophical or even aesthetic sense, and it certainly represents no new discovery as some critics have implied. Proust himself, taking note of comparisons between himself and the philosopher Bergson, which were made when Proust's work first appeared, pointed out that his distinction between the voluntary and the involuntary memory and his insistence on the overwhelming importance of the latter type for artistic creation are his own ideas and are not to be found in Bergson.

Another line of criticism has attempted to trace the madeleine-and-cup-of-tea incident to similar incidents in authors whose work Proust had closely studied—Ruskin and Chateaubriand. And indeed the theory of the effect of similar sensory perceptions in reawakening dormant memories is one that looks sufficiently familiar to all readers of romantic poetry and prose. Probably many passages parallel in important respects to the famous one of Proust's could be found in the literature of the nineteenth century. One passage which I myself have recently come across is from the Victorian story-teller, Wilkie Collins, whom Proust may never have read though his acquaintance with English literature was extensive and Collins's story *A Terribly Strange Bed* is one of the best known and frequently reprinted narratives of its period. The passage which I came across in Collins reads as follows: ". . . My thoughts began insensibly to wander. The moonlight shining into the room reminded me of a certain moonlight night in England—the night after a picnic party in a Welsh valley.

Every incident of the drive homeward, through lovely scenery, which the moonlight made lovelier than ever, came back to my remembrance, though I had never given the picnic a thought for years, though, if I had *tried* to recollect it, I could certainly have recalled little or nothing of that scene long past. Of all the wonderful faculties that help to tell us we are immortal, which speaks the sublime truth more eloquently than memory? Here was I, in a strange house of the most suspicious character, in a situation of uncertainty, and even of peril, which might seem to make the exercise of my recollection almost out of the question, nevertheless, remembering, quite involuntarily, places, people, conversations, minute circumstances of every kind, which I had thought forgotten forever; which I could not possibly have re-called at will, even under the most favorable auspices. And what cause had produced in a moment the whole of this strange, com-plicated, mysterious effect? Nothing but some rays of moonlight shining in at my bedroom window."

How close the tone, ideas, and feeling of this passage are to those of Proust must be left to the judgment of other readers of Proust (the comparison is easily made and the resemblance, at least on a number of points, seems to me striking), yet it must be doubted if Proust actually ever came across it, or, if he did, remembered it. The importance of Collins's passage is that it establishes the fact that a certain aesthetic point of view, which may be the origin of Proust's, was fairly commonplace in Victorian literature—that is to say, the literature of the age directly preceding Proust's in the language which, outside of French, he knew best and was most interested in. What is strik-ing in Proust, however, is not the aestheticism which he shares with other romantics but the intensity which he brings to the expression of it and which is entirely his own. Collins tells us the effect of the particular sensory perceptions he describes upon his involuntary memory, but Proust makes us feel the effort in-volved in connecting the taste of the cake dipped in tea to his boyhood experience of Combray. The evocation of the past to the nineteenth-century writer is lyrical and quite easy, but to the twentieth-century writer it is suspenseful and dramatic and difficult. Collins's description is that of an effortless medium, but Proust's vision is delivered only after agonizing labor. Of course, it is not the strain alone that gives art its value but the quality of what the effort produces. The texture of Proust's narrative, its sensitivity and style are incomparably superior to the rather conventional descriptions which I have quoted from Collins.

When the nineteenth-century writer thinks in terms of dramatic narrative (and this holds true of writers far greater than Collins), he thinks of outward and violent action (*A Terribly Strange Bed*, for example, deals with an attempted murder), but to the twentieth-century writers the most interesting and engrossing field of action often lies in the inward consciousness of the characters. Stephen Dedalus in Joyce's *Portrait of the Artist . . .* is radically transformed by his moment of vision of the girl on the beach which is completely unaccompanied by words or actions; Hans Castorp in Mann's *Magic Mountain* is transformed by his vision as he lies swooning in the snow; and similarly Marcel is transformed by the taste of the madeleine dipped in tea. These climactic moments do not have the slightest resemblance to the climaxes of melodrama, the murders, adulteries, and duels which are the staple means of expression in the older novel. The publisher who found Proust's narrative boring and intolerably slow because nothing much *happened* in it in any outward sense except that a gentleman turned over in bed from one side to the other, was perhaps still attuned to a more extroverted and less inwardly-oriented literature. The modern reader is more receptive to psychological, introspective nuances and Proust's narrative in this Overture (especially in the third and concluding section) seems to him filled with excitement. The reason for this is that Marcel is launched upon the most painstaking, treacherous and uncertain of voyages—the quest for self-knowledge and the finding of his true vocation in life. Self-knowledge to Proust implies a heroic, Herculean effort to reclaim vast tracts of one's past which have been inundated by oblivion and to bring them under cultivation by the conscious mind. Goethe's Faust, at the end of Part Two, undertook no greater task in reclaiming lost lands from the marshes and the sea nor did his success afford him more satisfaction than the outwardly quiet labors of Proust in digging for meaning through the memories of his past. In fact, it should be a truer criticism of Proust to say that his psychological drama in such an episode as the one I am discussing verges perilously upon melodrama than that he is not dramatic enough. There can be psychological melodrama as well as the familiar physical kind and to realize the meaning of psychological melodrama we have only to read these half-dozen pages, 53–58.

COMBRAY

From one cup of tea—and the taste of a bit of cake dipped into it—the whole town of Combray sprang to life again in Marcel's mind. The words of the sentence which concludes the Overture (in C. K. Scott Moncrieff's translation) are the following: "And just as the Japanese amuse themselves by filling a porcelain bowl with water and steeping in it little crumbs of paper which until then are without character or form, but, the moment they become wet, stretch themselves and bend, take on color and distinctive shape, become flowers or houses or people, permanent and recognizable, so in that moment all the flowers in our garden, and in M. Swann's park, and the water-lilies on the Vivonne and the good folk of the village and their little dwellings and the parish church and the whole of Combray and of its surroundings, taking their proper shapes and growing solid, sprang into being, town and gardens alike, from my cup of tea." (58)

Combray is an extended description of the country town where Marcel spent his vacations during his boyhood. Though it is enlivened by many social episodes, both within the narrator's household and in the larger arena of the town itself, the peculiar charm and distinction of this "chapter" (which is the size of an ordinary novelette) lie in its pastoral descriptions of flowers, fields, river, country church, and garden. Wordsworth once said that his sister Dorothy had given him eyes and ears—presumably for the subtleties of nature which she observed with such sensitivity and patience. I think that Proust is equipped to do something similar for almost all of us; certainly he has done it for myself. He opens our senses to the most delicate and fleeting shades of natural beauty. Even those with a healthy, humanistic scepticism (such as Socrates exhibits in the Platonic dialogue, *Phaedrus*) concerning the charms of botany will probably listen to him with interest and, at least momentarily, be converted to his Rousseauistic (or should I say Ruskinian?) gospel. "This is the land of lost content" —as A. E. Housman has it; this is the imaginative country and experience of youth which never return for anyone and which those who have once experienced it never think of without nostalgic longing and regret.

Irving Babbitt accuses romanticism of being what might be called a philosophy suited to vacationists rather than to the serious business of directing life in which vacations are, at best, merely exceptional interludes. Rightly understood and confined to its proper sphere, romanticism to him may have undeniable attractions. Now Proust is undoubtedly a romanticist in Babbitt's sense, and therefore I find it singularly appropriate that he should begin this section directly after the Overture with what may be called a "Pastoral Symphony." Here at the very threshold of his work which, in spite of what has been said, does contain a good deal of action, is a virtually untroubled expanse of inaction. Here is the picture of that early Paradise which cannot be regained (one of Proust's aphorisms is that "the only Paradise that is real is the Paradise we have lost") and which we cannot help but wish to regain.

We are told by Russian critics that Tolstoy's *War and Peace*, in spite of all the scenes of carnage and suffering in it which fully justify the first word in the title, is to be regarded as "the idyll of the Russian Nobility of the nineteenth century." Proust's *Combray* is the idyll of the French comfortable upper middle class of the latter part of the same century. Culture, wealth, leisure—these supply the necessary background of calm and security for the enjoyment of nature which is Proust's central concern here. But he would not be an important novelist or one capable of being exported across national and linguistic boundaries if he were not able in some way, like the Russian master, to suggest the universality of his subject. It may be that the unhurried, peaceful life of reading and contemplation of nature, of existence in a placid and stable social order in which the slightest external events echo and reverberate with the resonance of epic deeds and actions is the secret ideal of all of mankind.

What makes this assumption even more acceptable is that the hero and central figure in this section is Marcel as a boy, at that stage of life where it is entirely proper for him to be carefree and passively joyous and minutely observant. When this same attitude appears in an adult, who ought to be struggling and striving in the world, the reader is likely to sense it as a pathetic incongruity to the real needs of his situation. This is the case, for example, with

Ivan Goncharov's famous character Oblomov, who insists upon living the uneventful, idyllic life at an advanced age, long after he has any right to do so. Oblomovism as a term has therefore entered the Russian language to denote a form of spiritual illness—the disease of compulsive inaction. *Combray*, on the other hand, is the name of an "island" Paradise for vacations in the midst of France; at its center is a boy growing in awareness and intertwining in his sensibilities with all of the natural beauty that surrounds him, and this gives to his experience a sense of fitness and propriety which is purposely absent from Oblomov.

In the closing pages of *Combray* (237–238), the affinity between Marcel's view of life and that of Oblomov seems clearly apparent: "Whether it be that the faith which creates has ceased to exist in me, or that reality will take shape in the memory alone, the flowers that people show me nowadays for the first time never seem to me to be true flowers. The 'Méseglise Way' with its lilacs, its hawthorns, its cornflowers, its poppies, its apple-trees, the 'Guermantes Way' with its river full of tadpoles, its water-lilies, and its buttercups have constituted for me for all time the picture of the land in which I fain would pass my life, in which my only requirements are that I may go out fishing, drift idly in a boat, see the ruins of a gothic fortress in the grass, and find hidden in the cornfield—as Saint-André des Champs lay hidden—an old church, monumental, rustic, and yellow like a mill-stone; and the cornflowers, the hawthorns, the apple-trees which I may happen, when I go walking, to encounter in the fields, because they are situated at the same depth, on the level of my past life, at once establish contact with my heart."

The image of drifting idly in a boat, which Goncharov too uses so effectively in *Oblomov* to represent the quintessence of luxurious and passive enjoyment of life, recurs elsewhere in Proust's narrative. It is present in the description of the Vivonne River (219): "After leaving the park the Vivonne began to flow again more swiftly. How often have I watched, and longed to imitate, when I should be free to live as I chose, a rower who had shipped his oars and lay stretched out on his back, his head down in the bottom of his boat, letting it drift with the current, seeing nothing but the sky which slipped quietly above him, shewing upon his features a foretaste of happiness and peace."

The flower descriptions of *Combray* are full of exquisite grace and delicacy, of which the following phrases are a fair sample: ". . . the river flowing past, sky-blue already between banks still black and bare, its only companions a clump of daffodils, come out before their time, a few primroses, the first in flower, while here and there burned the blue lamp of a violet, its stem bent beneath the weight of the drop of perfume stored in its tiny horn." (214)

But more often he achieves his effects not by painting the external world but by finding the precise language to communicate the tranquilizing effect of the idyllic world he describes upon the narrator's mind: "I should have liked to be able to sit down and spend the whole day there, reading and listening to the bells, for it was so charming there and so quiet that, when an hour struck, you would have said not that it broke upon the calm of the day, but that it relieved the day of its superfluity, and that the steeple, with the indolent, painstaking exactitude of a person who has nothing else to do, had simply, in order to squeeze out and let fall a few golden drops which had slowly and naturally accumulated in the hot sunlight, pressed, at a given moment, the distended surface of the silence." (214)

The pleasures of good food and of good reading also enter into this picture of the idyllic life: "I discovered pleasures of another kind, those of being comfortably seated, of tasting the good scent on the air, of not being disturbed by any visitor; and, when an hour chimed from the steeple of Saint-Hilaire, of watching what was already spent of the afternoon fall drop by drop until I heard the last stroke which enabled me to add up the total sum, after which the silence that followed seemed to herald the beginning, in the blue sky above me, of that long part of the day still allowed me for reading, until the good dinner which Françoise was even now preparing should come to strengthen and refresh me after the strenuous pursuit of its hero through the pages of my book. And, as each hour struck, it would seem to me that a few seconds only had passed since the hour before; the latest would inscribe itself, close to its predecessor, on the sky's surface, and I would be unable to believe that sixty minutes could be squeezed into the tiny arc of blue which was comprised between their two golden figures. Sometimes it would even happen that this precocious hour would sound two strokes more than the last; there must have been an hour which I had not heard strike; something which had taken place had not taken place for me; the fascination of my book, a magic as potent as the deepest slumber, had stopped my enchanted ears and had obliterated the sound of that golden bell from the azure surface of the enveloping silence." (108–109) And then, as if carried to a crowning pinnacle of enthusiasm and nostalgia where prose is no longer an adequate instrument to convey his feelings, he breaks into a poetic apostrophe to Combray and to the segment of time past which he is in process of resurrecting.

The servant Françoise, who had already played a role in the Overture, dominates *Combray*. Very early in this section (64) her career as a whole is briefly outlined by the narrator—its great and eventful change was to be her transfer from the employment of Marcel's Aunt Léonie, after her death, to the employment of his immediate family—an outline which reveals that Proust has the whole story of his vast work firmly in hand and plotted in advance. There will be none of the improvisation (as distinguished from planned composition) which had characterized and weakened his first attempt to write a novel in *Jean Santeuil*.

Françoise is depicted by Proust as a reincarnation of the medieval peasant "who had survived to cook for us in the nineteenth century." (193–194) She is the very type of dogged fidelity to those she recognizes to be her legitimate masters. But though a type, she is, like every character in Proust, an individual as well—almost to the point of eccentricity. She is contrasted sharply with the superficially affable and bland modern servants who, perhaps just because they lack distinctive character, impress unwary strangers in spite of an "utter barrenness of spirit in which no amount of training can produce the least trace of individuality." (67) Individuality is the criterion of all human value to Proust, whether in the eccentric nobleman Charlus or the servant Françoise. And it is interesting to observe how he goes about establishing her individuality.

A preliminary stroke is the account (65–66) of the considerateness shown Françoise by the narrator's mother (an important indication of the latter's character, too, and paralleling an earlier kindness and perceptiveness which she had shown in the Overture to Swann, when she had engaged him in conversation on the subject of his daughter Gilberte, though a glacial silence still surrounded any mention of Swann's unfortunate marriage to Odette). Marcel's mother, by talking to Françoise about her parents, her daughter, and her son-in-law, touches her deeply with "the pleasure of feeling that her peasant existence, with its simple joys and sorrows might offer some interest, might be a source of grief or pleasure to someone other than herself." (66)

The conversation between Françoise and her mistress, Aunt Léonie (68–70), besides revealing the invalid's "Noah's Ark" view of the world (as Proust once described it in reference to himself), also shows a fine, diplomatic intelligence in the servant which enables her to retain control in a situation where it is she who is nominally controlled. If Françoise is a peasant, she also has a peasant's shrewdness in getting what she wants, unobtrusively, while appearing to be concerned solely with what her mistress desires. Her cleverness is demonstrated not only in relation to her superiors but (much less winningly) in relation to her inferiors, the various "assistant-maids" over the years whom she drives so mercilessly. One particular story along this line that is told by Marcel has to do with a maid who has managed to get herself quite illegitimately pregnant and whom Françoise (for this and other reasons) harries to the point where it is a wonder that she does not have a miscarriage. The time of the employment of this unfortunate is identified merely as "the year in which we ate such quantities of asparagus." (99–100) It is only much later that Marcel is able to make a connection between this and the fact, accidentally discovered, that Françoise had known that her "assistant" had been allergic to asparagus and became ill in handling it. (This incident recalls to my mind a similar instance of sadism from Scott Fitzgerald's *The Great Gatsby* involving the unhappy Daisy Buchanan, who finding that one of her servants is allergic to silver polish, sets him to polishing silver all day long.)

This is the dark side of Françoise's character, for like all the personages in Proust, her character has its lights and shades and it is by a judicious distribution of these that she is made to appear so life-like. Marcel becomes aware of this underside of her character when he surprises her one day in the act of killing a chicken and "beside herself with rage as she attempted to slit its throat beneath the ear, accompanied with shrill cries of 'Filthy creature! Filthy creature!'" (154) The scene is shockingly raw to the sensibilities of the boy: "I crept out of the kitchen and upstairs, trembling all over; I could have prayed, then, for the instant dismissal of Françoise." (155)

It is interesting to note here that this unattractive truth about the old servant is *surprised* by Marcel. He had thought of Françoise before that as possessing "saintly kindness and unction." Unpleasant truths of this sort are consistently surprised in the pages of *Remembrance*, and we must regard this surprise as a facet of his vision of the nature of man. Human beings are naturally secretive creatures. The boy surprises the inner truth about his invalid aunt Léonie one day just as she is awakening from a dream about her deceased husband who "was trying to make me take a walk every day!" (138) As she realizes that the horrible thought was suggested to her only in a dream, the boy overhears her thank God that her husband is no longer there to disturb her peace with his salutary advice. A much more important surprise is that by which Marcel accidentally discovers one day that Mlle. Vinteuil is a Lesbian and a sadist. Quite unintentionally he witnesses a scene through the open windows of her house in which she is engaged in a perverse sexual ritual with a female friend—a ritual which culminates in her friend's spitting on the portrait of Mlle. Vinteuil's dead father. (209–210) Some of the book's first readers felt that this startling scene had no justifiable place in the volume, which was half pastoral idyll and half normal heterosexual love affair (by this I mean the account of Swann's relation to Odette in the second half of the book), and that it ought to be excised from future editions of *Swann's Way*. Proust had to inform them that while the episode involving Mlle. Vinteuil and her Sapphic friend seemed to be a loose end without any reason for being in the volume at all, they would see eventually, when the whole work appeared, that it formed a necessary part of its structure.

One of the fascinations in rereading Proust is to see how adroitly he prepares his surprises by hints dropped long before in his narrative. So, well in advance of the revelation of her shameful secret, there had already been some stress (143) upon the mannishness of Mlle. Vinteuil's appearance. The exposure of the homosexuality of Charlus in later volumes is prepared by hints too numerous to mention. A revelation by "surprise" in the *Combray* section is the *snobbishness* of the engineer-poet, Legrandin. Snobbery, like homosexuality, will be developed at length in later volumes. Legrandin is a man whose ordinary appearance and behavior are so at odds with what he really is at the bottom of his soul that for a long time, even after clear evidence of his failing has made itself manifest, the conservatively-minded family of Marcel was unable to bring itself to believe that appearance and reality were in conflict here, as they are in the case of so many other people. Only repeated instances of offensive behavior on his part served eventually to overcome the family's doubts, and this experience is the occasion for a general observation by Proust which is equally applicable to all the surprises and reversals and misdirections of attention that sprinkle his pages and lend an air of mystery and suspense to *Remembrance:* "It was like every attitude or action which reveals a man's deep and hidden character; they bear no relation to what he has previously said, and we cannot confirm our suspicions by the culprit's evidence, for he will admit nothing; we are reduced to the evidence of our own senses, and we ask ourselves, in the face of this detached and incoherent fragment of recollection, whether indeed our senses have not been the victims of a hallucination; with the result that such attitudes, and these alone are of importance in indicating character, are the most apt to leave us in perplexity." (161)

One of Proust's strongest points as a creator of character is his ability to maintain a balance between the unique and the representative. When he tells us concerning the primitive Françoise that "apart from her own kinsfolk, the sufferings of humanity inspired in her a pity which increased in direct ratio to the distance separating the sufferer from herself" (155) we think that we recognize a trait that, if not universal, is still sufficiently widespread to be readily recognizable perhaps even in ourselves. But when he notes the peculiarity of some of Françoise's language and moral evaluations (for example, when she compares soldiers to lions, not as a way of praising their courage but with the intention of denigrating their brutality "for by her way of thinking, to compare a man with a lion, which she used to pronounce 'lie-on,' was not at all complimentary to the man"—page 110), we have the pleasurable sensation of knowing that he has caught her image in its complete uniqueness, in the way in which she is herself and no one else in the world. Every character in Proust can make the boast of Rousseau in his *Confessions:* "If I am not better than others, at least I am different."

Proust's narrative moves, though very slowly, and never more slowly perhaps than in the section *Combray*, since an idyll by its very own nature is virtually bound to stand still. One notices very quickly that for Proust it is true that, as Byron puts it in the concluding line of *Beppo:* "stories somehow lengthen when begun." In other words, digression is particularly tempting to him, and all the more so in this portion of *Remembrance* where "the necessary business" of the narrative is so small.

He has occasion, for example, to mention Marcel's great-uncle Adolphe (89) who used to occupy a room on the ground floor of Aunt Léonie's house until a quarrel with the boy's parents, of which the boy was the unwitting cause, drove him away. To explain the quarrel, Marcel has to tell us (90) that at the time in question he was a lover of the theater—a "Platonic" lover (90) as he puts it, because his strict parents thought him too young as yet to attend a performance. He goes on, then, for some pages (91–92) telling how enamored he was of the announcements of plays which are posted on public columns in Paris, how his first exchanges with a new school friend invariably concerned their favorite performers, and how the sight of an actress emerging from the *Théatre-Français* "had plunged (him) in the throes and sufferings of hopeless love" (92). These memories relate to Marcel's uncle, because his uncle "knew many (actresses) personally" and "used to entertain them at his house." (93) This type of acquaintance which had made his uncle an object of ironic comment to the narrator's strait-laced family built him up to heroic proportions in the eyes of the romantic boy, who determined to take advantage of his relationship to meet some of the theatrical personages who haunted his dreams.

With this idea in mind, Marcel calls upon his uncle Adolphe one day while the latter is entertaining a "lady in pink" (94). After much hesitation and soul-searching on his uncle's part, and after some prodding by the lady, who, it appears from her conversation, has seen Marcel's mother somewhere and is interested in meeting her son, he is admitted to the house and immediately feels some of the disillusionment (95) which it is his fate to feel always at the shortcomings of prosaic reality when it is compared with the gorgeous creations of his imagination. The lady in pink turns out to be "in no way different from other pretty women." (95) There is a conversation between the lady and

Uncle Adolphe (96-98) from which it appears that the Russian Grand Duke is an intimate friend of the lady—and so, in spite of appearances, she is different from other women Marcel has met. When he gets home (98–99), he tells the story of the visit and the meeting to his parents, who take an altogether different and more serious view of the matter, for they actively resent the introduction of their respectable child to a woman of questionable moral reputation. Marcel's "father and grandfather had 'words' with (Uncle Adolphe) of a violent order" (99) precipitating the family quarrel which he had referred to at the beginning of the episode and which lasted as family quarrels sometimes do, as long as his uncle lived.

And (bringing the digression back to the main line of the narrative about Combray) "so I no longer used to go into the little sitting-room (now kept shut) of my uncle Adolphe. . . ." (99) Though the "lady in pink" is not identified at this point in the narrative, several volumes later on we learn that she was Odette, and on second reading some of the striking characteristics of Odette (her affectation, for example, of sprinkling her speech with English expressions), which become familiar to us in the course of the narrative of her affair with Swann, are unmistakably present here. We see, then, that this "digression" is tied into the main line of development of *Remembrance* much more closely than had first appeared to be the case. This may help to explain why Proust is not quite as vulnerable as he appears to be to the charge which Byron makes against his own narrative method in *Beppo:*

> I find
> Digression is a sin, that by degrees
> Becomes exceeding tedious to my mind,
> And therefore may the reader too displease.

Of course, Byron is not really afraid of boring his readers in spite of all the digressions in which he indulges. A mind as lively, as various, and as interesting as his could not help being entertaining whatever the subject he chose to write about or whatever the departures he chose to make from that subject. The same thing is true of Tolstoy who, in *War and Peace*, sometimes gives the impression of a loquacious master of ceremonies who continually cuts into the time of the speakers whom he is supposed to introduce. Yet we forgive him, too, because of the liveliness and variety displayed in his privileged soliloquies. Proust, at least to my ear, has as fascinating a voice as Tolstoy's. His narrative is continually interspersed with aphorisms, Montaigne-like little essays on all sorts of topics, digressions which are all "carried off" and incorporated into the deeper unity of his work.

The names of characters who are to play important subordinate roles in *Remembrance* are introduced to us in *Combray* (112-113)—Marcel's fellow-student, Bloch, and Bergotte, the famous novelist who, together with Vinteuil the composer and Elstir the painter, is one of the three principal representatives of art in Proust's story. The less important representatives of art are the performers—the pianist at the Verdurins, Morel the violinist, and Rachel and Berma the actresses. One way of judging the changes that take place in the complete story of *Remembrance* is to compare Bloch here with the very much older Bloch of the last volume, *The Past Recaptured*. The early Bloch affects a hyperaesthetic pose. He is a defender of what Henri Bremond was later to call *la poésie pure*. It is not the intellectual meaning that interests him but the sound and suggestion contained in a line of poetry, and he is a complete iconoclast with regard to the greatest and best-established reputations in French literary history. In Racine and in Musset he finds only a few lines to admire, and these lines, if we are to believe him, are absolutely meaningless and consist simply of a succession of beautiful sounds. But in *The Past Recaptured* Bloch has become converted to a doctrine of uncompromising literary realism. He is just as opinionated and affected as he has ever been, but his affectation has taken a new form. He has become extremely democratic in his views (perhaps the Dreyfus case in which we see him take such a partisan role in the middle volumes of *Remembrance* has influenced him in this direction) and he condemns literature "meant for the idle class" which presumably includes such symbolist and "meaningless" or obscure poetry as he had been so passionately fond of in his initial literary incarnation as a student.

Bloch also serves to introduce the theme of the narrator's relationship to Jews in general. The narrator Marcel is so fond of Jews as friends as to arouse the satiric comments of his grandfather who implies that every time the boy brings a new friend home with him he is sure to be Jewish. Bloch is a relatively un-assimilated Jew whose relationship to French culture is an uneasy one; the conflicts which afflict him culminate later on in "self-hatred" which makes him abuse his fellow-Jews verbally with all the ferocity of an incurable anti-Semite. He is contrasted with Swann, the assimilated Jew who is portrayed as perhaps the most gentle and aristocratic character in the pages of *Remembrance*, though he is not so far assimilated as not to be aroused by the injustice done to Captain Dreyfus. Marcel's parents are represented from the very beginning as distrusting the affectations and sentimentality of Bloch, those "transports of the heart" which he loudly exhibits and which seem to them so little to be relied upon. Soon, Bloch realizes the worst fears he had inspired them with by sharing with Marcel some scandalous gossip about the latter's aunt, after which (since Marcel has, in turn, like a dutiful lad, relayed the news to his parents) Bloch is forbidden to enter the house again.

In *Combray*, too, we have the first appearance of a theme which is to play an important part in unifying the disparate materials of *Remembrance* as a whole—namely, the desire of the narrator of the story to become a writer (222). It may be thought that little suspense as to the resolution of this theme is possible since the very existence of the book before us postulates the positive outcome of the struggle. And yet, somehow, the question is treated with a great deal of vivacity. Marcel for a long time despairs of ever becoming a writer (222-224). That is because he finds no suitable philosophical or intellectual theory in his mind to serve as a framework for such a book, and he identifies talent with the possession of such intellectual powers. Yet at the very moment in which his hopes are at their lowest ebb because he senses his intellectual poverty only too well, his sensibility to the beauty of certain impressions—"a roof, a gleam of sunlight reflected from a stone, the smell of a road" (229)—argue the presence of a talent that has not yet succeeded in finding itself. His first really satisfying literary experience, the composition of a piece of prose on "the steeples of Martinville" (231 ff), arose precisely from such unintellectualized aesthetic perceptions. The little composition gives Marcel a feeling of joy he has never known before—"I found such a sense of happiness, felt that it had so entirely relieved my mind of the obsession of the steeples, and of the mystery which they concealed, that, as though I myself were a hen and had just laid an egg, I began to sing at the top of my voice." (234) It is this moment of joyful discovery that determines his fate, for he has found a vocation which is stronger than himself; he has stumbled upon an activity to which he can devote himself in good conscience, whether anyone else in the world recognizes the value of what he is doing or not.

The point here is that Marcel has started with an altogether inadequate idea of what art is. It is *not* primarily an intellectual activity but one that depends upon the feelings and perceptions. The superior intellectual is not necessarily a superior artist or even an aesthete. The aesthete, on the other hand, may be inferior intellectually speaking. Art, in other words, is "pure"—as Bloch had insisted from the first, and though Bloch himself later on changes his mind about this, the progress of the narrator in *Remembrance* is in the opposite direction: it is to deepen his realization of what *purity* means in relation to literature. Bloch, from being an admirer of Art-for-Art's-sake, becomes a defender of the realistic and naturalistic and "social" school of literature, but Marcel, in the last volume *The Past Recaptured*, insists more firmly than ever upon the fallacies in the approach of the naturalists to art and is more than ever convinced that the symbolists (and the philosophical idealism which is the assumption upon which they proceed, whether they consciously are aware of it or not) are on the right track.

The concluding section of *Combray* rehearses themes already introduced in the *Overture* and in turn introduces the material of the following section of the story, *Swann In Love*. The mother's kiss of the introductory section is now recalled once more. (238) The cup of tea (out of which "Combray sprang") appears again in the text. (239) The story of Swann's great affair with Odette begins with this passage in the last paragraph of *Combray:* "And so I would often lie until morning, dreaming of the old days at Combray, of my melancholy and wakeful evenings there; of other days besides, the memory of which had been more lately restored to me by the taste—by what would have been called at Combray the 'perfume'—of a cup of tea;

and, by an association of memories, of a story which, many years after I had left the place, had been told me of a love affair in which Swann had been involved before I was born. . . ." (239)

SWANN IN LOVE

This particular section of *Remembrance* (some 250 pages long) constitutes by common consent of critical readers perhaps the most brilliant gem in the diadem of Proust's fame. It seems fairly safe to say that whoever is not capable of recognizing the purity of the author's inspiration here, his marvelous sensitivity to nuances of feeling which everybody has experienced but few could express, his eloquence which stems from inward perception and is not mere extroverted rhetoric, is immune to the appreciation of his genius. It is only a love story, a romance if you will, but it is a romance that has few peers in literature and none that I can think of in modern literature. It is a story filled with the most thorough scientific analysis, which yet manages to retain its magic and poetry. Like the mystery of that painter's art which Swann and Elstir discuss in the book (329–331), it is ultimately unfathomable. One may read it again and again, memorizing every phrase and the position of every incident in the plot, and yet be able to account no more satisfactorily for the literary power one feels in it than one did before undertaking a minute study of the text.

I always think of Swann's story as Proust's equivalent of Wagner's Prize Song from *Die Meistersinger*. Wagner, it is said, wrote this beautiful melody (the rival almost of Schubert at his best) as a reply to his critics who had said that his music dramas, composed of intertwined leitmotifs, devoid of traditional arias, and constructed upon new principles, were as innocent of artistic form as "endless streams of macaroni." According to these critics, he had abandoned the traditional method of writing opera in favor of a new method which was really no method at all because he did not possess the required lyric gift. And so Wagner had decided to write a music drama centered upon the composition of a song, which was to be more ornately framed as a center of attention than any operatic aria had ever been. The critics and public were both invited to judge the lyrical gift of the composer under the most stringent conditions, and the composer was able to prove, once and for all, that if he chose to write in a new mode it was not because he could not master the old one and acquit himself with the highest honor according to its standards.

Now Wagner was much on Proust's mind while he was writing *Remembrance* and he spoke of his own composition's leitmotifs and suggested that, just as Wagner's form was not that of old-fashioned opera but a completely new combination which be called music drama, so the form of *Remembrance* was not that of the familiar novel (even the epic novel such as Tolstoy's) but a hitherto untried mixture of the novel, autobiography and history in the form of memoirs. But in the first volume of this multi-volumed effort, Proust chooses to narrate an uninterrupted romance, which possesses an unmistakable beginning, middle and end like every other story. *Remembrance* is a behemoth of a composition, which is the literary counterpart of Wagner's *Ring*— that is to say, an artistic undertaking the vast extent of which in itself is enough to constitute it one of the wonders of the world—but *Swann In Love* is designed perhaps to stop the mouths of those sceptics who were sure to claim that if the writer chose to brew a mixture of novel, autobiography and history, it was because he lacked the capacity to compose a pure example of any one of these genres.

The tone of *Swann In Love*, like that of other modern treatments of the subject (I am thinking of Somerset Maugham's *Of Human Bondage*, for example, which appeared just two years after the French publication of *Swann*), is somewhat antiseptic towards romantic illusion, though it is itself basically a romance. To compare Proust's work with Maugham's, by the way, seems to me illuminating. It is intended as no reflection upon the English novelist to say that, compared with Proust's, his work seems lacking in fineness of perception, or that it is occasionally burdened with melodramatic strokes (the complete wrecking of Philip's apartment at one point by Mildred, for example) which are more suitable to the effects possible on the stage rather than to the more restrained and "subjective" form of the novel. But there are similarities as well as contrasts between Maugham in *Of Human Bondage* and Proust in *Swann In Love*. In both books, it is a question of the *enslavement* (suggested by Maugham's title) of a sensitive, intellectually superior man by an inferior, rather stupid woman. Actually, the bondage which Maugham speaks of is (like that discussed in the fifth book of Spinoza's *Ethics*) the bondage of a man to his own emotions. Like hypnosis, romantic love is a condition which has initially at least to be consented to. After one has lapsed into a trance, to be sure, the option of withdrawal from the situation is forfeit. Swann is certainly responsible at the beginning for what happens to him. He has reached a "dangerous age" and wonders what it is like to "live solely for love" (as had happened to characters in the books he read). One must never forget that "one seeks in love before everything else a subjective pleasure." (253) If it is any consolation to the lover, then, it is a fact that he is compelled by a necessity which operates in himself rather than by one which originates outside himself, as it appears to do on the surface. And yet this knowledge will not help him to free himself from the toils of a Mildred (in Maugham's story) or of an Odette (in Proust's).

It should be noted that, as in the case of other important affairs in the pages of *Remembrance* (Marcel-Albertine, Saint Loup-Rachel, Charlus-Morel) the relation between Swann and Odette involves a wealthy man on one side and a poor woman (or else a poor man, in the homosexual affair of Charlus and Morel) on the other. Swann, Proust says clearly enough, belongs among the idlers of society, or, more precisely, "to that class of intelligent men who have led a life of idleness." (248) Swann never forgets this fact and, in the midst of his most exquisite tortures at the hands of his mistress, he is thankful that his private fortune has made him financially independent and that he is able for this reason to contribute to her upkeep (458), a condition which may keep her from breaking off with him completely.

The affair between Swann and Odette is intimately connected from the beginning with the milieu provided by the "salon" of the Verdurins, and so the story begins with a vivid sketch of "the little clan" created by these upstarts. (242–244) The Verdurins are wealthy bourgeois who, because they have been excluded by birth from fashionable, aristocratic society which they pretend to believe is populated entirely by "bores," have built up a social group of their own, which includes an unrecognized painter, a talented pianist, a scholar, a rising young professional man (the physician Doctor Cottard), a relative, Saniette, and the demimondaine Odette de Crécy. It is a salon created jointly by the gregariousness of the human animal and the presence of a great deal of money. The Verdurins, though from the point of view of money they belong to the same class as Swann does, have not managed to negotiate the steps of the social ladder as adroitly as he has done, and this failure has embittered them to the point where they refuse to admit the existence of the hierarchy which has rejected them. It is only Swann's adventurous sexual pursuits, in other words, which have brought him into such low company, and it is his higher aristocratic connections which eventually prove his undoing here.

After the description of the salon, there follows (245–246) an account of Swann's introduction to the Verdurins by Odette and after that (247–249) some observations on the character and social habits of Swann—his romantic enjoyment, for instance (247), of the feeling of social mobility. Like other storytellers (and dramatists too, as Aristotle pointed out) Proust has begun his tale "in the midst of things"—in the crowded, colorful, and vulgar drawing room of the Verdurins. And after making sure of catching our attention and interest, he returns to an earlier period (252) and notes how fateful it was that the mutual friend who introduced Odette to Swann had pretended that she was "harder of conquest than she actually was." This love was not born at first sight—Swann is very deliberate, indeed, in his approach, for the fact is that Odette seemed to him when he met her to be endowed "with a style of beauty which left him indifferent." (252) He falls into the habit of seeing her regularly, we judge, out of boredom or sheer spiritual inertia.

In the beginning, it is Odette who acts as the pursuer of Swann (253). She tells him that time drags when he does not see her (254), and he is compelled to make polite excuses to explain his absence of real eagerness. (The fact that Odette is the pursuer reverses the traditional role of her sex, but this may be explained by the fact that she is in a far less secure position in society than Swann. Some critics, no doubt, who insist on seeing in Proust's admitted homosexuality the key to all his literary creations—and not simply those which are frankly and explicitly concerned with sexual aberrations—may suppose that he has changed the sex of Odette here as they say he did later on in the affairs involving Gilberte and Albertine—changes which left some incongruities behind them—but it seems to me that it is not necessary to go so far as this and it is possible to see in the social disparity between Swann and Odette the satisfactory explanation for the reversal of the customary courtship roles played by men and women.)

Swann's excuse for not calling upon her more often at this stage is that he is engaged in writing an essay on the painter Vermeer which in reality he has long ago abandoned. (254) Odette incidentally shows herself to be so ignorant and lacking in culture (the Bohemian atmosphere at the Verdurins and their aesthetic affectations have evidently done little to improve her mind) as not to have heard of Vermeer and she inquires if he is still alive! (255) Swann is so easy and self-confident in his attitude that he is able to joke about the possibility of forming a hopeless passion for Odette, and Odette is so servile and submissive as to assure him her time is always at his disposal, that she is "always free if you want me." (255)

But even at this early stage, the dangerous possibility is mentioned (256) that from having a very limited place in the romantic dreams of Swann, an "accident" might precipitate Odette into occupying these dreams to the exclusion of all others, and in that case (since love is a subjective phenomenon) Odette's physical imperfections and her distasteful attributes might no longer have any importance to Swann. At this point, we return to the Verdurin salon where Swann has allowed himself to be taken and introduced by Odette. We see the "little clan" viewed through the tolerant eyes of Swann, who impresses his hosts with his remarkable social ease (260) which he has acquired in much more rarefied circles of society (a fact that he takes good care to keep well hidden from the Verdurins who should find it hard to forgive him for enjoying such privileges.) In these social scenes we glimpse not only the buffooneries of Doctor Cottard, of the painter (who is called M. Biche—Mr. Darling—but is revealed to us as the great artist Elstir in a subsequent volume), and of the hypocritical Verdurins themselves, but we become familiar with the characteristically sensitive accents of Swann himself. Swann's speech (263) is interspersed with expressions which he seems to place between quotation marks, almost as if he were reciting a text from the later Henry James. The intention appears to be, as in James, to sterilize the common language, which he is compelled to use, with the antisepsis of irony. This, as we are to recognize later on, is the characteristic manner of speech in the wittier circles of the Faubourg Saint Germain, particularly in that most fashionable of drawing rooms which Swann used to frequent, the Duchess of Guermantes'.

The social scenes serve as the background for the introduction of the Vinteuil Sonata (268 ff) and particularly of the "little phrase" within it (272) which is to be associated indissolubly with the love of Swann and Odette. The sonata is played one evening by the pianist of the Verdurin circle, and when Swann, upon whom the music had already made a great impression in the past without his being able to identify it by name, asks him about it he learns that the sonata has created a stir among avant-garde musicians though its fame has apparently not yet reached the general public. (275) Swann remembers having known a Vinteuil as a neighbor and country music master at Combray, but he refuses to associate so mediocre a person with the composer of such a glorious work. (275–276) Still, he considers the possibility that the man he has known may be a distant relative of the composer. Swann, in other words, has not yet learned the lesson that man as a social being and man as an immortal soul capable of divine aesthetic creation are incommensurable concepts. It is a lesson that Proust is never tired of repeating with what amounts almost to a self-conscious emphasis.

Proust is very patient and skillful in tracing the process by which Odette the pursuer (280–281) gradually relinquishes her active role to Swann, who succumbs to the insidious influence of habits of seeing her which he had thoughtlessly contracted. Slowly, it is *he* who begins to be uneasy at the possibility that at some time she may become satiated with his company. . . . Swann, however, is far as yet from being tied firmly to Odette at this time and is still carrying on an affair with a little working girl (281) whom he holds in his arms in the carriage which is taking him to a rendezvous with Odette at the Verdurins'.

Yet at the very moment that Swann thinks himself footloose and free with reference to Odette, the "little phrase" from Vinteuil's Sonata, which he hears so often now in her company at the Verdurins', is casting its spell, is in the process of becoming the "national anthem" of his relationship with Odette. (281–282)

The *habit* of seeing Odette every evening is inexorably walling him in; almost unwittingly he takes to treasuring certain keepsakes from her: a chrysanthemum which she "impulsively" plucks from her garden and which he locks in "a secret drawer of his desk." (283) It is as if he is blithely building a prison of associations all about himself without realizing that at a given moment the walls will be high enough and strong enough to make it difficult for him to escape. The remarkable feature of Proust's art is how he is able to follow the sequence of feelings step by step making each one seem inevitable and yet making it believable that his hero should not have known what was happening to him until it was too late to do anything about it.

Odette, when Swann meets her, lives amid luxurious appointments and commands the services of a footman. (284–285) These, we gather, must be the spoils of her former conquests. But it is not long before Swann is "lending" her money, the extraction of tribute from him being carried out with such address that it is long before Swann realizes that he is helping to support her and that she belongs to the general category of "the kept woman." Odette, an actress, is extremely self-conscious of the impression she makes at every moment, and her tastes run to the artificial even among flowers. Thus, she prefers to surround herself with chrysanthemums and orchids precisely because they look so *unnatural*, "being made, apparently, out of scraps of silk and satin." (285) She is full of affectations and superstitions. (286) Proust finds evidences of her character where few writers should think of looking for it—for instance, in "that florid handwriting, in which an affectation of British stiffness imposed an apparent discipline upon its shapeless characters, significant, perhaps, to less intimate eyes than his, of an untidiness of mind, a fragmentary education, a want of sincerity and decision." (287)

In these pages (287–288), Swann notes for the first time Odette's striking resemblance to a figure in a painting by one of his favorite masters—Botticelli. Swann, who has long had the habit of seeing the people about him in works of art which he has spent a lifetime in studying, is excited by his discovery that his friend Odette's face is very similar to that of Jethro's daughter in one of the frescoes by Botticelli. There follows one of the most important transmutations in Swann's feelings about her, since he is now able to rationalize and justify those feelings.

(289–290) He has no natural or native feeling, as we have seen, for Odette's style of feminine beauty; nevertheless, he is impressed by the fact that one of his favorite painters had found this style lovely enough to enshrine it in permanent form in his art. Proust's analysis of the affections is never better than in those passages where he traces the interaction (in an aesthete such as Charles Swann) between art and love. (290–291) Yet it may not be aesthetes only who are victimized in this fashion by their tastes; everyone is subject to the same process more or less, as La Rochefoucauld implies in one of his cynical maxims to the effect that many a man would never have fallen in love had he not read about it first.

Imperceptibly, Swann's bondage to his habit of seeing Odette nightly grows. (291–292) The accidental breaking of the habit lays bare the existence of his enslavement (like a fatal disease discovered in an advanced stage of development). The truth is evident to M. Verdurin in the stricken look that appears on Swann's face one evening when he comes to call for Odette too late and she has already left without him. Verdurin, with characteristic delicacy of expression, remarks to his wife after seeing the expression that appeared on Swann's face when he learned that he had missed his friend: "I think we may say that he's hooked." (293)

There follows (295–296) a description of Swann's feverish "hunt" for Odette through the streets and restaurants of Paris. How little men know of themselves until a crisis occurs. (295) For a moment, life becomes "more interesting" (296) to Swann as a result of the pain caused him by the unexpected absence of Odette. On p. 296, Proust gives us a remarkable analysis of the misery of the human situation in general, as he sees it—an analysis which, like Schopenhauer's philosophy (for which we know that Proust acquired an early taste), reduces life to a monotonous alternation between pain and boredom.

It is in this section of the story that Proust writes a memorable paragraph on the genesis of love in a state of anxiety; the particular anxiety is that of Swann, desperately searching for the absent Odette, but, as is so often the case in Proust, he rises to a more general point of view where his observations seem equally applicable to the experience of other men: "Among all the methods by which love is brought into being, among all the agents which disseminate that blessed bane, there are few so efficacious as the great gust of agitation which, now and then, sweeps over the human spirit. For then the creature in whose company we are seeking amusement at the moment, her lot is cast, her fate and ours decided, that is the creature whom we shall henceforward love. It is not necessary that she should have pleased us, up till then, any more, or even as much as others. All that is necessary is that our taste for her should become exclusive. And that condition is fulfilled as soon as—in the moment when she has failed to meet us—for the pleasure which we were on the point of enjoying in her charming company is abruptly substituted an anxious, torturing desire whose object is the creature herself, an irrational, an absurd desire, which the laws of civilized society make it impossible to satisfy and difficult to assuage—the insensate, agonizing desire to possess her." (298–299)

Just as Swann is ready to abandon his fruitless search for her, he suddenly comes face to face with Odette. (299) And then for the first time, in the carriage on the way to her house, the two lovers embrace and kiss. (300–302) The embrace is a result of an improvisation by Swann while leaning over Odette to pin a flower, a cattleya, which has been loosened on her bodice by an unexpected jolt of the carriage. The far-reaching consequences of this innocent action result in the creation of a new expression in the private language of the lovers—"to do a cattleya"—by which ever afterwards they designate the act of physical possession which for the first time occurs on this particular evening. (303) It is completely Proustian that the mention of this fact should be accompanied by a cynical aphorism which tells us that possession of women "even of the most divergent types . . . (becomes) an invariable and monotonous experience."

Such a sentiment prepares us for the disillusion to follow, because once the ice is broken, Swann's physical possession of Odette becomes a habitual experience. (304) The association of the "little phrase" from Vinteuil's Sonata with the love affair becomes ever closer, since Swann no longer has to rely on the pianist at the Verdurins' to play it for him—Odette now plays it (vilely) on the piano in her apartment. The effect of the music upon Swann is described as "anaesthetic." (307) Swann, a sybarite as well as an aesthete, makes Odette kiss him while playing the phrase on the piano. (308) As in the work of other philosophic naturalists, there is for Proust an intimate relation between the animal and the spiritual components of man—Swann enjoys kissing and biting Odette, he tells us, while dreaming of Botticelli's art.

Under the influence of his awakening sensual feelings towards Odette, Swann is resensitized to all sorts of other experiences of nature which had hitherto left him cold and indifferent. (309) But a less pleasant moral effect of his strong feelings is that he is able to deceive himself concerning the nature of Odette and to regard her quite unjustifiably as "good, simple, enthusiastic, idealistic." (310) As a by-product of the vital renewal brought to him by love, Swann is now able to return to his long-neglected composition of a critical essay on Vermeer. (310–311) Of course, Swann is continually being confronted with the fact of Odette's intellectual limitations, but he tampers with his own system of values and succeeds in minimizing the importance of her lacks to himself. (312–313) He also continues to associate Odette with the society of the Verdurins and convinces himself that their house provides a really "charming atmosphere." (320–321) Swann "unconsciously (allowed) gratitude and self-interest to filter into his intelligence and to influence his ideas." (322) Because Madame Verdurin has been able to play the role of go-between so adroitly, she appears to him to be "a great and noble soul." He is able to describe the Verdurins quite sincerely to one of his friends as "magnanimous creatures." Instead of being disgusted by the excesses and affectations of Madame Verdurin (of which Marcel has supplied the reader with numerous examples) Swann claims with a straight face that "she has a profound understanding of art." (322) Such is the strength of his instincts demanding rationalization, such is his moral weakness for which he will be called upon to pay dearly.

And yet even with this sacrifice of his integrity, Swann does not succeed in winning completely the confidence of the Verdurins, since they sense a kind of reserve about his attitude and cannot help learning from time to time that he is a part of a much more fashionable life than the one which they lead. One of the other guests at their evening parties, Forcheville (who is also a friend of Odette's), innocently refers in their presence to Swann's well-known friendships among the aristocracy. (334–335) Directly challenged in this manner, Madame Verdurin feels that she is called upon to assert her authority and with the attitude of a Grand Inquisitor stamping out a heresy (336) asks Swann to admit candidly to the assembled company that some of his famous friends in the Faubourg Saint Germain are really uncouth bores. However, Swann is too sensitive and proud and truthful a person to do what is so often done in the smart society depicted in Proust's pages—that is, to speak badly of people behind their backs at the same time that one is polite and even obsequious to them in their presence. Even though he realizes that he is hurting his own position, he refuses to give the Verdurins the satisfaction they desire by deriding his fashionable friends (as Forcheville who is an aristocrat by birth himself but of a much coarser fiber than Swann is only too willing to do). Thereupon, the Verdurins are really displeased with Swann, discuss him rudely after he has left (343), and we realize that his days as a welcome guest in their house are numbered. Soon, indeed, "disgrace threatens" him at the Verdurins (345), though he remains oblivious to the danger.

Meantime, he is getting ever more deeply involved with Odette. He is now supplying her with 5,000 francs a month (347) and yet he is described as being so unselfconscious of this that if people had said to him: "It's your money that attracts her," he would not have believed them. (346) He is completely disarmed by the expression he occasionally detects on Odette's face, which somehow reminds him of his mother. (347) At times, Swann still shows some realization that objectively speaking Odette is a rather mediocre woman, but since she seems to be fascinating and desirable to other men (like Forcheville, for example) he takes pride in her partiality for him. (351).

It is at this crucial point in the affair that Swann suffers his first attack of virulent jealousy (352–353). He suddenly thinks, without any "reason" whatever, one night after she has dismissed him a little earlier than usual with the plea that she is not well, that she is really intending to entertain another lover in his stead after he has left. So Swann laboriously makes his way back across the city of Paris to her street and is thunderstruck to find her windows brightly lighted up and to hear two voices behind her shutters! In a frenzy, he raps on the shutters to force her to open them and to reveal the identity of the man with whom she has been betraying him. But as the shutters are opened, he looks into a room which he has never before seen and into the faces of two strangers. He has simply mistaken the house next to Odette's for hers, because in his previous visits to the street he had associated the only light still burning with her house. What an absurd and ironical anti-climax! Surely it is one of the happier and more surprising strokes of Proust's inventive faculty, even if it bears some of the marks of first-hand experience. What it reveals about the state of Swann's mind and the depth of his commitment to his mistress is hardly humorous. What he has suffered psychologically is as serious in its way as a physical heart-attack, and it is just as unexpected in its onset. Pirandello once said that facts are like empty sacks; it takes a great many other facts around them to make them stand up. This attack of jealousy is a fact; it is made credible by the density of other facts with which Marcel has abundantly surrounded it in his narrative. In retrospect, it seems inevitable.

From now on, jealousy becomes the great theme of Proust's entire work. If readers who appreciate that work were asked what particular psychological phase of human experience he excels in rendering, I think that it would be his depiction of jealousy that many, perhaps most, of them would single out for praise. Jealousy is, to Proust, "the shadow of love" (357), and he is as much a master of shadow as a means of projecting light in his picture as Rembrandt is. There is no love, in his pages, which does not have its counterpart in jealousy; a love which cast no shadow should be for him, like a physical body which cast no shadow, unreal.

Though this fit of jealousy on Swann's part ends in reassurance, it is quickly followed by more palpable causes of uneasiness on his part. When he visits Odette at an unexpected hour one afternoon, he evidently disrupts other plans and arrangements which she is careful to keep secret from him. (359 ff) Alerted to a new and hitherto unsuspected aspect of Odette's personality—as a liar (360), Swann one day surprises an expression on her face which is identical with that which he had seen once when she was telling an untruth to Madame Verdurin to cover a clandestine arrangement with Swann himself. (268)

Swann now experiences one by one the terrors of the lover's hell. Though a man of scrupulous honor, he is prepared to stoop to anything, even spying, in order to learn the truth about Odette's activities. He manages to read (with great difficulty through the envelope which he holds against the light) a letter that Odette has entrusted him to mail to Forcheville. (365) Jealousy now grows morbid in him, courses wildly and uncontrollably through his mind, and fastens itself upon every man in the hotel at which he and Odette are staying. (367) Madame Verdurin chooses this weakest, most vulnerable of moments to break socially with Swann and to refuse to invite him to her evening parties where he could count on meeting regularly with Odette. (368–369) The cruel, treacherous blow immediately reverses Swann's attitude to the Verdurins; his previous insincerities and rationalizations on the subject are only too painfully evident to him now, and shame compounds the hurt which their perfidy has inflicted. (370 ff) Swann's hysterical ranting against the Verdurins sometimes reaches a pitch which reminds the reader of the insane hyperboles that mark the conversation of the Baron de Charlus in later volumes. (371–373) This is true, for example, when he chooses to express his disgust with the style of a certain form of architecture by referring to buildings as "petrified excretions." (379) But rage avails him nothing. After Madame Verdurin's stubborn ukase has gone out against him, poor Swann is expelled and completely forgotten by "the little clan."

As a result of the ironic reversal brought about by time, the Verdurin drawing room, which had served the purpose of bringing Swann and Odette closer together, becomes a barrier between them. (374–375) In the crisis Swann stands revealed as a man who unfortunately does not know himself. (375) Odette is not clever enough to follow in detail the fantastic intellectual ironies of his conversation with her (fantasies which make him sound more and more like Charlus), but she does grasp the central fact that he loves her and is mortally jealous of her. (376–377) Such an excess of passion in one of a pair of lovers, Proust points out, always has the effect of absolving the other from the obligation to love in return. (356–357) The seesaw has changed its position completely. In the beginning, it was Odette who acted as the pursuer; now it is Swann who is in complete and hopeless despair and Odette who is in flight from him. Ironically, too, it is at this moment that Marcel records some physical changes that have taken place in Odette, who has grown stouter. (378) But it hardly matters what happens to the objective Odette once the subjective image of Odette in Swann's mind has begun to grow steadily more obsessive.

The narrator injects himself into the story here by comparing Swann's anxieties and anguish with his own sufferings at Combray while waiting for his mother to come and kiss him goodnight. The comparison suggests not only the pattern of the Freudian analysis of the psyche, though it does suggest that inescapably, but the fact that the texture of all human life is perhaps simpler than we think it is and falls into a comparatively few underlying motives of deprivation, unhappiness, pain. Odette's whimsical and unpredictable kindnesses to Swann (386–387) only add to his uneasiness; yet he cannot help suspecting that a state of calm and peace between them instead of continual tension would make an unfavorable atmosphere for his romantic attachment to her: "When Odette ceased to be for him a creature always absent, regretted, imagined; when the feeling that he had for her was no longer the same mysterious disturbance that was wrought in him by the phrase from the sonata, but constant affection and gratitude, when those normal relations were established between them which would put an end to his melancholy madness, then, no doubt, the actions of Odette's daily life would appear to him as being of but little intrinsic interest. . . ." (388)

Jealousy in Swann becomes a chronic state in which relief is illusory. (389–390) Marcel patiently chronicles each thought which crosses Swann's mind with reference to Odette (291), each "swing of the pendulum" in his affection for her (292), each fluctuation and reversal of feeling (394–395), each tragicomic contretemps: "Sometimes several days had elapsed, during which she had caused him no fresh anxiety; and as, from the next few visits which he would pay her, he knew that he was likely to derive not any great pleasure, but, more probably, some annoyance which would put an end to the state of calm in which he found himself, he wrote to her that he was very busy, and would be unable to see her on any of the days that he had suggested. Meanwhile, a letter from her, crossing his, asked him to postpone one of these very meetings. He asked himself why; his suspicions, his grief again took hold of him. He could no longer abide, in the new state of agitation into which he found himself plunged, by the arrangements which he had made in his preceding state of comparative calm; he would run to find her, and would insist upon seeing her on each of the following days." (395–396)

Marcel compares the lover to a morphinomaniac or a consumptive (399) and indicates that Swann's malady has entered the incurable stage. Odette who, when she was pursuing Swann, had assured him that she was always free to see him, now that he is hopelessly tied to her, is never free. (403–404) Swann begins to hear more and more scandal about the past life of Odette. (405–407) He is, however, helpless to detach himself from her. The tables have been turned so completely in favor of Odette that she never bothers telling him until the last possible moment if he will be able to see her and then only when she is certain that there is not a more exciting engagement to which she can look forward. (407–408) When Odette is away from him, Swann is happy only when he knows that she is in the company of his friend Charlus (409); we are not to learn for some volumes of *Remembrance* that the reason for this is that Charlus is a homosexual whose tastes and temptations are not in conflict with those of the heterosexual Swann. Odette's actual presence is, to Swann, like a drug which brings him temporary relief though its effect in the long run is to aggravate his disease. (410) Finally, on page 411 we see a Swann reduced to complete hysteria, if not something worse. He cries inexplicably, feels cold for no ostensible reason, and wishes he were dead! If he wishes to live it is only in the hope of surviving to a time when he will no longer be in love with Odette. This page (411) is surely one of the most terrible in the whole of Proust; here we have the dreadful climax of the shattering affair with Odette as we see how credible it is that in some 150 pages Swann has been brought from a state of complete indifference to the nadir of despair where his mental anguish is so unbearable that he looks hopefully for signs on his body of some fatal physical disease which will remove him from a world that has become sheer torture to him!

Odette is described in this section of the story as filled with self-assurance in the presence of Swann where she had once felt only timidity. (414) He dares not look in drawers of his desk where he has put away the chrysanthemum and the other mementos of her love. (417) Pages 417–456, a lengthy description of a musical evening party at the house of one of Swann's less smart hostesses of the Faubourg Saint Germain, the Marquise de Saint Euverte, is in a sense a digression from the direct line of narrative concerning Swann's love for Odette. It helps to prepare the revelation that comes to him there during the playing of Vinteuil's Sonata as to the complete hopelessness of his position in relation to her. Hitherto, in spite of all his sufferings he had been sustained by the illusion that things might still change for the better; now he knows that she will never love him again. (457) That evening party at the Saint Euvertes' is one of the most remarkable examples of Proust's art—it is the first of a series of such scenes in the Faubourg Saint Germain in drawing rooms which progressively ascend the steps of the social hierarchy (Madame de Villeparisis, the Duchess of Guermantes, and the Princess of Guermantes). It deserves extended commentary and analysis of its own which should be out of place here since it would interrupt a chronicle of the development in the attachment of Swann to Odette. It must be said, however, that Proust's power of portraying a social scene of this sort is quite comparable to the power Tolstoy displays in rendering such gatherings as that at Anna Pavlovna Scherer's at the beginning of *War and Peace*. Proust is able to combine the liveliness of such a scene with a sense of strict order and control. It is a very difficult combination of qualities to sustain, and he does it with the expert skill and lack of strain of a juggler, who is able to keep a dozen balls in the air (characters and shifting scenes) without dropping one of them.

In the first stages of his love for Odette, Swann had taken up his work on the essay on Vermeer which he was writing, but later he apparently abandoned it again. Now, in the last stages of the affair, he takes it up once more in the hope of finding escape from his obsession. (457) Having already, as we have seen, wished himself dead, he goes on to wish Odette dead, too. (459) He thinks it remarkable that in her peregrinations about the city of Paris, she does not meet with some accident, and he feels a cordial sympathy for Mahomet II who stabbed one of his wives as soon as he found himself in love with her in order, according to his biographer, to regain his spiritual freedom.

Another milestone in the experience of Swann is reached with his receipt of an anonymous letter denouncing the immorality of Odette. (461) Certain details in the letter betray an intimate knowledge of Swann's life, and in thinking about which one of his friends could have been responsible for writing it Swann is shocked to find how little one really knows concerning the character and potentialities of even one's best friends. Swann oscillates (462–464), almost like a person suffering from a mental illness, between suspecting nobody and suspecting everybody. There are good reasons for thinking that none of the people he has trusted is capable of such wanton cruelty, and on second thought there are equally good or even better reasons for thinking that they are all capable of it. The anonymous letter mentions, among other transgressions of Odette, the Lesbian relationship she is supposed to have had with Madame Verdurin. At first, Swann dismisses the idea as inherently absurd, but later (466–468) he remembers a statement of Odette which seemed to point to the possibility of its truth.

He subjects Odette to a cross-examination (468 ff) which should more properly perhaps be called a "brainwashing" and at last he succeeds in extracting from her a half-hearted confession (470) which shocks him by going far beyond the worst suspicions he has ever entertained. Swann then realizes that it is "insane" (471) to desire to possess another person completely, as he has wished to do. A second "confession" by Odette (473) prompts Swann cynically to conclude that vice is far more common and widespread than the innocent and inexperienced suppose. (474) These confessions relate to Lesbianism, but another accusation in the anonymous letter is proved correct when Odette admits that she has been approached by procuresses. (478) Odette, in replying to Swann's searching questions, is compared by Marcel to "a headsman wielding an axe." (480) Perhaps he might with some justice have been compared to Oedipus for the relentless job of detective work he does which can only lead to his own destruction! His questions rob him of his fondest, dearest memories of the past by revealing the unsuspected double life that Odette had been leading at the very time she was making professions of the deepest affection to Swann. And she reduces Swann to a level where he can be accurately described by Marcel's adjectives: "craven, weak, spiritless . . . crushed." The whimsical favors and marks of affection which Odette chooses to bestow upon him are as cruel as her more frequent denials. Swann, at last, reaches the point of believing so strongly in her perversity, corruption and evil that he thinks her quite capable of hiding another lover in their room while they are making love in order visually to inflame his rival's ardor! (482)

In desperation and complete demoralization, Swann even takes to patronizing the brothels of Paris again (482–483), but, like other devices of distraction, this one too fails to work. The women there, after all, "did not know Odette" (483), and this is enough for Swann to lose interest in them quickly. But Odette herself comes to his rescue in this extremity by deciding to go away from Paris on a series of yachting voyages with the Verdurins (484), and she stays away for more than a year. What everything else which he had tried in an effort to achieve detachment from her had failed to accomplish, habit finally accomplishes. After a while, Swann finds that he experiences progressively less and less need of Odette. After raging for so long, the "disease" of his love is in the process of vanishing into nothingness. The *coda* of his love-affair sets in with the same quality of surprise and unexpectedness with which it had begun. Life in general in the pages of Proust as in those of other romantic writers is a realm of inexplicable mystery and wonder, and nothing in life is more wonderful and mysterious than the feeling of love, or so completely unaccountable. The detachment from Odette becomes complete as the result of an accidental meeting between Swann and Madame Cottard on a bus. (485–487) Madame Cottard, who had been along with the Verdurins on their yachting trips, assures the incredulous Swann that Odette really thinks so highly and continually of him that she never once stopped talking about him while they were away. Swann, who had naturally supposed that his name was never mentioned in the presence of the Verdurins, is astonished by this news, but Madame Cottard appears to him to be too simple-minded and sincere a woman and too circumstantial in her account for him to be able to doubt the truth of what she has said. An extended absence, the intervention of habit, and finally these kind words all serve to wean Swann away from his cruel need of Odette—a need which had cost him his peace of mind and very nearly his life itself. And thus, the greatest love of Swann's life and one of the greatest stories of love in literature draws to a close. The final knell of his passion is sounded in a strange dream that Swann has concerning Odette and the Verdurins. (490) In this dream he sees her objectively for the first time since he had fallen in love with her (that is to say, since he had succumbed to a subjective state in which the imagination predominates over reality). When he awakens from the dream, he is a changed man, and as he is being shaved that morning he says to himself wonderingly: "To think that I have wasted years of my life, that I have longed for death, that the greatest love that I have ever known has been for a woman who did not please me, who was not in my style!" (494) He can once again see Odette as she is in herself and not as she is transfigured by her resemblance to a Botticelli portrait. Swann's aesthetic pursuits have separated themselves from his emotional life, and the confusions to which he has been subjected by their conjunction are at an end.

A footnote to the affair, which becomes evident in later sections of *Remembrance* and was indeed implicit in the narrative from the very beginning, deserves to be mentioned. It is that Swann marries Odette long after he has ceased loving her in the romantic sense of the term. He marries her for reasons of expediency; he has had a child with Odette and since she is unscrupulous enough to use the child, Gilberte, as a weapon against her erstwhile lover, Swann undertakes to disarm her and to gain permanent possession of the daughter, whom he now loves more than the mother, by marrying Odette. Love and marriage, here and elsewhere in Proust's narrative, are entirely dissociated from each other.

PLACE-NAMES—THE NAME

This fifty-five-page section of *Swann's Way* is a transition to the next volume in the series (*Within A Budding Grove*) rather than a real end of a story. In line with its transitional intention, it has elements which point backward to the earlier section of the story and it has other elements which clearly point ahead to the story that is to follow. I am tempted, in fact, by a superficial comparison that might be made between this last "chapter" and the ending of Tolstoy's *War and Peace*, which also has a curious and inconclusive character, because it too was desirned to bridge the gap to a sequel which unfortunately was abandoned by its author, Tolstoy's abortive novel *The Decembrists*. Had that novel been written, the transitional nature of the historical speculation which now somewhat inappropriately concludes the epic tale of Napoleon's reverse in Russia in the winter of 1812 should be clear. But Proust's later volumes were not merely planned, they were actually executed and so it is possible to put each segment in its proper place in the scheme of his work.

At the beginning of this transition (495), the narrator returns to the theme of sleeplessness he described in the first pages of the book. Only now, instead of recalling Combray, as he did in the opening subdivision of the story (by way of prelude to the extensive portrayal of the life of that country town), Marcel mentions Balbec, the northern French beach resort noted for its displays of nature in the raw, great storms, and wild seacoast (496) which will serve as the setting for the greater part of the subsequent volume. But along with this most striking and sensational aspect of Balbec, as it had appealed to the imagination of his boyhood, Marcel recalls that he had also been intrigued by Swann's emphasis upon the artistic and architectural aspects of the old Norman town (497), its great church, painting, etc. So Swann weaves his way into this portion of the narrative, too, though its main part in the subsequent volume will not be concerned with him at all, nor even with his daughter Gilberte, but with Albertine and Saint-Loup. The familiar figure of Swann serves to tide the narrative over to the new and unfamiliar figures later on.

But the allusions in Proust and the interconnection of parts of his work are subtler and more indirect than this explicit reference to Swann and Balbec. For Swann is also present, at least by implication, in Marcel's recollection (498) of the fascination which railway timetables had for him as a boy when he dreamed of seeing for the first time Balbec, Venice, Florence—a fascination which will recall to every reader of Proust the anguished perusal of railway timetables by Swann himself at the very height of his tempestuous affair with Odette when his mistress temporarily absented herself in the country, away from him with the Verdurins. It was Marcel's parents' promise to him as a boy to let him travel in Italy (499) that first released his capacity for dreaming. And what a romantic capacity that proved to be. What magic resided in "mere" names for the young Marcel, names that became so much more gorgeous than reality to him that they "aggravated the disenchantment that was in store for me when I set out upon my travels." (500) The sorcery was, in large part, the result of his reading; his idea, for example, of *Parma* had been almost supernaturally transfigured for him after reading Stendhal's *Chartreuse*. (501) Marcel's imagination at that faraway time in his youth had performed feats comparable to those described by Rimbaud in his sonnet on the color of vowels: "Bayeux, so lofty in its coronet of rusty lace, whose highest point caught the light of old gold of its second syllable; Vitré, whose acute accent barred its ancient glass with wooden lozenges; gentle Lamballe, whose whiteness ranged from egg-shell yellow to a pearly grey; Coutances, a Norman Cathedral, which its final consonants, rich and yellowing, crowned with a tower of butter; Lannion with the rumble and buzz, in the silence of its village street, of the fly on the wheel of the coach; Questambert, Pontorson, ridiculously silly and simple, white feathers and yellow beaks strewn along the road to those well-watered and poetic spots; Benodet, a name scarcely moored that seemed to be striving to draw the river down into the temple of its seaweeds; Pont Aven, the snowy, rosy flight of the wing of a lightly poised coif, tremulously reflected in the greenish waters of a canal; Quimperlé, more firmly attached, this, and since the Middle Ages among the rivulets with which it babbled, threading their pearls upon a grey background, like the pattern made, through the cobwebs upon a window, by rays of sunlight changed into blunt points of tarnished silver. . . ." (502–503)

Reality, in fact, is a drab thing to Marcel without the embellishment of the imagination (504). And when illness interdicts the realization of the boy's dream of an Italian journey, he is left with the consolation only of a powerful imagination working upon names like Florence and Venice. (508) The doctor who treats him tells his parents that he must abstain from all undue excitement including that of going to the theater for the first time to see the famous actress Berma. Instead, Françoise, who has become part of the household of the narrator since the death of Aunt Léonie, is charged with taking him out to play on the Champs-Élysées. (508) It is there that he hears another name that is magical to him being called—that of Gilberte Swann. (509) He is invited to play in a game with her and her friends (510) and soon begins to experience all the anxieties of a lover with regard to her (511) that her father had once experienced with

Odette. He asks himself such questions as—will she or won't she come to play today, because of the weather, a party, her mother, etc.? He no longer recognizes any object in life "save not to let a single day pass without seeing Gilberte." (516) The parallels between her and her mother are innumerable—for example, just as Odette, in the early halcyon days of her affair with Swann, had pressed a chrysanthemum upon him as a token of her affection (a token which, later on, when she no longer loved him, seemed like an ironic mockery to him), so Gilberte gives an agate marble to Marcel which he cherishes. (520)

Such parallels may possibly suggest that Proust is writing a satire upon a romantic love—reducing it, in mock-epic style, to a kind of children's game. But the reader would be wrong who interpreted this to be Proust's intention. He seems interested rather in trying to say that the impulses which eventually flower into full-blown romantic love are constant in human life—from the mother's goodnight kiss, through the growing boy's attachment to a little girl friend, to the mature Swann's enslavement by an Odette. No one is either too old or too young to be made a fool of by love, but that is not because love itself is foolish. On the contrary, it is, along with art, one of the very few worthwhile and serious things in human life. This was the message that Swann had found embodied in Vinteuil's Sonata: "When it was the little phrase that spoke to him of the vanity of his sufferings, Swann found a sweetness in that very wisdom which, but a little while back, had seemed to him intolerable when he thought that he could read it on the faces of indifferent strangers, who would regard his love as a digression that was without importance. 'Twas because the little phrase, unlike them, whatever opinion it might hold on the short duration of these states of the soul, saw in them something not, as everyone else saw, less serious than the events of everyday life, but on the contrary, so far superior to everyday life as to be alone worthy of the trouble of experiencing it." (451)

Gilberte shows unmistakable signs of being as fickle as her mother. There are days on which she is kind to Marcel, other days when she is moody and seems sorry to see him. (522) Marcel, unlike his family at Combray with its "caste conception" of society, is impressed with the lofty social friends of Swann who occasionally accompanies his daughter to the Champs-Élysées. (524–525) Gilberte evidently leads a fashionable social life, where she is an intimate of the great novelist Bergotte and others whom the boy admires, far above the sphere open to Marcel. (527) Of course, there are some respects in which a boy's love will differ from that of an older, more experienced, more disillusioned man—for example, in the directness and naïveté of his wish fulfillments. Thus, Marcel romantically dreams that any day now he is destined to receive a letter from Gilberte in which she is going to confess that she loves him and has been concealing the fact from him. (528) Needless to say, there is nothing in reality to correspond with such a thought and the letter never comes. Marcel rationalizes his love for Gilberte when she makes him a gift of a precious book by her friend Bergotte, just as Swann had justified to himself his admiration for Odette by the resemblance he detected between her and a figure in Botticelli. (528–529) The name and every association of the name Swann grow obsessive in the thoughts and conversation of Marcel, because of his love for Gilberte. (533) He even sinks, with complete unselfconsciousness, to the absurdity of wishing he were as bald as Swann! (534) Madame Swann, too, naturally benefits from the enhancement of Marcel's imagination—he admires her as she walks each day in the fashionable Allée des Acacias of the Bois de Boulogne which "was thronged by the famous Beauties of the day." (538–539) It is perhaps interesting to note that Marcel discusses the "ephemeral" attractions of fashion as it is displayed in the Allée des Acacias in so rapt, so exalted a tone (presumably reflecting the lofty feelings of his boyhood on the subject) that, as if he were composing a poem, he rises on occasion to the level of using epic simile in the manner of Homer, Virgil, Dante: "As from a long way off, the sight of the jutting crag from which it dives into the pool thrills with joy the children who know that they are going to behold the seal, long before I reach the acacia-alley, their fragrance, scattered abroad, would make me feel that I was approaching the incomparable presence of a vegetable personality, strong and tender; then, as I drew near, the sight of their topmost branches, their lightly tossing foliage, in its easy grace, its coquettish outline, its delicate fabric, over which hundreds of flowers were laid, like winged and throbbing colonies of precious insects; and finally their name itself, feminine, indolent and seductive, made my heart beat, but with a social longing, like those waltzes which remind us only of the names of fair dancers, called aloud as they entered the ball-room." (539)

But illusion is separated only by a trifling interval from disillusion in the pages of Proust (as it is said that from the sublime to the ridiculous only a single step need be taken), and Marcel comes down to earth with a resounding thump when he learns accidentally that Gilberte's parents, M. and Mme. Swann whom he had idealized in his mind, "did not like my playing with her." (540) The abrupt deflation of illusion (Swann's disillusion at the end of the section *Swann In Love* is probably the best example) regularly signalizes the ending of a narrative movement in Proust and the beginning of a new movement. So it is here too. The love affair with Gilberte is, of course, far from having run its course, but it does not claim our attention again until the next volume. We return, in the coda of *Swann's Way*, to the present tense of the Overture—that is, to the time when the narrator, in middle age, is looking back upon his life and walks once more in autumn in the Allée des Acacias, trying to recapture the impressions made upon him there by the experiences of his lost youth. He calls to mind the dress and riding-carriage of Odette Swann as he used to see them many years ago during "the happy days when I was young and had faith." (547) The feeling in Proust's pages at this point seems akin to the mood evoked by Wordsworth in his great "Ode on Intimations of Immortality From Recollections of Early Childhood." The eyes of all men dim with age and lose the freshness of vision which imagination had once lent to them. Now, as Marcel the aging narrator looks around him, there are nothing but modern motor-cars and chauffeurs to be seen in that celebrated "Garden of Woman," the Allée des Acacias. Nowhere save in memory are the smart victorias, coachmen and grooms of his youth. Styles of dress have changed radically too—"hats . . . immense, covered with fruits and flowers and all manner of birds." The new women he sees before his eyes are all "just women, in whose elegance I had no belief, and whose clothes seemed to me unimportant." (548) Marcel, in short, has at this stage of his existence (before discovering his true artistic vocation, as he is to do in the volume

The Past Recaptured) grown as obtuse and unimaginative as Wordsworth's Peter Bell at the time when "a primrose by the river's brim/ A yellow primrose was to him/ And it was nothing more." His spontaneous boyhood poetry has forever departed from him and he is left a dull, prosaic man. So he is brought to reflect upon the central contention of all idealistic philosophies that the divine spark illuminating the world must originate in ourselves and cannot come to us from the outside. At the end of *Swann's Way* the narrator has become merely another nostalgic, sentimental, and ineffectual *laudator temporis acti*. His position here, in other words, is very different from what it is to be at the end of *Remembrance* as a whole, after he has gone through the experience of having a mystic vision which reveals to him the connection between art and eternity and his own function as an artist in rescuing the world he has known from the destructive action of time.

We should notice how adroitly Proust manages to weave his motives and themes into the texture of his narrative. Thus, on the page next to the last, Marcel is ruminating on the fact that "he should have liked to be able to pass the rest of the day with one of those women, over a cup of tea, in a little house with dark painted walls (as Madame Swann's were still in the year after that in which the first part of this story ends). . . ." (549–550) And though the cup of tea here is not that of Aunt Léonie nor the one in which the magical madeleine had, by being dipped, produced a complete revolution in his sensibility, nevertheless those other cups of tea are inevitably recalled to our minds by this one.

The closing sentences in *Swann's Way* are marked by a pathos which clutches at our hearts—not quite as sustained or deep in quality as that of the coda of *Remembrance* as a whole yet nevertheless profoundly moving: "The places that we have known belong no*t* (all English editions that I have seen misprint this word as no*w*) only to the little world of space on which we map them for our own convenience. None of them was ever more than a thin slice, held between contiguous impressions that composed our life at that time; remembrance of a particular form is but regret for a particular moment, and houses, roads, avenues are as fugitive, alas, as the years." (551)

Here, then, is the impressive portal leading into the world of *Remembrance of Things Past*. It contains enough reminders of its author's architectural abilities and the quality of his sensibility to reassure the receptive reader concerning the genius which informs his masterwork in its entirety.

3. Within A Budding Grove

Within a Budding Grove TAKES PLACE IN PARIS AND IN BALBEC.
THE FIRST VOLUME OF THIS SECTION IS DEVOTED CHIEFLY TO PARIS,
the second volume wholly to events at the beach resort of Balbec.
Two youthful love affairs of the narrator Marcel are delineated—
the earlier one with Gilberte Swann in Paris, the later one with
Albertine Simonet beside the sea on the Channel coast. The first
affair is completed in this section, and though Gilberte continues
to be a character in later volumes, Marcel's passion for her is
ended here. The second affair with Albertine, however, is only
begun in this part of *Remembrance* and is not concluded till
many volumes later; it is the single most important affair in the
whole work. But the feeling which arises from the pages of
Within a Budding Grove is a mixture of disillusion and disappointment. This results not only from the amorous experiences
described but from many of the incidental ones. Marcel looks
forward to his first visit to the theater and to his first glimpse of
the great tragedienne Berma, but he is bitterly disappointed with
both. He looks forward to his meeting with the great novelist
Bergotte whose books he has admired so much, and the appearance of the writer proves commonplace and undistinguished. He
looks forward to a glimpse of the Gothic Church at Balbec which
is supposed to have a "Persian" appearance, and it turns out to be
something far beneath his expectations. *Within A Budding
Grove* is also the section in which Marcel is introduced for the
first time to the experience of a brothel by his friend Bloch and
meets there a little actress named Rachel who is destined to
occupy a large place not in his own life but in the life of one of
his best friends.

The opening section is largely concerned with a dinner given
by the narrator's family for M. de Norpois, an associate of

Marcel's father in the public service. M. de Norpois, an extremely wealthy aristocrat who has made a career of diplomacy, affects the narrator in a number of ways, and to understand his influence we have to know something about him. Norpois is a man who has served with distinction under the Second Empire before being called back into service by the Third Republic, and we are told "that Bismarck rated his intelligence most highly." His temperament is described as "negative, methodical, conservative" and in one comprehensive word: "governmental." His speech— a caricature of the impassive, poker-faced, fence-sitting, double-dealing, non-committal, high-sounding, "correct" gobbledy-gook traditionally associated with official diplomacy—is admirably parodied by Marcel. The author's facility of mimicry of various types of people seems inexhaustible. Norpois is made to talk in the monotone of a dull parliamentary journal on foreign affairs, and in spite of his shrewdness, keen observation and ability (within limits) to report accurately what he has seen, the truth transpires at every moment that he exaggerates his own importance as well as that of the role he plays in life, and that he is in the last analysis only a "stuffed shirt."

But it is this very quality, granted the impressive reputation he enjoys, which enables him to do the narrator one good turn and more than one ill-turn. For by virtue of the fact that Norpois impresses the boy's parents (their own stuffiness and especially that of the father is argued by their being taken in by such a stuffed shirt), he convinces them to allow him to go to the theater for the first time to see the actress of whom he has dreamed so much, Berma. (His disillusion as a result of this experience is beside the point here; it is certainly better, according to Marcel, to experience something and be disillusioned with it than never to have experienced it at all.) Norpois, the experienced man of the world, convinces the parents that seeing Berma is "an experience" which a young man ought to have. The strait-laced repressiveness of the household is evident from such a restriction against the theater as is assumed here. Perhaps because Marcel has formed excessive expectations in advance, perhaps because the experience has been delayed too long, perhaps because there is something about the Proustian temperament which inclines him to disillusionment in life, the impression he carries away from his first encounter with the stage is rather of the enthusiasm, and somewhat brutish ill manners, of the audience than of the art of the great actress he had come to see.

But Norpois has another and more destructive effect upon the self-confidence of Marcel, for although abstractly and in principle approving the choice of a literary career for a young man (as a way of entering diplomacy indirectly—for it is diplomacy that is the narrator's father's choice of a career for his son) Norpois is contemptuous of an example of his writing that Marcel is encouraged to show him and is even more contemptuous of the older writer Bergotte, who has touched Marcel's feelings intimately and represents the ideal upon which he has modeled himself.

Norpois gives the great world's first judgment upon the talent of the narrator and his taste; it is of some moment therefore that the judgment is negative. Even many years afterwards, as he recalls this first rebuff, it rankles in his soul and his comment on the mutual incomprehension that must always exist between men like himself and men like Norpois is bitter indeed: "He belonged to the class of men who, had we come to discuss the books I liked, would have said: 'So you understand that, do you? I must confess that I do not understand, I am not initiated,' but I could have matched his attitude, for I did not grasp the wit or folly, the eloquence or pomposity which he found in a statement or a speech, and the absence of any perceptible reason for one's being badly and the other's well expressed made that sort of literature seem more mysterious, more obscure to me than any other. I could distinguish only that to repeat what everybody else was thinking was, in politics, the mark not of an inferior but of a superior mind." (I, 41)

The portrait of M. de Norpois, etched in acid, is, like so many of the portraits in Proust, masterly in its caricature. The commonplaceness of Norpois's mind is caught in a series of quotations (I, 45–46) which are the climactic points of his utterance: " 'In the words of a fine Arab proverb, *The dogs may bark; the caravan goes on!*' After launching this quotation M. de Norpois paused and examined our faces, to see what effect it had had upon us. Its effect was great, the proverb being familiar to us already. It had taken the place, that year, among people who 'really counted' of 'He who sows the wind shall reap the whirlwind' which was sorely in need of a rest, not having the perennial freshness of 'Working for the King of Prussia.' " Norpois's idea of literature is communicated by his admiration for a man (who enjoys excellent social connections) who has published a book "dealing with the Sense of the Infinite on the Western Shore of Victoria Nyanza" and has followed that sensational production with a little book "on the Repeating Rifle in the Bulgarian Army; and these have put him in a class by himself."

One of the author's characteristic narrative habits is conspicuously in evidence during the account of the Norpois dinner, and that is his tendency to interrupt the main line of his narrative at any given point with digressions of such length that it is difficult to decide, on a first reading, exactly what the main line of the narrative is intended to be. The inordinately long interruption of the Norpois narrative has to do with the new and rather vulgar climbing personality which Swann has developed since his marriage to Odette has compelled him to begin his career of social conquest over again from the beginning, this time not in his own behalf but in behalf of his wife who is completely excluded from fashionable society.

Norpois's reason for rejecting the writings of Bergotte and also those of Bergotte's youthful disciple Marcel is that these writings are inspired by the idea of Art for Art's sake and that "at this period of history there are tasks more urgent than the manipulation of words in a harmonious manner." Norpois, then, is the spokesman here for a vulgarly moralistic, Philistine, naturalistic, socially responsible viewpoint concerning literature, which the whole of *Remembrance* is implicitly opposed to and which is explicitly condemned in the last volume of it, *The Past Recaptured*. Truth, for Proust, is as much the function of style (which is to the writer, he says, what color is to the painter, the product of a particular vision of the world), turn of phrase, manner, as it is of subject matter.

The Norpois episode is intricately woven in and connected with two episodes which follow: the resumption of Marcel's affair with Gilberte Swann (and his introduction into the Swann household) and his long expected meeting with Bergotte. Norpois, who is acquainted with the Swanns, hearing of the narrator's admiration for Madame Swann, gallantly offers to mention it to her on his next visit. The immoderate gratitude of the boy for this offer has the effect of making Norpois change his mind about carrying it out. What Norpois fails to do, however, is done by Doctor Cottard, who, acting under the mistaken impression that the Swanns already know and appreciate the young man, mentions him favorably on one of his visits and thus becomes, quite accidentally and unintentionally, the cause of bringing them together. The feeling conveyed by this unexpected juxtaposition is one of wonder at the variety, the inventive genius of life itself, its surprising, unpredictable developments which make all attempts to control it or even, in many cases, to understand it, futile. In matters of love especially (and it is because of his love for Gilberte that the narrator seeks an introduction to the Swanns) occurrences "appear to be governed by magic rather than by rational laws." (I, 102) It is one of the paradoxes of the romanticism of Proust that, though a great master of intellectual analysis, he is as sceptical of the ultimate value of analysis as Wordsworth himself!

The meeting with Bergotte is also connected in more than one way with this dinner for Norpois. There is, first of all, the contrast provided by their mutual contempt. Bergotte remarks of Norpois that "he has to keep his mouth shut half the time so as not to use up all the stock of inanities that hold his shirt-front down and his white waistcoat up." (I, 192) Then there is the comic contrasting effect which the different opinions of Norpois and Bergotte concerning the intelligence of their son have upon the parents of the narrator. These respectable people are predisposed in favor of Norpois; the somewhat Bohemian Bergotte stands for nearly everything that inspires them with an unaffected scorn. But when they learn that Bergotte has expressed a good opinion of their son whose talents Norpois has obviously slighted, their parental pride quickly effects an overturn in their opinion of Bergotte and they find much to admire in his talent, his intelligence, and his perspicacity.

As is often the case in *Remembrance*, some of the most interesting passages in *Within a Budding Grove* have to do with art itself. The peg upon which the reflections are hung is the reappearance in the narrative of The Vinteuil Sonata, which is played by Madame Swann for Marcel as she had once played it for her husband Charles. His subject in the following passage is the slow growth in the appreciation of difficult, unfamiliar works which seem for a long time to resist the audience: "The reason for which a work of genius is not easily admired from the first is that the man who has created it is extraordinary, that few other men resemble him. It was Beethoven's Quartets themselves (the Twelfth, Thirteenth, Fourteenth, and Fifteenth) that devoted half a century to forming, fashioning, and enlarging a public for Beethoven's Quartets, marking in this way, like every great work of art, an advance if not in artistic merit at least in intellectual society, largely composed of what was not to be found when the work first appeared, that is to say of persons capable of enjoying it." (I, 146–147) And he concludes the passage with a sentence which brings to my mind one of T. S. Eliot's. Marcel's sentence reads: "What artists call posterity is the posterity of the work of art." Similarly, in one of Eliot's early and most celebrated essays he tells us that "Some one said: 'The dead writers are remote from us because we *know* so much more than they did.' Precisely, and they are that which we know."

Concerning the work of Bergotte, Marcel remarks: "Genius, and even what is only great talent, spring less from seeds of intellect and social refinement superior to those of other people than from the faculty of transposing, and so transforming them. To heat a liquid over an electric lamp one requires to have not the strongest lamp possible, but one of which the current can cease to illuminate, can be diverted so as instead of light to give heat. To mount the skies it is not necessary to have the most powerful of motors, one must have a motor which, instead of continuing to run along the earth's surface, intersects with a vertical line the horizontal which it began by following, is capable of converting its speed into ascending force. Similarly the men who produce works of genius are not those who live in the most delicate atmosphere, whose conversation is most brilliant or their culture broadest, but those who have had the power, ceasing in a moment to live only for themselves, to make use of their personality as of a mirror, in such a way that their life, however unimportant it may be socially, and even, in a sense, intellectually speaking, is reflected by a genius consisting in the reflective power of the writer and not in the intrinsic quality of the scene reflected. The day on which young Bergotte succeeded in showing to the world of his readers the tasteless household in which he had passed his childhood, and the not very amusing conversations between himself and his brothers, on that day he climbed far above the friends of his family, more intellectual and more distinguished than himself; they in their fine Rolls Royces might return home expressing due contempt for the vulgarity of the Bergottes, but he, with his modest engine which had at last left the ground, he soared above their heads." (I, 181)

This idea that the special accomplishment, talent, genius of a person has little or no connection with his general culture is repeated by Proust a number of times, notably in connection with Doctor Cottard whose endowment for diagnosis is extraordinary though his social personality is unendurable and his general intelligence undistinguished. The real worth of a person is the result not of cultivation or indiscriminate curiosity or social "advantages," but of a quite peculiar, perhaps necessarily narrow gift, and this gift is not easy to recognize. Doctor Cottard's orders are disobeyed by the narrator's family when it has not yet recognized the infallibility of his intuition, which took account of symptoms too subtle to be noticed by the eye of most doctors.

But the really central subject of the first volume of *Within a Budding Grove* is the continuation of Marcel's boyhood affair with Gilberte. This is the second of the great quintet of love affairs (Swann-Odette, Marcel-Gilberte, Marcel-Albertine, Saint Loup-Rachel, Charlus-Morel) developed in *Remembrance*, which are all variations on a single theme. This theme—whatever the age of those in love and whatever the conventionality or unconventionality of their loves—is concerned with the hopelessness, the unavoidable unhappiness in which they are all involved. This unhappiness grows out of the natural recalcitrance of the human will, which makes it impossible for two human beings to understand completely or be in harmony with each other over any extended period of time.

At the beginning of this part of the story, Marcel had despaired of ever being invited to Gilberte's home, but at last, in consequence not of his conscious manipulations but of the chance intervention of Cottard, an invitation from the Swanns arrives. For a time, it brings him into close, almost continual contact with her and her family, so that Madame Swann is able to speak of Marcel as her daughter's greatest "chum." But then new causes of estrangement between them arise (the principal one appears to be the boredom of Gilberte and her craving for novelty), and ironically Marcel retains the privilege of visiting her home and conversing with her mother but is forced to do so only when Gilberte is absent. Marcel begins a series of complicated intellectual and psychological maneuvers (feigning indifference, writing letters he knows to be false) designed to reawaken the interest of Gilberte in himself. But these attempts to influence the heart and will by means of clever and cold intellectual suggestion are doomed in advance. No great things in love or in art can be achieved by the head alone, according to Proust. Repeatedly in his accounts of love—it is possibly the most characteristic note struck in these accounts—he shows us a man of great ingenuity, sensitivity, and subtle finesse completely helpless before the blank, stupid, irrational resistance raised against him by one who seems in every way inferior but is irresistibly strong with a feeling of distaste for him.

After staying away from Gilberte wilfully for a long period, Marcel succumbs to the temptation of trying to see her again. He sells a valuable heirloom in order to have the money to gratify all her wishes. (Marcel quotes with approval La Bruyère's observation that "It is a mistake to fall in love without an ample fortune." This is a mistake Proust's characters never make, though their possession of ample financial fortunes does not succeed in rescuing them from the general human lot of suffering.) By an odd and fateful coincidence, Marcel, on his way to effect a reconciliation with Gilberte, catches a glimpse of her leaving her house in the opposite direction in the company of what he takes to be a young man (though volumes later, it is revealed that it was a girl who had accompanied Gilberte). Crushed anew by his jealousy, Marcel is as yet young enough and strong enough to adhere to a new resolve not to attempt to see his beloved again, and the habit of not seeing her (which is almost more than he can bear at the beginning) eventually results in detaching him from her. The subtlety of the analysis of the succession of slow stages in such a process of oblivion confirms once more the observation made by Joseph Conrad, who wrote of *Remembrance:* "I don't think there ever has been in the whole of literature such an example of the power of analysis, and I feel pretty safe in saying that there will never be another." (*Marcel Proust —An English Tribute*, London 1923)

Two years later, having arrived "at a state of almost complete indifference to Gilberte," Marcel goes with his grandmother to the seashore resort of Balbec. Here, a new set of surroundings and habits give the final blow to the remaining traces of his first love. He feels as if he has recovered from a serious illness: "My journey to Balbec was like the first outing of a convalescent who needed only that to convince him that he was cured." (I, 309)

This trip has other tortures in store for him, however. For one thing, it is his first prolonged separation from his mother. And Balbec Church, which he had looked forward to seeing with so much anticipation, is almost as great a disappointment as the actress Berma had proved to be. On the other hand, the unanticipated Grand Hotel of Balbec, in spite of the torture it involves for Marcel to adjust himself to its novel physical surroundings, proves to be very interesting. The manager of the Hotel, "a sort of nodding mandarin," is a distinct Character, a kind of male Mrs. Malaprop in his abuse of language, and Aimé, the headwaiter, the boy who operates the elevator in the Hotel, and the other guests are all hardly less eccentric.

These guests include "a chief magistrate from Caen, a leader of the Cherbourg bar, a solicitor from Le Mans" and, in addition to these provincial worthies, at least one man who is a genuine curiosity, who has the servants call him His Majesty "and had indeed proclaimed himself King of a small island in the South Seas, inhabited by a few savages." (I 356–357) The narrator's interest is aroused also by a country gentleman and his daughter, M. and Mlle. de Stermaria, the representatives "of an obscure but very ancient Breton family." (361) Among the visitors to the Hotel, he recognizes a nobleman of the district, the son-in-law of his family's snobbish neighbor Legrandin in Combray, the Marquis de Cambremer. But the most important of the guests is Madame de Villeparisis, who had once gone to school with Marcel's grandmother. After some mysterious hesitation on his grandmother's part, the acquaintance is renewed and it gives the other guests a much higher idea of Marcel's social status than they have hitherto had. Madame de Villeparisis, who is the mistress of M. de Norpois (though this bit of scandal is as yet unknown to the narrator) becomes the instrument of introducing him into a much more elevated social sphere than the one we have seen him move in thus far. She introduces him and his grandmother to the Princesse de Luxembourg (his first "Royalty") who treats them with a condescension such as she might have displayed to animals in the zoo, and then later on to two of her own relatives who are to play important roles in his life: the Marquis de Saint-Loup and the Baron de Charlus, a most mysterious character whom Marcel had already encountered in a railway station where he had taken him to be, because of his eccentric behavior, either a thief or a lunatic! The first extended sketch of Charlus's character—that is to say the most important character, along with Swann and Marcel, in the whole of *Remembrance*—appears at this point in the narrative (at the opening of the second volume of *Within a Budding Grove*).

With a new character like Saint-Loup, Marcel follows a plan which is outlined in a passage from this volume: "Thus it can be only after one has recognized, not without having to feel one's way, the optical illusions of one's first impression that one can arrive at an exact knowledge of another person, supposing such knowledge to be ever possible. But it is not, for while our original impression of him undergoes correction, the person himself, not being an inanimate object, changes in himself; we think that we have caught him, he moves, and when we imagine that at last we are seeing him clearly, it is only the old impressions which we had already formed of him that we have succeeded in making clearer, when they no longer represent him." (II, 242)

The world, as Proust conceived it, is in as complete a state of flux as ever it was for philosophers like Heraclitus or Bergson. Saint-Loup at first seems glacially aloof and distant to Marcel, who has looked forward to meeting him. But this is soon revealed as merely a false appearance. Underneath the forbidding aristocratic manner, which he had inherited from his mother, is a warm-hearted, enthusiastic young man who is extremely interested in the thought of Nietzsche and of Proudhon and asks for nothing better than pure intellectual pleasures. No one is less snobbish than he—his social position is too secure for him to give it a thought. Snobbery is likely to be characteristic of the Verdurins and of Legrandin—that is to say, the insecure, social climbers of the world.

The same "optical illusion . . . of first impressions" is even more evident in the narrator's meetings with Charlus, whose furtive looks, abrupt reversals of mood, and general strangeness present a problem both to Marcel and the reader, for which there is no trace of a plausible solution until the beginning of *Cities of the Plain*, some volumes later on. The narrator also meets his old Combray friend Bloch at Balbec, and the latter is now shown as part of a close-knit and far from cultivated or sympathetic Jewish family. Marcel and his new friend Saint-Loup dine at the Blochs' and from that encounter a satiric picture of the menage emerges—Bloch's sisters who tastelessly ape his affected, Homeric manner of speaking, his father who is in no way superior but whom the son idolizes, and his uncle, M. Nissim Bernard, a habitual liar whom no one in the family takes seriously.

Some indications appear early of the extent to which Saint-Loup is being made to suffer by some little actress who exploits him without respecting him. The identity of this mistress is not revealed here, and later on it is to be one of the stunning surprises of the story to Marcel. The young nobleman makes every effort to be agreeable to both Marcel and his grandmother. He proposes on one occasion to take photographs of the grandmother, who welcomes the idea and takes a lot of trouble preparing to pose for the picture. Her attitude annoys the narrator who is not used to seeing her give way to the promptings of vanity, which is the motive he reads into her action. It is only much later that he realizes that his grandmother was already seriously ill at this time, having suffered the first signs (which she kept carefully hidden from him) of the malady that would soon destroy her. Her real reason for wanting to be photographed while still looking well was that she wished to leave the picture as a memento to Marcel. The incident is another example of the insistence throughout *Remembrance* on the insuperable difficulty of getting to know even those people who are closest to us. When Marcel realizes the truth about this situation much later on, it is too late; his grandmother has long been dead. The meaning of many such incidents is summed up by the narrator in a subsequent volume when he writes: "Man is the creature that cannot come forth from himself, who knows others only in himself, and who, if he asserts the contrary, lies." The ex-

treme subjective idealism of this view, as I have remarked elsewhere in this book, trembles on the edge of solipsism.

Last Part of *Within a Budding Grove* (vol 2, pp. 121–356)

SEASCAPE, WITH FRIEZE OF GIRLS

This last part of the volumes of *Within a Budding Grove* is
concerned for the most part with Marcel's late-adolescent love
for Albertine, which balances his boyhood love for Gilberte at
the beginning of this section. Albertine Simonet, like Gilberte
Swann, is part of a group, and in courting her the narrator becomes involved necessarily with the girls around Albertine, this
"little band" to which she belongs. It is a much more distinctive
group than the one that surrounded Gilberte and is indeed almost comparable to the "little clan" at the Verdurins' which had
supplied the setting for Swann's love for Odette.

Marcel is passing through a period of youth in which, to use
his own words, one sees beauty everywhere. (121) Proust never
allows us to forget that, as the German idealistic philosophers
put it, "there is no object without a subject." Desire projects
the attractive aura around certain images of the external world,
which the superficial, the materialistically-minded, and those
whose imaginations are poverty-stricken assume has an existence
in itself. In fact, one of the principal functions of the narrative
here and the source of its dramatic interest is Marcel's exposure
of the illusions surrounding his initial glimpse of Albertine and
her friends.

The "little band," as it first appears to him, consists of five or
six young girls "like a flight of gulls which performed with
measured steps upon the sand." (122) One is pushing a bicycle;
two are carrying golf clubs. (123) These girls seem to enjoy
"mastery over their limbs which comes from perfect bodily condition and a sincere contempt for the rest of humanity." (123)
They are "exuberant with youth" or rather, to put it precisely
as he does: "They could not set eyes on an obstacle without
amusing themselves by crossing it, either in a running jump or
with both feet together, because they were filled to the brim,
exuberant with that youth which we need so urgently to spend
that even when we are unhappy or unwell, obedient rather to

the necessities of our age than to the mood of the day, we can never pass anything that can be jumped over or slid down without indulging ourselves conscientiously, interrupting, interspersing our slow progress—as Chopin his most melancholy phrase—with graceful deviations in which caprice is blended with virtuosity." (126)

One of them in particular seems more ruthless and daring than the others as she leaps over a terrified old man on the beach, brushing his yachting cap with "her nimble feet," while another girl comments "with more sarcasm than sympathy": "Oh, the poor old man; he makes me sick; he looks half dead." (127) No wonder that their nature, as he is first able to surmise it by watching their actions from afar, seems to Marcel to be "bold, frivolous, and hard." (125) They appear to be repelled by "shyness, awkwardness, constraint" and attracted to all that is characterized by "grace, suppleness, and physical neatness." In fact, they strike the observer as pagan deities, miraculously restored to life: "noble and calm models of human beauty . . . like statues exposed to sunlight upon a Grecian shore." (125)

Coming down to earth again from such high-flown, far-fetched fancies, Marcel locates them more realistically in his imagination as being in all probability "the very juvenile mistresses of professional bicyclists." (128) And he adds: "In none of my suppositions was there any possibility of their being virtuous." It is a flimsy screen of facts indeed upon which the young man's fantasy begins to play. Marcel imagines them to be healthy perhaps because he is lacking in health himself; he fancies them to be bold and anarchically free because these qualities are complementary to his own very strict, Puritanical upbringing: "My grandmother had always watched over me with a delicacy too timorous for me not to believe that the sum total of the things one ought not to do was indivisible or that girls who were lacking in respect for their elders would suddenly be stopped short by scruples when there were pleasures at stake more tempting than that of jumping over an octogenarian." (128–129)

It is clear that he is attracted to the "little band" first of all because he presumes them to be in important respects the opposite of himself. Aesthetically even more than sensually, he feels himself drawn towards "these young flowers . . . like a bower of Pennsylvania roses adorning a garden on the brink of a cliff."

(135–136) Adding to their attractions is Marcel's conviction that it will be difficult, perhaps impossible, for him to make their acquaintance. He is aware of no possible bridge to bring him to them, and the sight of their buoyancy, health, self-sufficiency more than half convinces him that they should be contemptuous of him if they did get to know him. One of the most potent ingredients in the early stages of love, according to Marcel, is "the risk of an impossibility." (182) Prostitutes, whose predictable reactions could be provoked by paying for them with money, were without effect on his romantic imagination precisely because of the absence of uncertainty. "There must be, between us and the fish which, if we saw it for the first time cooked and served on a table, would not appear worth the endless trouble, craft and stratagem that are necessary if we are to catch it, interposed, during our afternoons with the rod, the ripple to whose surface come wavering, without our quite knowing what we intend to do with them, the burnished gleam of flesh, the indefiniteness of a form, in the fluidity of a transparent and flowing azure." (133) In the beginning, Marcel's desire has hardly differentiated among the members of the group. It is the group itself that attracts him: "I was in love with none of them, loving them all." (183)

The line of narrative involving Marcel and the girls is interrupted temporarily to make room for another significant episode and experience of Marcel's youth—getting drunk for the first time. This happens in a smart restaurant at neighboring Rivebelle where he is taken to dine by his friend Saint-Loup. He vividly describes that intensity of living dangerously in the present moment alone, without regard to the past or the future, which distinguishes a state of intoxication. (159–160) All prudence is lost sight of in such moments; sobriety had assured him that "it is not the activity of the present moment but wise reflections from the past that help us to safeguard the future." (158) Yet drunkenness, though mad, has some undeniable attractions—especially for youth. The concentration upon the fleeting moment is the very essence of poetry and romance. Escape from the burdens of responsibility is just what is being sought. Everything that Marcel is searching for by immersing himself in the contemplation of beauty—whether in the form of flowering young girls or of art—seems to be his for the asking while he is drunk.

But the excursion to Rivebelle with Saint-Loup has another purpose in the story which makes it truly functional rather than merely digressive. For it is while dining at Rivebelle one night that the two young men meet the famous painter Elstir, about whom Marcel has heard from Swann. (173) It is disillusioning to Marcel to learn that Elstir is the silly painter who had been nicknamed M. Biche in the Verdurin circle in the days of Swann's affair with Odette. But since that frivolous social phase of his existence, Elstir has retired from the "world" into "an isolation with a savagery which fashionable people called pose and ill-breeding, public authorities a recalcitrant spirit, his neighbors madness, his family selfishness and pride." (176–177) In this state of solitude, he practices his art more profoundly and seriously than he was ever able to do while his thoughts were preoccupied with society, and his fame has recently been rising among connoisseurs of painting both at home and abroad. Surprisingly, Marcel and Saint-Loup find Elstir receptive to their request to be allowed to join him, but that is because to him they are not members of society primarily but disinterested lovers of art. That they are young recommends them too so far as the artist is concerned, for "Elstir loved to give, to give himself. Everything that he possessed, ideas, work, and the rest which he counted for far less, he would have given gladly to anyone who could understand him." (176)

He invites them to come to his studio but so obsessive has Marcel's concern with the "little band" of girls become that he takes a long time in acting upon the invitation and finally goes reluctantly only because his grandmother urges him to do so. There, however, a pleasant surprise awaits him, for as he looks out of the studio window he sees the bicyclist of the little band and learns from Elstir, who knows the whole group well, that her name is Albertine Simonet and that they are the daughters of "a set of respectable people, extremely rich and belonging to the world of industry and business." (199) What a comedown this is from his romantic dreams concerning their dissolute disreputableness. They belong to that bourgeois segment of society to which he himself belongs and which holds much less attraction for him than "the mystery of the lower orders" or that of an aristocratic society "such as the Guermantes frequented." (200) The "disillusion" is so startling that it almost makes him lose interest in them completely: "And no doubt if an inherent quality, a rank which they could never forfeit had not been conferred on them, in my dazzled eyes, by the glaring vacuity of the seaside life all around them, I should perhaps not have succeeded in resisting and overcoming the idea that they were the daughters of prosperous merchants." (200)

Elstir is now important to Marcel solely as a possible intermediary to introduce him to the girls. (204) But feeling that this introduction is sooner or later inevitable has the effect of making him lose much of his interest when it had seemed to him unattainable. (215) This last passage is particularly good in its subtle analysis of the rhythms of human desire—its ebb when a sought-after object is reached and its passionate flow in the direction of all that escapes one's grasp. At last, Elstir kindly arranges a tea party at which Marcel meets Albertine. (236) Close-up, she is very different in his eyes from what she had appeared to be at a distance; she is "not implacable so much as almost frightened." (241) There follows a passage on the optical illusions inseparable from first impressions. (242)

He is disappointed to find her so little different from the girls he already knows. (244) When he is introduced a little later on to a second girl of the group, Andrée (253–254), he is even more astonished to find how different she is from what he had thought she was like on first seeing her. For it was she who had leaped over the prostrate figure of the terrified old banker on the beach. Now he sees that she is "delicate, intellectual, and this year far from well." (268–269) Later, he adds to this description by calling her "neurotic" and "too much like myself." (339) In spite of these disillusions, however, he feels his affections still engaged. He wonders what could possibly be the taste of Albertine's cheeks—"uniform pink, violet tinted, creamy, like certain roses whose petals have a waxy gloss." (262) He determines on a bold approach to her while he is thinking about her in her absence but finds his own conventional conditioning too strong for him and reverts to his usual timidity in her presence. (253) He seeks refuge in numbers—that is to say, the "little band" in its entirety, and "presently I was spending all my time among these girls." (266) He abandons Elstir, Saint-Loup and in fact every sort of social intercourse that takes him away from his girls. (267–268) He loves every minute of the childish games (King of the Castle and Who Laughs First) which he plays with these delightful creatures in "the rosy dawn of adolescence." (285) He finds the company of these girls superior to that of his more intellectual friends because "it was not based on the lie which seeks to make us believe that we are not irremediably alone." (289).

In the midst of one of these games, Albertine as a jest passes Marcel a note which says: "I love you!" Taking it in earnest, he determines that it is she with whom he is going to have his affair. Though none of the girls he now knows are the Dionysiac creatures he had at first imagined them to be, he discovers in Albertine a "craze for amusement" which causes him mentally to compare her with Gilberte and to conclude that there is a family resemblance between the women that a man loves in his life. These beings are all of them without exception "fitted to gratify our senses and to wring our hearts." (270) But Marcel has become a more sophisticated amorous strategist since his affair with Gilberte, and he cleverly plays off Andrée against Albertine. (316–317) At the same time, he tries to throw Andrée herself off the scent so far as his real feelings are concerned. (318) He has learned to trust nobody when it comes to these.

A climax in this opening phase of his relationship with Albertine (the most extensively developed affair in the pages of *Remembrance*, reaching across many volumes) comes when he learns that she intends to spend a night at the Grand Hotel where he is staying because she wishes to catch the train leaving Balbec early the next morning. (319–320) She invites him to come to her room on that evening, and he interprets her invitation to mean that she intends to permit the complete consummation of their love. He feels all the more certain of this when he enters her room and finds that she is in bed with a slight cold. The sight of her in this recumbent posture is too much for his self-control: "Leaving her throat bare, her white nightgown altered the proportions of her face, which, flushed by being in bed or by her cold or by dinner, seemed pinker than before . . . Beyond her, through the window, the valley lay bright beneath the moon. The sight of Albertine's bare throat, of those strangely vivid cheeks, had so intoxicated me (that is to say had placed the reality of the world for me no longer in nature, but in the torrent of my sensations which it was all I could do to keep within bounds) as to have destroyed the balance between my life, immense and indestructible, which circulated in my being, and the life of the universe, so puny in comparison. . . . Death might have struck me down in that moment; it would have seemed to me a trivial, or rather an impossible thing, for life was not outside, it was in me." (324–325) The effect of such vehement passion as Marcel experiences is identical with that produced by alcohol, of which he had said earlier: "Intoxication makes real for an hour or two a subjective idealism, pure phenomenism; nothing is left now but appearances, nothing exists save as a function of our sublime self . . . Unfortunately the coefficient which thus alters our values alters them only in the hour of intoxication . . . The people who had lost all their importance, whom we scattered with our breath like soap-bubbles, will tomorrow resume their density. . . ." (160–161)

It takes but a moment for Marcel to be awakened from this particular dream of felicity. He hears Albertine's startled cry: "Stop that or I'll ring the bell!" (326), but he has gone too far to draw back at what he interprets to be but a feint of coyness and as he consummates the kiss he hears with horror "a sound, precipitous, prolonged, shrill. Albertine had pulled the bell with all her might." (326) Being thus deflated so rudely by reality, Marcel's interest in Albertine abruptly collapses. They remain "friends," but she tells him that none of the other boys she knows should ever have dared what he has tried to do. She has never seemed so completely different from the wild girl of his early imaginings as she does at this moment. If the affair is ever to resume with a "second movement" it will have to be in another time and place than this one. And in fact it is not resumed until later volumes when he returns from Balbec to Paris. His disillusion as to the possibility of possessing Albertine has the effect of detaching him from her temporarily.

The coda of *Within a Budding Grove* is concerned with the end of the summer at Balbec, the setting-in of autumn weather when the girls and most of the other guests leave the hotel. (350) New relationships spring up between the remaining guests who have spent the summer together without getting to know each other. But now, in a common effort to stave off boredom, all social and conventional barriers suddenly seem of no account. (352) And it is on a subdued and rather sad note of emptiness that this volume ends. There has been much bustle and activity in it, high hopes, strong feelings, yet the dominant tones left in our memory are those of disappointment and disillusion. All the sound and fury of youth (which are rendered by Proust with painstaking fidelity) have in the end signified not very much. But this very paucity of significance is itself significant. The search by Marcel for meaning in life has not come to a dead end. It is the end of one movement of feeling only; he has reached a position which calls for a regrouping of forces and a development in a new and different direction. There are to be more emotional setbacks to his hopes before he makes that break-through into a meaningful life of literary creation which is de-scribed in *The Past Recaptured* and which represents the ultimate answer to his personal problems for which the other solutions conventionally suggested (friendship, society, love, professional occupation) have failed to be adequate.

In attending to the main business of the plot and characters of this book, we must try not to lose sight of the texture which so largely contributes to its aesthetic quality. The metaphorical richness of such a descriptive passage as the following can be literally *eye-opening* in its effect upon the reader who has not fully appreciated some of the quieter aspects of pictorial art: "I would now gladly remain at the table while it was being cleared, and, if it was not a moment at which the girls of the little band might be passing, it was no longer solely towards the sea that I would turn my eyes. Since I had seen such things depicted by Elstir, I sought to find again in reality, I cherished, as though for their poetic beauty, the broken gestures of the knives still lying across one another, the swollen convexity of a discarded napkin upon which the sun would patch a scrap of yellow velvet, the half-empty glass which thus showed to greater advantage the noble sweep of its curved sides, and, in the heart of its translucent crystal, clear as frozen daylight, a dreg of wine, dusky but sparkling with reflected lights, the displacement of solid objects, the transmutation of liquids by the effect of light and shade, the shifting color of the plums which passed from green to blue and from blue to golden yellow in the half-plundered dish, the chairs, like a group of old ladies, that came twice daily to take their places around the white cloth spread on the table as on an altar at which were celebrated the rites of the palate, where in the hollows of oyster-shells a few drops of lustral water had gathered in tiny holy water stoups of stone; I tried to find beauty there where I had never imagined before that it could exist, in the most ordinary things, in the profundities of 'still life.' " (235)

One of the by-products of a reading of Proust, it seems to me, is that he sensitizes us not only to the most delicate nuances possible in literary art but that he communicates to us an appreciation of the language of other arts as well.

4. Guermantes Way

PART I

THE LARGEST PORTION OF THIS VOLUME IS GIVEN OVER TO A DE-
SCRIPTION OF A SOCIAL OCCASION AT THE HOUSE OF MADAME DE
Villeparisis, whose drawing room is the third to which the narrator Marcel introduces us. The first was that of Madame Verdurin, the second that of the Marquise de Sainte-Euverte. Madame
de Villeparisis' salon, being that of a member of one of the most
aristocratic families in France, the Guermantes, takes us further
into the magic circle, though we are still at some distance from
the center.

Guermantes Way I opens with the narrator's family installed
in a new apartment in Paris in the Hotel de Guermantes, but
though physically he is a neighbor of the famous Duchess who
has haunted his romantic dreams about the old aristocracy of
France, he is still a world away from her, socially speaking. The
Duke and Duchess, who are his landlords, lead an entirely inaccessible, mysterious, fascinating life "behind a barred threshold," close by and yet infinitely distant. A number of little shops
are described as flanking the court of honor in the Hotel de
Guermantes, leaving Marcel uncertain as to whether they are
"alluvial deposits washed there by the rising tide of democracy"
(10) or residues of an earlier feudal age. The servant Françoise
shows great interest in the doings of "the people below" (11),
that is in the Duke and the Duchess. She strikes up a lively conversation with one of the little shopkeepers in the courtyard,
Jupien the tailor (14), who is to have a large role to play later
on in revealing the perversion of the Baron de Charlus, to the
narrator. Jupien seems to be a bundle of contradictions—on the
one hand, cynical and cold (17), and on the other, filled with
feelings of kindness, pity, and generosity. In addition, he is the
possessor of a refined literary taste.

Marcel dreams of entering the "ideal" realm of the Faubourg Saint Germain.(31) It is "ideal" to him since he realizes that "only imagination and belief can differentiate from the rest certain objects, certain people, and can create an atmosphere." (32) Marcel is vividly aware of the inescapable truth of Kantian idealism. He reflects that "the line of demarcation that separated me from the Faubourg Saint Germain seemed to me all the more real because it was purely ideal." (31) And he is quite convinced that he will never be able to set foot inside the society of the Faubourg, in spite of his physical proximity to it. (32)

But soon there arrives an invitation from the Marquise de Villeparisis (35) whom he has met at Balbec, and though she is not at the very apex of the aristocracy she is a Guermantes and a very considerable first step in the direction of the fashionable life. The description of the occasion on which he accepts this invitation occupies the larger part of the second half of *Guermantes Way I*. Meanwhile, Marcel visits the theater where he is able to see the nobility in public and to gauge the reaction of other people. (40 ff) He overhears one of the spectators comment, for example, that the title Princesse de Guermantes is absurd—as in a certain sense it no doubt is, since such titles have been long defunct in republican society. (47) And yet, such attitudes seem to him somewhat like that of the fox to the grapes out of his reach; he can feel the stirrings of envy in himself for the demigods whom he sees moving in a privileged sphere (49) and he judges that others, no matter what their professions, must experience similar feelings. Snobbery is far more widespread, according to Marcel, than we commonly suppose; in fact, it appears to him, in some form or other, inseparable from human nature itself. "Posterity," he says, "has not changed since the days of Homer and Pindar" and for this posterity "the enviable things are exalted birth, royal or quasi-royal, and the friendship of kings, the leaders of the people and other eminent men." (263)

Marcel confesses such feelings in himself when he tells us that, in the theater that night, he would have preferred to have the opinion of the performance of *Phèdre* held by the Princess and Duchess of Guermantes rather than that of any critic who was merely an intellectual like himself, because the opinions of the Princess and the Duchess, however inferior intellectually and aesthetically they might be, should provide him with "an invaluable clue to the nature of these two poetic creatures." (63) Looking up at the theater boxes where the aristocracy is seated, Marcel feels "as though (he) had seen, thanks to a miraculous rending of the clouds that ordinarily veiled it, the Assembly of the Gods in the act of contemplating the spectacle of mankind." (70) And how thrilled Marcel is when his "landlady," the Duchess, waves at him in glad recognition from her box, a gesture in sharp contrast to her usual indifference in greeting him before this magical evening—an icy indifference which returns to her manner immediately afterwards as though the interlude had never occurred or was without the slightest social importance. (70–71)

Extreme and unbalanced cases of snobbery like that of Legrandin in the first volume (and in this one, too) or of the Marquise de Gallardon give Marcel the occasion for some delightful satire. In *Guermantes Way I*, there are two brief but sharply etched portraits in this category. One is that of Madame de Cambremer and her careful calculation as to whether the speed of her social campaign to reach the upper regions of the aristocracy will surpass the speed of the mortal disease from which she knows herself to be suffering. (66) The other is the exactly parallel case of the Prince von Faffenheim who, in the latter half of *Guermantes Way I*, tries to get the support of Norpois for election to a very exclusive intellectual Institute, and who, knowing himself to be suffering from a fatal heart ailment, reflects pathetically: "If I wait too long, I may be dead before they elect me. That really would be unpleasant." (358) Such are the instances of worldly vanity when snobbery, like jealous love, attains to the proportions almost of a mental disease. Generally speaking, however, snobbery is treated as a foible rather than a vice; only a man who is incurably vicious like Legrandin rages against snobbery as "the unforgivable sin that St. Paul must have had in mind."

It is in response to an invitation from Saint-Loup that Marcel leaves Paris for the garrison town of Doncières where his friend is stationed. (87) Saint-Loup, it seems, is in difficulties with his own girl (91) whom Marcel has not yet seen. Marcel, too, is disturbed by anxieties of various kinds (114–115), and so the two young men find distraction in each other's company and conversation, as well as in that of the other officers of the regiment. Here, the conversation turns to the Dreyfus Case—in which Saint-Loup, unlike so many in his class of society, shows himself to be in favor of a retrial of the convicted man (136, 141 ff), apparently under the influence of his mistress who is an actress and the friend of many intellectuals. Quite naturally also, the talk in the officers' mess turns to the subject of war and military science and strategy (141 ff, 143, 146–149, 151–153). Ironically, in this period, twenty years prior to World War I, Saint-Loup prophesies that "with the terrible advance of artillery, the wars of the future, if there are to be any more wars, will be so short that, before we have had time to think of putting our lessons into practice, peace will have been signed." (153) The irony is underscored when, many volumes later, Saint-Loup falls on the battlefield almost at the very opening of hostilities, so that though the war is to be hard-fought and longdrawn-out (in spite of weapons more terrifying than artillery), for Saint-Loup personally it is destined indeed to be very short. The important point for the present, however, is that in the midst of such talk Marcel feels relieved of his painful obsession with the Duchess of Guermantes (154) whose great name, beauty, and variable degrees of cordiality and coldness have plunged him into an "agony" which he compares to that which he once suffered over Gilberte and, earlier still, over his mother's goodnight kiss at Combray. (158)

The Duchess, who seems so inaccessible to Marcel, is the aunt of his friend Saint-Loup who keeps a photograph of her in his room (100). Marcel tries to get his friend to use his influence with his aunt, to speak well of him to her (131), to get a dinner invitation for him to her house (132), to give him her photograph (133). But all these machinations are in vain; when Marcel gets back to Paris he finds that the Duchess, in spite of the extravagant recommendation of her nephew, still refuses to invite him to her home (189) and that when he resumes his greetings to her on her morning walks his unflagging persistence annoys her as much as ever. (191–192) At Doncières, Marcel had seen certain caricatures of his own impulses to snobbery in the form of "sons of rich business or professional men who looked at the higher aristocratic society only from the outside and without penetrating its enclosure." (119) These were the army associates of Sergeant Saint-Loup, whose origins lay in an altogether less exclusive segment of society, and who avidly discuss all of his comings and goings, his habits of dress, etc. Marcel discerns a tendency towards social mixing (a somewhat leveling, democratic tendency which is to become more pronounced as *Remembrance* progresses) between members of the nobility in the army and those upper middle class republicans "who had clean hands and went to Mass." (129)

Interfused with the social theme is the story of Saint-Loup's relationship to his mistress, which is cut after a familiar pattern in Proust: a rich man in love with a girl far below him socially. At this stage of the affair, Marcel's friend is on a seesaw of feeling with his girl, reminiscent of Swann's affair with Odette— he is full of anxiety as long as he is convinced that she wishes to break off with him (91), but as soon as she shows signs of wanting a reconciliation he becomes cool and reassured and does not know if he really wishes her to return to him. (164) As everywhere in Proust, powerful sentences difficult to forget appear in the text: "It has been said that silence is a force; in another and widely different sense it is a tremendous force in the hands of those who are loved." (160) Like Swann, Saint-Loup reaches an extreme of misery at last where nothing in the world is important to him except his mistress. He is so completely possessed that he loses all sense of proportion or even of decency and looks forward to a brilliant, rich, loveless marriage in order that he may afford to go on keeping her in the style to which she has been accustomed by him. (208–209) Saint-Loup is yet another image that makes us realize the meaning of the phrase about a man ruining himself for love. What, then, is Marcel's astonishment when he is introduced to this supposed paragon among women and she turns out to be none other than *Rachel when from the Lord* (as he has nicknamed her in imitation of his grandfather's habit of working people's names into the titles of operatic arias) who had once frequented the higher-class brothels of Paris and whom he had himself turned down when she was offered him by a procuress for the paltry sum of twenty francs. (211–212) Now he watches Saint-Loup spending hundreds of thousands of francs for the privilege of being tortured and betrayed by her. The spectacle furnishes Marcel an additional occasion for reflections on the subjective nature of love. (212–213) The changes of mood between the lovers are positively dizzying; immediately after the most brutal quarrels they are ready to make love. (230) Rachel is portrayed as cruel not only to her lover but to others as well—for example, when she arranges to have some of her theater cronies hiss a rival actress off the stage in tears. (233–234) In the wake of passionate scenes of lovemaking, there follow ugly jealous quarrels, really sordid scenes between Robert and Rachel. When Rachel addresses herself to an effeminate dancer backstage (243) in the presence of her lover and suggests that the three of them might get together some time for heightened sensations, a sulphurous atmosphere of corruption and lasciviousness rises to the reader's nostrils reminiscent of that which accompanies some of the more shocking tableaux of Roman decadence in the *Satyricon*.

The third and largest subdivision of *Guermantes Way I* is devoted to the party at Madame de Villeparisis'. When Marcel received an invitation from her, his father advised him to accept it since in her drawing room he may meet Ambassador Norpois again (199) and perhaps benefit by more of his advice concerning a literary career. But before turning to this subject, let me note for a moment an important narrative hint which is dropped by the author at the moment of Marcel's return from his stay with Saint-Loup at Doncières. He comes into the house unexpectedly and sees his grandmother before she is aware that he is in the room. Under these circumstances he has a very keen, clear perception of her as "a dejected old woman whom I did not know." (188) The moment in which he sees her thus is a moment of privileged vision—like that which James should have called an epiphany, a manifestation which enables him to penetrate surface appearances to the profound truth that lies hidden beneath them. Nothing more is made of the incident at this point but the somber note that is struck clearly prepares the reader for the revelation of the grandmother's mortal illness before the present volume has run its course.

The social standing of Madame de Villeparisis (in spite of her great family connection with the Guermantes) is, for some reason that Marcel finds it hard to fathom, doubtful in quality. (248) Her drawing room is not quite exclusive enough to be really fashionable. (263) This ambiguous position may be due to any one of various reasons that come to Marcel's attention in the course of time. It may be that, like some of the ladies of noble birth who frequent her house, she has been ostracized at some time in her life for some grave instance of misconduct, probably of a sexual kind. (265–267) It may be because, as Charlus informs him maliciously, she has married a commoner who had simply appropriated the title Marquis de Villeparisis to which he had no shadow of a claim. (403). It may be simply because she is an intellectual and artistic woman, a "bluestocking" who paints pictures, writes memoirs, and has been too free with her invitations to people of no standing socially who had appealed to her for some personal reason. For in the perpetual masquerade and costume ball that is called fashionable life the most whimsical, arbitrary standards are applied to make or break people. Of course, there is an appeal from the groundless opinions of snobs (like Madame Leroi) to the verdict of posterity, which (reading the memoirs of Madame de Villeparisis) will not realize that her social standing was somewhat under a cloud. (263) Thus literature redresses the balance, does justice to those who have been dealt with unjustly, and places the contemporary in the perspective provided by the permanent and unchanging.

At the very moment that Marcel was visiting Madame de Villeparisis "it was true that the social kaleidoscope was in the act of turning and that the Dreyfus Case was shortly to hurl the Jews down to the lowest rung of the social ladder." (257) The use of the image of the kaleidoscope indicates how accidental and fundamentally unimportant social changes appear to be in Proust's eyes. All human relations, in fact, are to him "as eternally fluid as the sea itself." (370) In *Remembrance* the Dreyfus Case serves him as one more device or instrument of analysis which enables him to understand and sometimes to lampoon his characters. He is fascinated by the curiosities and contradictions which the case helped to expose in the human personality as well as in society.

There is, for example, Madame Sazerat, an old Combray neighbor who is the exact opposite of Marcel's father, for she is an anti-Semite *and* a Dreyfusard at one and the same time (397–398) while Marcel's father who is not an anti-Semite is nevertheless an anti-Dreyfusard. Every character in Proust has his own reasons for being either a partisan of Dreyfus or opposed to him, or else for adopting an attitude of neutral indifference to his fate. It is an extremely various picture of humanity that Proust draws. Bloch, who is now a successful playwright, turns up in the Villeparisis drawing room. (273–274) He engages Norpois in conversation on the subject of the Case, hoping to draw out some "inside information" through the Ambassador's connection with the government. But Norpois is so consummate a diplomat and so successfully straddles the fence that Bloch mentally places him now in one camp, now in the other. (320) He expresses approval of the characters of both Colonel Picquart and of Lieutenant Henry, who are in deadly opposition to each other. It is clear that Norpois is not at all concerned with the guilt or innocence of the prisoner or of his personal tragedy, but solely with the way any expression of his opinion may adversely affect his own political position.

The Duchess sees in the Case merely an opportunity to display her well-known wit. To her, the issue seems less moral than aesthetic: "In any case, if Dreyfus is innocent he hasn't done much to prove it. What idiotic, raving letters he writes from that island. I don't know whether M. Esterhazy is any better, but he does show more skill in his choice of words, a different tone altogether. That can't be very pleasant for the supporters of M. Dreyfus. What a pity for them there's no way of exchanging innocents!" (328) Madame de Villeparisis, who had herself introduced Bloch to Norpois because she wished to please the playwright with an eye to one of her future entertainments, suddenly decides that he may indiscreetly compromise the official position of her lover and determines on the spur of the moment to show Bloch the door. (339–340). Almost simultaneously, as if in confirmation of Marcel's observation on the turn of the social kaleidoscope, Madame Swann makes her entry into the Villeparisis drawing room. She has come a long way since the first volume when Swann's marriage to her was considered so disgraceful that not only his aristocratic acquaintances but even his middle-class ones, like the narrator's family, refused to invite her to their houses. And she has made her advance on the strength of her proclaimed anti-Dreyfusism. (346) Odette is embarrassed at meeting Marcel again, because he can remember the time she told him that she was convinced of Dreyfus's innocence. (362) Being married to a wealthy gentleman of Jewish extraction like Swann, whom we are to find quite prominent in the ranks of the Dreyfusards, the motivations of Odette are so complex that it is extremely improbable that, even if she had possessed the required intellectual capacity, she should have formed an objective, disinterested judgment in the matter. It is evident, however, that the opinion she has arrived at finally is helpful in furthering her social career, and she is only one of a host of obscure ladies of questionable origin who, by joining the various patriotic, nationalistic, anti-Semitic societies have found a long-sought key to open the doors of the Faubourg Saint-Germain.

But all these characters are simple-minded in their approach to the Case compared with the Baron de Charlus. As on every other subject, Marcel finds him to be nothing if not original. Charlus regards all Jews in France as foreigners; a Jew to him simply cannot be a true Frenchman. Consequently, runs his singular line of reasoning, Dreyfus could *not* have committed treason to France, as he was charged with doing, since he owed his allegiance in the first place not to France but to some mythical entity which Charlus calls "Judaea." Towards France, according to the eccentric nobleman, Dreyfus was at most guilty of a "breach of the laws of hospitality." (396) Charlus's remarks on this and on other subjects are made in language so violent and extreme that Marcel characterizes it as "almost insane." In fact, it is difficult to understand the qualification implied in the word "almost." The reader as well as the narrator are still in the dark at this point concerning the secret key to the Baron's character —namely, his sexual aberration. As soon as we have learned of his homosexuality, we are enabled to understand much that has hitherto puzzled us. We become aware of the fact that the continual risks he runs of being cast out of respectable society give an edge of sadistic cruelty to his behavior, particularly so far as other pariahs are concerned.

Marcel's own sympathies in the Case are made abundantly clear. M. Reinach, who helped to vindicate the accused man, scored, he says: "the most astonishing victory for rational policy (a victory against France, according to some) that the world has ever seen." (406) We hear echoes of the great national discussion even on the level of the servants in the book. The butler of the Guermantes is an anti-Dreyfusard (like his masters), while

Marcel's butler is pro-Dreyfusard. (406–407) We are reminded of the division and quarrels of the servants of the Montagues and Capulets in *Romeo and Juliet*.

The theme of homosexuality, though it is still not explicitly in the foreground of attention in this volume, is making its way toward the place which it is to occupy in the volumes of *Cities of the Plain*. The Duchess whispers a scandalous accusation against the Prince of Bulgaria, implying that his tastes in love are not quite normal. (332) Earlier, in a scene preceding Madame de Villeparisis' party, Robert de Saint-Loup had been approached in the theater by a homosexual who had made an indecent proposition to him, which he had resented violently enough to beat the man. (240)

But the most important development along this line is tied up with the unfolding character of the Baron de Charlus. Charlus's "way with the ladies" (366–367) is in part the natural result of his having so much in common with them and in part the exaggerated pose of one whose real emotional interests lie in a very different direction. Charlus invites Marcel to come and visit him at home (381), an invitation that seems to disturb Madame de Villeparisis profoundly when she learns of it. (390) She insists that Marcel leave while her nephew's attention is occupied for a moment elsewhere, but Charlus pursues him as soon as he sees him leaving (391) and regales him with some of his typically fantastic conversation. (392) Charlus in this passage obscurely hints at his own abnormality (as we realize in retrospect) by speaking mysteriously of "a freemasonry . . . that numbers in its ranks four of the reigning sovereigns of Europe." (399) His view of the therapeutic effect of sexual aberration is given in the sentence: "There are maladies which we must not seek to cure because they alone protect us from others that are more serious." Charlus, as I have said, is nothing if not original. Beyond proposing to train Marcel in the secrets of "diplomacy," Charlus does not carry out his intentions this particular evening. He leaves Marcel abruptly in order to take a cab home; he had previously passed up several cabs until one came along whose driver seemed hopelessly drunk so that Charlus was compelled to take the reins from him. And still, in spite of all these wild eccentricities and very broad hints, the narrator does not suspect the reason for his behavior. This is not because he is dull or imperceptive but because one of the valuable lessons we learn from Proust is that people are able to see only those things which they are looking for. Unprepared by their own experience for an unexpected revelation, they remain blind to the most glaring pieces of evidence (which, later on, they cannot understand how they overlooked) and, if they are especially stubborn (like Marcel's father), they refuse to credit the testimony of their own senses when it does not conform to their preconceptions.

After the Villeparisis party Marcel goes home to find his grandmother gravely ill. From the vain imaginations and trivialities and gossip of fashionable society, we are brought down with a painful thud to the hard ground of reality. Various doctors are called into consultation—first of all, Doctor Cottard, whose reputation as a diagnostician has grown enormously. Then there is the eminent specialist Dr. du Boulbon, recommended to Marcel by the novelist Bergotte as one of the few physicians with whom it is possible to converse intelligently upon literature. Dr. du Boulbon was a pupil of the famous psychiatrist Charcot, who had predicted great eminence for him in the study of the human mind. (414) He does indeed turn out to be a great talker and is especially eloquent on the subject of the connection between creativity and mental illness. (418–419) Unfortunately, he is one of those doctors who tend to interpret all disease in terms of their own special interests. He is a sort of medical monist. All illness to him originates in the sufferer's mind —he defends a psychosomatic theory, which had not yet been named. And he succeeds in convincing the family of Marcel, though not the grandmother herself who is the patient, that all her troubles are nervous in origin rather than organic as they had feared. Somewhat in the fashion of the celebrated charlatan Coué, he persuades them that if she but says to herself that she is well and behaves as if she were, she will be well. Though she does not credit the soundness of the diagnosis, she does stoically follow his orders to take exercise, goes out for a walk in the Champs-Élysées (the literal meaning of this name is perhaps designed to have a symbolic significance at this point) and, after a satirical encounter there with the snobbish proprietor of a comfort station (whose values she compares to those of the Verdurins and the Guermantes in conversation with Marcel), she suffers a stroke and has to be taken home by her grandson. (425–428) On this melancholy note, *Guermantes Way I* ends.

PART 2

This volume begins and ends with somber reminders of human mortality. The first forty-eight pages describe the cruelly drawn-out illness and death of Marcel's grandmother. At the end of *Guermantes Way II*, it is the fatal disease and impending death of Swann that claims our attention. The whole intervening portion of the book is given over to continued descriptions of social frivolity and snobbery (we are slowly approaching the absolute center of the Faubourg Saint-Germain) and undoubtedly the contrast of the spectacle of the vanities of life and the inevitable suffering brought by old age, illness, and death is intended, in its contrasting lights and shades to introduce a philosophical perspective into the picture.

There are more detailed parallels between the beginning of this section and its end which should be pointed out since they help to unify and, by repetition, to emphasize the meaning of the book. In the opening pages, Professor E., a physician who is a friend of Marcel's father, when called upon in an emergency to examine the grandmother after her stroke, consents to do so only in his office (in spite of the fact that he is told that she is hardly well enough to leave her carriage) and pleads an important social engagement as an excuse for not visiting her at home: "Call at your house! Really, sir, you must not expect me to do that. I am dining with the Minister of Commerce. I have a call to pay first. I must change at once, and to make matters worse I have torn my coat and my other one has no buttonholes for my decorations." (2) After the examination, which reveals a desperate case of uraemia "for which there was not the slightest hope" the Professor shows his visitors out of the office: "I had shut the door behind me, and a footman was showing us into the hall when we heard a loud shout of rage. The maid had forgotten to cut and hem the buttonholes for the decorations. This would take another ten minutes." (8) This scene is similar in detail to the much better-known, often-discussed and admired scene at the end of *Guermantes Way II* when the Duke and Duchess, on their way to a costume ball, are informed inconsiderately by their guest Swann that the doctors have given him only a few months to live and that he will therefore be unable to accept their invitation to accompany them on a trip to Italy the next year, since he will in all probability be dead for several months by that time. They pretend not to believe that he is serious about this, because that would interfere with their own immediate pleasures. The Duke, who is much the coarser of the two, is especially pressing in his refusal to allow his wife to delay another minute to comfort Swann. At the very last moment, however, an unexpected mishap occurs (like that of the uncut buttonhole) when the Duke notices that the Duchess is wearing black shoes with a red dress and he makes her go up to her room to change her shoes, while he frets at the delay of ten minutes to his dinner. He consoles their dying friend as they take their departure for dinner, by calling out to him in a loud voice: "You, now, don't let yourself be taken in by the doctor's nonsense, damn them. They're donkeys. You're as strong as the Pont Neuf. You'll live to bury us all!" (395)

Swann accepts the attitude of his friends as perfectly understandable, because the world he lives in, to use the narrator's own expression, is a world in which "each of us is indeed alone." And though the Duke, the Duchess, and Professor E. are extreme examples of callousness, Marcel himself cannot help chiding his stricken grandmother, as they are on their way home from the doctor's office, because she has failed to acknowledge a greeting from their Combray neighbor Legrandin, whom they have just passed in the street: "I, who was not yet detached from life, asked my grandmother if she had acknowledged his greeting, reminding her of his readiness to take offence. My grandmother, thinking me no doubt very frivolous, raised her hand in the air as though to say: 'What does it matter? It is not of the least importance.' "(4)

The forty-eight pages dealing with the grandmother's illness and death are among the best in the book (comparable to those concerned with the death of Bergotte in *The Captive* which are so often anthologized). Though at times perilously close to the edge of sentimentality (11), the section as a whole is grimly, one may almost say painfully, realistic. Little of the horror of sickness is spared the reader. Her uraemia at one time affects the grandmother's eyes (28–29) and she becomes temporarily blind. Then she goes deaf, though she regains her sight. The doctor prescribes leeches as a treatment—a martyrdom to the grandmother who has always abhorred crawling things; now she has to suffer them silently on her very brow! There are convulsions (35), injections of morphine (40), oxygen (39). The agony reaches such a pitch that the poor distracted woman makes an attempt on her own life by trying to jump out of the window. (30)

And always there is the startling contrast between these things and the triviality of those who are in good health. Proust knows medical men very well, both because he himself was an invalid and because he had two physicians in his immediate family— his father and his brother. He excels in his satire of medicine. The specialist x (17–18), who is called in because the advertisement of his abilities is so widespread and because wish-fulfillment is the order of the day when death threatens, is a nose-specialist who traces all ailments back to the human nose just as we have seen Dr. du Boulbon earlier attributing them to the mind. The specialist may not be able to do anything for the grandmother, but he does succeed in passing on the colds and coughs of his other patients (stuffed into his bag, which Marcel humorously compares to the bag of Aeolus) to Marcel's whole family. Another humorous passage (Proust delights in mixing together the pathetic and the funny) relates to Dr. Dieulafoy, who enjoys a semi-official status socially for certifying the final stage of hopelessness in any illness, and who exhibits a sort of conjuror's nimbleness in making the envelope containing his honorarium vanish into his pocket. (44) As for the familiar Cottard, he is portrayed as a kind of general or strategist in the field of disease. (14)

Around the deathbed, there is small talk about the weather. (42–43) A little further away, the servant Françoise is taking fittings for her mourning dress. (33) The Duke of Guermantes's snobberies and silliness are, of course, completely unaffected by torments which he cannot imagine or sympathize with. (35–36) The grandmother's eccentric sisters, informed concerning her fatal illness, refuse to leave their native Combray, since they have discovered there a musician who gives excellent chamber music concerts, which they judge to be far more elevating to the soul than watching by an invalid's bedside should be. (18) A half-brother of the grandmother, who has been in religious orders in Germany, covers his face as he is standing by her bed and spies on Marcel through his half-open fingers to see whether or not his grief over her illness is real! (39–40) Marcel's friend Saint-Loup unaccountably chooses this vulnerable moment to send him a message (evidently provoked by his mistress Rachel's maddening infidelities and lies) accusing him of perfidious behavior. Unfeeling life goes on all around in its usual way for everyone except Marcel and his family. Only the novelist Bergotte, who is himself seriously ill, seems disinterested in his concern and spends several hours each day in the house talking to Marcel.

Early in the section, the author prepares the "sculpting" metaphor which is to conclude the chapter so memorably. Marcel, looking at his grandmother's suffering face, has a vision of "her features, like clay in a sculptor's hand (which) seemed to be straining. . . ." (15) The image is finally resolved in the sentence which concludes the section: "On that funeral couch, death, like a sculptor of the middle ages, had laid her in the form of a young maiden." (48) Death had been the sculptor from the very beginning of her illness, kneading the grandmother's flesh cruelly in preparation for this final, unexpected, aesthetic reversal. The art-simile (that is, his habit of comparing life to art in an attempt to heighten its reality) is impressively used by Proust in this metaphor at the end of the opening part of *Guermantes Way II*.

In the section which follows the grandmother's death, the largest part is devoted to a dinner at the Duchess of Guermantes's to which Marcel has been invited for the first time, but this is preceded by a sizable introduction in which many hints for future developments of the narrative are dropped and many other familiar themes and characters are momentarily taken up again.

An intimation of Marcel's future success in finding his vocation (which is the dramatic subject of *The Past Recaptured*, the last volume of *Remembrance*) is given when we learn that he has submitted an article to the newspaper *Figaro* and is impatiently awaiting its appearance in print. (51) Robert de Saint-Loup breaks off with his mistress Rachel and resumes cordial relations with Marcel, of whom she had made her lover wantonly jealous. (52) And Albertine, who has been absent during *Guermantes Way I*, comes to call upon Marcel. (56) The mention of Albertine's name is accompanied by images of the sea, against which he had first seen her outlined on the beach at Balbec. (57) This seems to be as good an illustration of a literary equivalent of the leitmotif in Wagnerian music-drama as one would ask for, since the leitmotif is a melody or musical phrase always accompanying the appearance or mention of a character. Images of the sea seem to be appropriate as an indication of Albertine's changeable nature.

The last time he had seen Albertine she had rebuffed his advances with decided vigor. But he senses the changes that have evidently taken place in her in the interim—changes indicated by a daring new vocabulary and sophisticated turns of expression which reveal maturity and cause him to hope for a more favorable outcome should he renew his advances. (62-63) Marcel stresses the importance of imagination in love and contrasts romantic with merely carnal possession. (72-73). He is not deceived in his hopes, for she now proves much more amenable to his desires. He describes a moment of complete physical satisfaction analogous to an unforgettable moment in his boyhood affair with Gilberte when he had found a similar release. (78-79) His description suggests a curious analogy, on the purely physical level, between the reactions of an organism to pleasure on the one hand and to death on the other: "Obliterating every trace of her customary anxieties and interests, the moment preceding pleasure, similar in this respect to the moment after death, had restored to her rejuvenated features what seemed like the innocence of earliest childhood." (79)

There is a short re-entry into the drawing room of Madame de Villeparisis (85 ff) which acts as a bridge to the much more exclusive drawing room of her niece, the Duchess. After turning down two separate invitations to dine with the Duchess in the house of Madame de Villeparisis (90-91), Marcel at last receives a coveted invitation to visit the Duchess herself (who is rumored—falsely as it turns out—to be about to separate from her Duke). Wondering how he might have earned such a high and unexpected honor, Marcel compares himself ironically to Mordecai at the moment when he was suddenly singled out for favor by King Ahasueras. (95–96)

Conversation in the Villeparisis drawing room points to the increasingly puzzling character of Charlus. Marcel is astonished to learn from the Duchess, for example, that the Baron has told her that he does not know Marcel and should very much like to meet him! (97–98) Almost immediately afterwards, he hears from his friend Bloch a strange story about how Charlus, who has never been introduced to him, met him in the street recently and kept staring pertinaciously at him as though he recognized him and "was anxious to know him personally." (101) Marcel cannot attribute this anecdote merely to Bloch's inordinate vanity; it has the ring of truth.

Hints of homosexuality continue to be dropped here and there, as it were by the way. For example, in a digression concerned with the marrying habits of young nobles like Saint-Loup and his friends (131 ff) we hear of one blissfully wedded and prolific male invert "spending the intervals of procreation in the pursuit of soldiers." (134) Some pages later, Charlus, who has recently denied all knowledge of him, sends Marcel a message through Saint-Loup asking him to pay him a visit on the evening of the Guermantes's reception. (143) He replies that he will do so after the reception is over.

This reception is the main business of the book. (149 ff) Marcel makes his first false step there by so losing himself in contemplation of certain paintings by Elstir that are the property of the Duke and Duchess (152–157) as to hold up the scheduled dinner for almost an hour. Clearly, to be so devoted an aesthete is somewhat at odds with the fulfillment of one's social duties. The place of art in fashionable society is honorable but strictly limited, and one who enjoys art sincerely must do so in a place apart and by himself; Swann had had something of the same experience while listening to Vinteuil's Sonata in the drawing room of the Marquise de Saint-Euverte long before.

From the beginning, the moral atmosphere of the Faubourg Saint-Germain is associated with thoughts of decadence and vice in the mind of Marcel: "One pretended not to know that the body of one's hostess was at the disposal of all comers, provided that her visiting list showed no gaps." (159) He is satirical, too, on the subject of the unromantic origin of the fabulous wealth of the Princesse de Parme, (164–165) a quite inferior, dimwitted lady who moves in the loftiest of social spheres. But it is human nature in general rather than the abuses of particular persons at which he seems to aim his barbed criticism. Snobbery and exclusiveness, stupidity and cruelty are universal human qualities, and in the very act of exposing the fashionable Faubourg to ridicule he reflects that in the future, in which radical leveling seems likely to be more and more the order of the day, society may become "secretly more hierarchical as it becomes outwardly more democratic." (203)

One of Proust's purposes in this section is to contrast the wit of the Guermantes with the stupidity of their kinsmen, the Courvoisiers. (183 ff) The Dutchess's sallies justify the comparison that has been made between her and Stendhal's immortal Duchess in the *Chartreuse de Parme*. The Courvoisiers are understandably jealous of the social successes she is able to score through the unfair advantage of verbal intelligence. (220)

Proust also analyzes carefully the contrasts and contradictions in the characters of the Guermantes themselves: "The Guermantes—those at least who were worthy of the name—were not only of a quality of flesh or hair, or transparency of gaze that was exquisite, but had a way of holding themselves, of walking, of bowing, of looking at one before they shook one's hand, of shaking hands, which made them as different in all these respects from an ordinary person in society as he in turn was from a peasant in a smock. And despite their friendliness one asked oneself: 'Have they not indeed the right, though they waive it, when they see us walk, bow, leave a room, do any of those things which when performed by them became as graceful as the flight of a swallow or the bending of a rose on its stem, to think: "These people are of another race than ours, and we are, we, the true lords of creation"?' Later on, I realized that the Guermantes did indeed regard one as being of another race, but one that aroused their envy because I possessed merits of which I knew nothing and which they professed to regard as alone important. Later still I came to feel that the profession of faith was only half sincere and that in them scorn or surprise could be coexistent with admiration and envy." (180)

Though Marcel shows some aesthetic admiration for the surface appearances of the aristocracy, the more profound reality about the worldly life is that it is characterized by "idleness and sterility." (224) It is the spiritual vacuum of her life that makes the Duchess profess her paradoxical, insincere opinions on literature and music (223) and arouses in her "the morbid need of arbitrary novelties." (224) The unstable and farfetched opinions of the Duchess concerning art give the author an opportunity to digress from the Guermantes to the state of literary criticism in general which also seems to him to be characterized by a "morbid need of arbitrary novelties." He speaks scathingly of "our criticism run mad . . . this depravation of taste (which) . . . will barter the whole of Molière for a line from *L'Étourdi* or (which) pronounces Wagner's *Tristan* a bore . . . except (for) a 'charming note on the horns' at the point where the hunt goes by." (225)

Returning to the Duchess, Marcel notes "the impossibility of finding pleasure when one does nothing else than seek it." (226) The Duchess is a bundle of contradictions. She is an anti-Dreyfusard, for example, apparently because she feels that this opinion is expected of her, yet she is too intelligent to believe in the guilt of Dreyfus, and in an effort to strike a balance between these different positions she makes something of a sensation by refusing to do homage to a nationalist general by standing up when he enters the room, and she does her best to discourage political discussion at social affairs. (233) The Duchess is certainly to be forgiven much because of what she suffers from the brutality of her husband whose habit it is to compensate his mistresses when he casts them off by inviting them to become part of his wife's salon. (236–237) The Duchess revenges herself—upon her servants—whom she uses as scapegoats, since the lord and master who is the real object of her wrath is out of reach of her vengeance. Her tone is characteristically malicious, even when she is talking about the aunt to whom she owed so much in her girlhood, the Marquise de Villeparisis. (269)

Someone in the course of conversation mentions Charlus's inconsolable grief over the death of his wife (272–273) whom Charlus himself had described to Marcel in the preceding volume as "the loveliest, the noblest, the most perfect creature." (G.W.I, 400). It seems that he has made "a regular cult of her after her death." The Duchess caustically observes that Charlus has "a

woman's heart" and that he mourns his wife as he might mourn
"a cousin, a grandmother, a sister. It is not the grief of a husband." (273–274) Her husband the Duke, who is also the brother
of Charlus, shows his displeasure with what he takes to be her
gratuitous reflections upon his brother's virility. This is one more
in the series of clues casually dropped as to the mystery of M.
de Charlus, though the evidence, from the narrator's point of
view, is still confusing and inconclusive.

An instance of the literary leitmotif occurs in the Duchess's
conversation when she happens to mention the name of Swann
and immediately says: "Life is a dreadful business" which are
the words she had used many years before when she encountered
Swann at the Saint-Euverte party in the first volume (286 cf. S.W.
443). It is as if the thought of her old friend, his sadness and sickness, always elicits the same response from her.

On page 294, the Prince de Guermantes (who has surprises in
store for the reader and stands at the very apex of the aristocratic
society of the Faubourg Saint-Germain) is mentioned for the
first time as a man who still lives mentally within the Middle
Ages, very stiff, very proper, completely unbending. (294) Society is the natural ground for false rumor and slander to grow
in. The Turkish ambassadress who is a tireless spreader of gossip
warns the narrator concerning the homosexual proclivities of the
Duke (a complete fiction). Charlus, according to her, is deeply
distressed by his brother's morals! (316–317) The Duke's conversation on genealogies is perhaps the most memorable of Marcel's experiences on this particular evening. (308 ff) One of the
differences that he notes between the middle class and the aristocracy is that the ancestry of the former is lost in obscurity,
while that of the latter, being known in many cases for centuries,
adds a dimension to our knowledge of people bearing famous
old names and titles. (320) In spite of all their shortcomings of
which he helps make us keenly aware, Marcel expresses his preference for both nobles and peasants, as against the merely
wealthy bourgeois. (331–332)

After the Guermantes's dinner party, Marcel goes to call on
Charlus, as he had promised Saint-Loup he would do. He is kept
waiting in the ante-room of the Baron for half an hour. (334 ff)
When he is finally admitted, he notices the Baron's tall hat and
cape upon a chair as if he has just come in. Charlus does not even

ask him to sit down before launching into an insolent and haughty diatribe denouncing him for unknown crimes and threatening to break off relations completely with him. The narrator is at a loss to understand these insane rantings which proceed for pages on end and are so distinctive that every reader of Proust feels as if he knows Charlus's tone of voice. What Marcel does grasp, however, is that he has to do here with a man who is evil—one who is "capable of doing murder." (338)

The fantastic hyperboles of Charlus in such a mood are impossible to convey without direct quotation. Here is one of his interchanges with Marcel at the very height of his paroxysm of rage: "I told you that I had taken a hundred steps towards you; the only effect of that has been to make you retire two hundred from me. Now it is for me to withdraw, and we shall know one another no longer. I shall retain not your name but your story, so that at moments when I might be tempted to believe that men have good hearts, good manners, or simply the intelligence not to allow an unparalleled opportunity to escape them, I may remember that that is ranking them too highly. No, that you should have said that you knew me, when it was true—for henceforward it ceases to be true—I regard that as only natural, and I take it as an act of homage, that is to say something pleasant. Unfortunately, elsewhere and in other circumstances, you have uttered remarks of a very different nature.' 'Sir, I swear to you that I have said nothing that could insult you.' 'And who says that I am insulted?' he cried with fury, flinging himself into an erect posture on the seat on which hitherto he had been reclining motionless, while, as the pale frothing serpents stiffened in his face, his voice became alternately shrill and grave, like the deafening onrush of a storm. (The force with which he habitually spoke, which used to make strangers turn round in the street, was multiplied a hundredfold, as is a musical forte if, instead of being played on the piano, it is played by an orchestra, and changed into a *fortissimo* as well. M. de Charlus roared.) 'Do you suppose that it is within your power to insult me? You evidently are not aware to whom you are speaking? Do you imagine that the envenomed spittle of five hundred little gentlemen of your type, heaped one upon another, would succeed in slobbering so much as the tips of my august toes?' " (341–342)

This outburst is followed by the celebrated scene in which

Marcel, infuriated beyond measure but unwilling to strike an older man, takes the top hat of Charlus from the chair on which it is lying quietly, tramples it on the ground, and then systematically and deliberately rips it to pieces. Whereupon, Charlus, without losing his composure but speaking a little more softly and calmly, orders his footman to replace it with another! (344) Charlus now contradicts himself from moment to moment in his attitude to Marcel in such a manner as to suggest that the Duchess's earlier expressed opinion that her brother-in-law had a trace of madness in him was a charitable understatement. (348) Before parting from Marcel, after an irrevocable "final" rupture, Charlus suddenly introduces the subject of the Princesse de Guermantes into the conversation. (351–352) According to him, there is absolutely no comparison in rareness and quality between the Princess and her cousin, the Duchess. He also adds bitingly that he (Charlus) alone can pronounce the "Open Sesame" which will secure entry into her drawing room for the narrator. The possibility of being introduced to the Princesse de Guermantes seems to be the last bait which Charlus deigns to hold out before the snobbish curiosity of the narrator.

Two months later, without any further contact with Charlus, Marcel receives an invitation to attend a reception at the Princesse de Guermantes's which is so completely unexpected that at first he thinks that some practical joker is playing a trick on him. (335) He can hardly believe the invitation genuine since he has thought of the head of the House of Guermantes as characterized by a quite exceptional "exclusiveness . . . (and) almost fossilized rigidity of aristocratic prejudices." (359) In his doubts and dilemma he turns for help to the Duke and Duchess but finds the former adamant in his refusal to check the authenticity of the invitation lest it should seem (if the invitation proves to be spurious) that he is seeking to have a real one sent to Marcel. The Duke, as a rule, is helpful to nobody but himself. He expects to be at the same reception that evening and to go on afterwards to a costume ball where he is to be dressed as Louis XI while his wife is to be attired as Isabel of Bavaria. To complete his joy, he "had made the most exciting assignation with a new mistress." (370) Unfortunately, on the evening in question (which is the same as that on which Marcel makes his call), the Duke's cousin

Amanien is lying so desperately ill that he is not expected to live till morning—which would mean that the Duke would be compelled to go into an official period of public mourning and his plans should be ruined. He has a stratagem, however, with which to avert the worst (that is to say, missing the masquerade). After a final checkup late in the afternoon to make certain that his cousin is still breathing, the Duke dismisses his servants with strict orders not to disturb him till the next morning. There will be time enough then to pay his respects to his relative.

While Marcel is making his call on the Duke and Duchess, Swann, whom Marcel has not seen for some time, also comes to call. Marcel notices at once that Swann looks strangely "altered" and very ill. (370–371) He is the only one who notices the change in Swann apparently; neither the Duke nor Duchess take it into account until Swann himself speaks of it. While alone with Swann for a moment, Marcel, who knows that he is a passionate Dreyfusard, asks him the explanation for the fact that the Guermantes are all anti-Dreyfusard. Swann doesn't hesitate a moment in answering that it is because "at heart all these people are anti-Semites." (374) Swann, in these closing days of his life, "was returning to the spiritual fold of his fathers." (374) This process of "recasting (was) entirely to his credit." (375) According to Swann, the Prince de Guermantes was quite unusually anti-Semitic, and yet Swann too was going to attend the reception in his house that evening because the Prince, an old school friend of Swann's, had written to ask him to come so that they might talk together concerning some unnamed subject. Dreyfusism has had a very marked effect upon all of Swann's political and literary judgments. He now likes Clemenceau, for example, though he had once regarded this republican politician (in the fashion of the Guermantes circle) as a British spy; also, it seems to him that the nationalist author "Barrès had lost all his talent" of late. (376)

The incident involving the red shoes of the Duchess which I have already mentioned, her bewilderment and incredulity and helplessness in the face of Swann's announcement of his impending death, the Duke's bluff assurances to the stricken man: "You'll live to bury us all!"—all these things are in the best vein of Proustian satire. In the closing pages of *Guermantes Way II*, we approach the midpoint of the narrative of *Remembrance* as a whole and come to what some readers have regarded as the very keystone of the Proustian arch, the introductory section of *Cities of the Plain* which forms an interlude preceding the account of the reception at the Prince and Princesse de Guermantes's to which all the characters at the end of *Guermantes Way* (the Duke and the Duchess, the narrator Marcel and Charles Swann) are converging.

5. Cities of the Plain

THE FIRST FORTY-FIVE PAGES OF THIS BOOK CONSIST, WITH A MINI-
MUM OF NARRATIVE DRAWN OUT IN THE EXAGGERATED RETARDA-
tions of a slow-motion camera, of an essay on homosexuality.
It has been shown that the initial impetus to undertake *Remembrance* came in the author's determination around 1908 to compose some articles dealing with homosexuality suitable to the
pages of a newspaper, relying for topical interest upon some
recently uncovered scandals in the highest reaches of European
society—the Eulenberg affair in the court of the German Emperor, Wilhelm II (which is mentioned in passing in the second
volume—page 129—of *Cities of the Plain*). Some of the material
in this opening chapter seems also to have been excerpted, as I
point out elsewhere, from Proust's abortive study *Contre Saint-
Beuve*.

Proust's philosophy is naturalistic, and he is ingenious in discovering likenesses between the vegetable, animal, and human
realms. The Baron de Charlus, "a pursy figure . . . his hair visibly
gray," and Jupien the tailor whom he accidentally encounters in
the courtyard of the Hotel de Guermantes are assimilated by
Marcel's observation to the plant he has been watching with bo-
tanical curiosity with its "offered and neglected pistil" patiently
waiting for the rare insect required to come and fertilize it." (2)
I have reversed the order which provides the significant parallels,
since in this dramatic situation the part of the bee ("humming like
a great bumble-bee"—p. 8) is played by Charlus while the part of
the plant (more particularly an orchid) is enacted by Jupien the
tailor, who is vividly described as standing fixed underneath the
Baron's meaningful look "like a plant." (5) The latter is compared explicitly to the orchid awaiting the arrival of the bee. (6)
Marcel himself is not unaware of the impression his description

is likely to make upon the traditionally-minded reader, for he says of the posture which Jupien assumes to attract Charlus (his backside provocatively stuck out): "I had not supposed he could appear so repellent." (6) Yet he adds a moment afterwards: "The scene was not, however, positively comic; it was stamped with a strangeness, or if you like a naturalness, the beauty of which steadily increased." (6) The description of something as both repellent and beautiful is not a mere instance of complacent self-contradiction or of the "multitudes" (to adopt Whitman's word declaring his independence of foolish consistency) which the narrator contains; it is rather the result of looking at the same object from different points of view. When Jupien's pose seems repellent to Marcel, he is no doubt taking the normal man's point of view, confronted with the ocular evidence of sexual perversion, but when he describes the scene between Charlus and Jupien as beautiful he is approaching it from the point of view of the human botanist thrilled by the curious spectacle life presents to his observation as a scientist who refuses to pass moral judgment upon its extraordinary variety. To the humanist, the series of "violent, inarticulate sounds" (12) which emerge from Jupien's shop where the two men have retired to complete their transaction may seem hideous to the point of being alarming because of their suggestion that men and animals are not so far removed from each other as we should like to think, but to the naturalist they seem like an agreeable confirmation of his hypothesis that forms of life, superficially so different from each other, are basically alike.

Marcel reminds the reader pointedly that he had long ago observed a preview of this scene between Charlus and Jupien when he had looked through the unshaded window at Montjouvain at Mlle. Vinteuil, the composer's daughter, and her Lesbian friend. (10) That scene had appeared to Proust's earlier readers to stick out like a sore thumb from the idyllic pages of the Combray portion in *Swann's Way*. Some of his more religiously-minded literary admirers like the poet Francis Jammes had argued with him to remove it altogether from his narrative. But now, the function of that earlier scene is much clearer in terms of the architecture of *Remembrance* as a whole (as Proust had assured them it would be in refusing their requests). Until this time, what Marcel had seen at Montjouvain seemed a unique and unparalleled form of behavior instead of being an instance of a fairly wide-spread vice. The scene in the Guermantes's courtyard causes a revolution in Marcel's vision of the Baron (18); much that had seemed odd, inexplicable, even mad in his behavior can now be explained simply as the consequence of his sexual compulsion. For instance, he now possesses the key to his behavior in that memorable scene in which he had been enraged to the point of smashing Charlus's top hat. He realizes that in addition to those persons (usually in a social class below him) with whom Charlus can satisfy his sensual urges directly through physical inter-course (as with Jupien) "there were in fact certain persons whom it was sufficient for him to make come to his house, hold an hour or two under the domination of his talk, for his desire, quickened by some earlier encounter, to be assuaged. By a simple use of words the conjunction was effected, as simply as it can be among the infusoria. Sometimes, as had doubtless been the case with me on the evening on which I had been summoned by him after the Guermantes dinner party, the relief was effected by a violent ejaculation which the Baron made in his visitor's face, just as cer-tain flowers, furnished with a hidden spring, sprinkle from within the unconsciously collaborating and disconcerted insect. M. de Charlus, from vanquished turning victor, feeling himself purged of his uneasiness and calmed, would send away the visitor who had at once ceased to appear to him desirable." (40–41)

As is proper to a full-dress essay on a large subject, Marcel divides it into parts. Thus, he speaks of the gregarious examples of homosexuality (25) and contrasts them with the "solitaries." (27) He speaks of the penalties of non-conformity to social custom (32) and of the fact that a man may belong in the ranks of a group whom *consciously* he shuns: "For no one can tell at first that he is an invert or a poet or a snob or a scoundrel." (33) He also continues his references to the *Arabian Nights* when Charlus, in conversing with Jupien, compares himself to the Caliph roaming about the streets of Bagdad in the guise of a com-mon merchant. (14) Homosexuals, says Marcel, live in a world in which "the most wildly improbable tales of adventure seem true, for in this romantic, anachronistic life the ambassador is a bosom friend of the felon, the prince, with a certain independence of action with which his aristocratic breeding has furnished him, and which the trembling little cit would lack, on leaving the duchess's party goes off to confer in private with the hooligan; a reprobate part of the human whole, but an important part, suspected where it does not exist, flaunting itself insolent and unpunished, where its existence is never guessed, numbering its adherents everywhere, among the people, in the army, in the church, in the prison, on the throne. . . ." (24)

What I missed in my first reading, distracted by the naturalistic comparisons, is the real accent of personal feeling which is the most impressive attribute of this chapter on second reading. This comes through particularly in the passages in which Marcel treats homosexuals of every variety as members of a single race apart and compares their plight movingly with that of another minority that has been subjected to various sanctions, persecutions and pressures by the majority through the centuries, namely the Jews. The two groups seemed to him comparable in that they were equally outcasts, and he was able to illuminate the situation of one of them through analogies with that of the other (just as many liberals in America now are able to understand indirectly the feelings of the Negroes by comparing them to other social pariahs). The Proustian apostrophes to the "race" of homosexuals are cast on the level almost of Miltonic eloquence with which Satan addresses the hosts of fallen angels in *Paradise Lost:* "Race upon which a curse weighs and which must live amid falsehood and perjury, because it knows the world to regard as a punishable and a scandalous, as an inadmissible thing, its desire, that which constitutes for every human creature the greatest happiness in life; which must deny its God, since even Christians, when at the bar of justice they appear and are arraigned, must before Christ and in his Name defend themselves, as from a calumny, from the charge of what to them is life itself; sons without a mother, to whom they are obliged to lie all her life long and even in the hour when they close her dying eyes; friends without friendships despite all those which their charm, frequently recognized, inspires and their hearts, often generous, would gladly feel, but can we describe as friendship those relations which flourish only by virtue of a lie and from which the first outburst of confidence and sincerity in which they might be tempted to indulge would make them expelled with disgust, unless they are dealing with an impartial, that is to say sympathetic mind, which however in that case, misled with regard to them by a conven-

tional psychology, will suppose to spring from the vice con-
fessed the very affection that is most alien to it, just as certain
judges assume and are more inclined to pardon murder in inverts
and treason in Jews for reasons derived from original sin and
racial predestination." (20–21)

After the introductory "essay" on homosexuality, *Cities of the
Plain* reverts to the point of the story which had been reached
at the end of *Guermantes Way II* where, as we recall, the Duke
and Duchess, Marcel and Swann had all been on their way to
the reception at the palace of the Prince de Guermantes. Marcel
still feels uncertain whether or not the invitation he has received
is a hoax. (47) This first reception at the Princesse de Guermantes's is generally reckoned one of the finest "set pieces" in
Remembrance; some readers have thought it the very finest example of its author's evocative power. In it, the long climb
upward from the drawing room of the Verdurins, through
that of the Saint-Euvertes, the Marquise de Villeparisis, and the
Duchess of Guermantes, which has traversed the various tiers of
French high society is at last complete. The pilgrimage has
reached its ultimate goal; one cannot rise higher in the Faubourg
Saint-Germain. If this Holy of Holies, too, turns out to be somewhat empty, that is not Marcel's fault. He is telling us simply
what he finally found on this expedition to the apex of fashionable French society. The challenge to the exploit was there—in
palpable reality as well as in a young man's romantic imagination
—and he rose to its requirements. When I use the word empty, I
mean to say devoid of real spiritual significance though not without charm and color and fascinating objects of interest such as
we find in all the salons depicted by Proust. That is, if one turns
one's attention from the "vapid conversation" (51) of the
Princesse de Guermantes and her "Royalties" and Ambassadresses
to the hidden streams of eccentricity that flow just below the
surface of this concourse of life as of every other, one may find
ample sources of amusement and possibly instruction and insight
into the realities of human nature.

Now that Marcel's eyes are at last unsealed to the hidden life
of the Baron de Charlus, he becomes aware that the society
around him (perhaps society in general) is swarming with illicit
lusts. He tells us in passing the story of a casual street affair

between the usher of the Princess who announces his name at the reception (which finally relieves his fear that he has been the victim of a practical joke) and one of the loftiest young noblemen in France, the Duc de Chattellerault (48–49). But most of the comedy at this party (and it is basically, like the other parties described, an exercise in comedy) is supplied, as might be expected, by the eccentric, the truly singular Charlus, whether it is in conjunction with M. de Sidonia who shares, if not his sexual weakness, his habit of "soliloquizing in society" (54–55) and sets up a dreadful cacophony with him—both talking at once and neither listening to the other, or with the diplomat, M. de Vaugoubert, minister to the court of King Theodosius, who has an irregular past and is a "confidant" (59) of Charlus though his political ambition has for many years had the effect of making him conform strictly to the recognized rules of society and has made him, at least outwardly, virtuous. (61) M. de Vaugoubert, as a comic figure, is ably seconded by the redoubtable Madame de Vaugoubert, who is said at the Ministry to wear the trousers in the family, while her husband wears the petticoats. (64) Charlus, incidentally, is described in this scene as being like a Harmony in Black and White by Whistler (who actually painted a portrait of Robert de Montesquiou—generally regarded as the principal model for Charlus—which is now part of the Frick Collection in New York and which may accurately be described in this fashion) and he is shown exchanging some spicy scandalous gossip along the lines of his special interests with Vaugoubert. (91 ff)

But, of course, Charlus and his cohorts and "confidants" are not the only ones present at the party. Marcel is surprised to meet Professor E. there—that physician who had diagnosed his grandmother's stroke but had been too busy to visit her at her home. Professor E., who is eager to learn if his fatal prognosis on that occasion has indeed been fulfilled, is a "man of a distinctly common type," (56) and his presence in such exclusive surroundings is explained by the fact that he has just cured the Prince of a nearly fatal case of septic pneumonia. The exception made in his favor proves the rule that governs the Princesse de Guermantes's salon and makes it the most rigorously exclusive one that Marcel has yet visited. Standing at the very pinnacle of society, the Princess can afford to be exclusive even in comparison with her very smart cousin, the Duchess, who is permissive almost to the point of being liberal in her eyes by consenting to entertain wealthy Jews and Jewesses like Mme. Alphonse Roths-child and Baron Hirsch whom the Princess would never deign to invite; the Duchess also admits into her salon upstart Bona-partists and even outright Republicans whom the Prince, a con-vinced and unbending Royalist, would never think of permitting his wife to invite. (95)

After several unsuccessful attempts and much bitter reflection on "the cowardice of people in society" (69-70) like Mme. de Sourvré, for example, who refuses to introduce Marcel to the Prince, he finally discovers someone almost by accident who is willing to perform that necessary amenity and finds his host's greeting, as he has expected it would be from what he has heard of him, "stiff, solemn, haughty." (77) The demeanor of this snobbish nobleman makes quite credible the malicious rumor which is circulating at the party that the Prince has taken his old school-friend Swann off to the further end of the garden in order "to shew him the door." (78) Marcel is shocked by this bit of intelligence which reaches him in several different versions, seeming to put the fact beyond question, and his effort to check the accuracy of the report at first hand with Swann himself supplies perhaps the main business of the evening in the narrative of Marcel.

The account of the Princess's reception contains a great many entertaining vignettes. There is one of the Marquise de Saint-Euverte (herself the hostess at the great reception described in the latter part of *Swann's Way*) recruiting or reminding half-hearted or reluctant guests of her own well-advertised enter-tainment the next day, which the Duchess (who has just dis-covered a pressing engagement at that very time) refers to as "her great annual beanfeast." (96) An invitation to the Saint-Euverte garden party is very much sought after by those who exist on the fringes of high society, like the provincial Mme. de Cambremer (who, after a certain number of years, has been quietly dropped by her hostess), but it is treated with unutter-able scorn by the thrice-noble, ultra-fashionable Charlus, who goes into an obscene speech on the subject—knowing perfectly well that Mme. de Saint-Euverte herself is within earshot: "Would you believe it, this impertinent young man . . . asked me just now, without any signs of that modesty which makes us keep such expeditions private, if I was going to Mme. de Saint-Euverte's, which is to say, I suppose, if I was suffering from the colic. I should endeavor, in any case, to relieve myself in some more comfortable place. . . . The proximity of the lady is enough. I say to myself all at once: oh, good lord, someone has broken the lid of my cesspool, when it is simply the Marquise opening her mouth to emit some invitation. And you can understand that if I had the misfortune to go to her house, the cesspool would be magnified into a formidable sewage-cart. . . ." (139–140) But the Marquise who cannot help overhearing him, pretends that she does not, begs his pardon obsequiously as she brushes past him and spiritlessly inquires of Marcel: "Tell me, what have I done to offend M. de Charlus? They say that he doesn't consider me smart enough for him." (141)

We are reminded over and over again that courage is far from common in society. The Duchess of Guermantes dreads the possibility of having to say hello to her old friend Swann in these anti-Semitic surroundings where she thinks he is in disgrace and she is relieved to learn that "there was no risk of having to converse in public with 'poor Charles' whom she preferred to cherish in private." (101) As for the Duke, he thinks it positively ungrateful on the part of Swann to have turned Dreyfusard. (107–108) "I would have answered for his patriotism as for my own. Ah! He is rewarding us very badly: I must confess that I should never have expected such a thing from him. I thought better of him." (109) The Duchess mentions Swann's pathetic desire to introduce his wife and daughter to her before he dies (which she has heard about indirectly) and treats the idea as the most intolerable bathos and sentimentality: "A writer with no talent would have only to say: 'Vote for me at the Academy because my wife is dying and I wish to give her this last happiness.' There would be no more entertaining if one was obliged to make friends with all the dying people." (112)

There is a brief sketch of the Marquise de Citri who, beginning with a fashionably blasé attitude, has ended by finding everything in the world—both in society and in art—a crashing bore! (120–122)And there is the amusing spectacle of Saint-Loup, still blissfully unaware of his uncle's vice and thinking of him as the formidable "womanizer" that he pretends he is, telling some stories about Charlus and Mme. Molé which (now that we are aware of the true state of affairs) seem artfully designed by the Baron himself to camouflage his incurable homosexuality. (127)

Swann's account of his interview with the Prince (which is as important in this party as the playing of the Vinteuil Sonata was during the Saint-Euverte party described in *Swann's Way*) begins as early as p. 124, but it is not completed for a long time because it keeps being interrupted by various personages and incidents that distract the attention of Marcel. These interruptions serve two purposes—first, they help to convey the activity, the liveliness, the sheer bustle of the party going on around the speaker—the difficulty of achieving any privacy or detachment in the midst of society—and second, they break up the tedium of a long exposition. In this latter function, they resemble the technique used by a dramatist—Shakespeare in *The Tempest* and in *Hamlet*—when he is confronted with the necessity of telling a long story about an action in the past and breaks it up (by means of questions and self-interruptions) into smaller units.

Swann tells Marcel that the malicious rumors about the Prince showing him the door are completely without foundation. Quite the contrary—the Prince has asked to see Swann because privately he has reached the same conclusion about the celebrated Case as his old friend. Not only that but his wife has quite independently arrived at the same conclusions and secretly subscribed to the Dreyfusard press because, not knowing what her husband was thinking, she did not want to alarm him. Even the priest who is his confessor agrees with him. (151) We now see how deliberate have been all the previous misdirections as to the character of the Prince de Guermantes in order to enhance the effect of this surprising reversal. We learn that there are Dreyfusards and anti-Dreyfusards of all shades and degrees of persuasion. To the fanatical Bloch, for example, who spends days in the court and, in order not to miss a single minute of the proceedings, brings sandwiches with him, the gentle Swann, in spite of his Dreyfusism, seems "lukewarm, infected with Nationalism and a militarist." (156–157)

But if there are surprising reversals of form, as in the case of the Prince, there are no less surprising instances of steadfastness, inertia, and running true to form in society. Running entirely true to form is the Marquise de Gallardon of whom there had been a delightful vignette in *Swann's Way* at the Saint-Euverte party. (S.W. 426 ff) This distant and a little disgraced relation of the Guermantes has not changed one whit in all the years since we have seen her; she is still absorbed in her favorite resentful meditations on the Duchess's neglect of her (165–166), and Oriane's unexpected courtesy and attention to her in the closing moments of the great reception exercise the same magical effect in turning her opinions inside out as they might have done years ago at the Saint-Euvertes. (169). A comparison of her role in *Swann's Way* and here in *Cities of the Plain* shows just how firmly Proust planned his story.

After the reception, as Marcel is expecting a call from Albertine (at a quarter to twelve at night), there is a comic caricature of the Duke, whose activities for the night are just beginning and who is on his way to his "delightful assignation" at the masked ball, refusing to believe the report brought to him in person by two of his relatives that his cousin Amanien, who had been lying so desperately ill, has breathed his last and that it is necessary to go into mourning at once. "He is dead!" the Duke cries in consternation. "No, no, they exaggerate, they exaggerate," and he continues his preparations for the ball. (173–174) The humor is so broad, the exaggeration so palpable in a passage of this kind that it quite justifies the comparison between Proust and Dickens which Edmund Wilson has suggested.

Marcel's disappointment at Albertine's failure to come to him when he is expecting her brings back thoughts of his unhappiness at the failure of his mother to come to say goodnight to him as a child in Combray. (184) He has a premonition that Albertine's life is so mysterious that only by imprisoning her could he hope to keep her under a watchful eye. (185) In the closing pages of this section, Marcel becomes ever more vividly aware of how unstable and fluctuating are the relationships of this world. There is a story of how the boorish Duke goes on a vacation to a resort where he meets three lovely Italian ladies who, with their beauty, birth and brains, convince him that his stubborn stand against Dreyfus is unenlightened and completely absurd. (193 ff) And Madame Verdurin, we are told, is gradually edging up into the fashionable world, in spite of the predominant Dreyfusism of her clan (in which the Sorbonne professor Brichot alone takes a Nationalist stand), because of her influential patronage of the increasingly smart Russian Ballet. (199) An uncle of Swann has died and left Gilberte 24,000,000 francs, "which meant that the Faubourg Saint-Germain was beginning to take an interest in her," since even the highest aristocracy is not above the need on occasion of transfusing bourgeois cash into its family financial veins. (204) All these changes—individual and social—seem senseless to Marcel (195), and the best image to express the meaningless succession of events and experiences is still that of the kaleidoscope.

The section following entitled *The Heart's Intermissions* (211 ff) tells of a second trip to Balbec in which the central episode involves an account of how, bending over to unbutton his shoes one day, Marcel suddenly and *blindingly* remembers the way in which his grandmother once performed this menial service for him (217). It is now a year after her death, and yet it is the first time he has realized her absence with real feeling, since the calendar of facts does not correspond mechanically with the calendar of our feelings about the facts. He dreams of his grandmother often after this. Judging from the hard point of view of the Duchess of Guermantes, one might say I suppose that Marcel *wallows* in the excess of his own sentiments (223, 224, 227). If ever he comes close to the brink of sentimentality it is in these pages, and perhaps even those not as callous or hard-hearted as the Duchess may be excused for thinking that he doesn't altogether escape the danger of toppling over the edge. The tears which Rousseau and the "Graveyard School" of English poetry brought back into literature in the eighteenth century are shed very copiously in this passage. Proust does not share the typical modernist's fear of allowing the simplest of human emotions to show themselves unashamedly in his protagonist.

CHAPTER 2 (255 FF)

If Sodom is to be understood as synonymous with the affinity of men for members of their own sex, Gomorrah, as the epigraph from Alfred de Vigny at the head of this volume makes clear, is the term for the perversion of women, more commonly known as Lesbianism or Sapphism. Marcel's distrust of Albertine and his suspicions of her Gomorrahn tendencies date from a chance remark made by Cottard to him, while watching her dance in the Casino with her breasts touching those of her partner Andrée. (272–273) Perhaps a good deal of Marcel's difficulties in love may be traced to his conviction that woman is "simply an accident placed so as to catch the ebullience of our desire." (319) This observation is of the same tenor as that made much earlier when he thinks of women as "different means to attain an identical pleasure." Brooding upon his mistress's possible abnormality, Marcel invents the idea of telling her that she has been accused of having unnatural relations with her friend Andrée. (323–324) She indignantly denies it, and Marcel has nothing substantial to go on, though he is conscious of living in an atmosphere in which much that had once seemed to him impossible is not really improbable. He had observed at the Princesse de Guermantes's that there is "no vice that does not find ready support in the best society." (161) There is a public scandal at this time about the unseemly behavior of a girl cousin of Bloch's and a retired actress. (336–337). Nissim Bernard, Bloch's uncle, is exposed as a member of Charlus's fraternity and the narrator knows him to be keeping an *embryo* waiter "as other men keep a chorus-girl from the opera." In short, Marcel feels uncertain about Albertine and vaguely unhappy about her. To be unhappy in love seems to Marcel, on the basis of his own experience and on the basis of what he has seen of Saint-Loup and heard about Swann and Odette, the normal state of affairs. He almost comes to the radical conclusion at this time that there is no such thing as reciprocal love: "I felt even then that in a love which is not reciprocated—I might as well say, in love, for there are people for whom there is no such thing as reciprocated love—we can enjoy only that simulacrum of happiness which had been given me at one of those unique moments in which a woman's good nature, or her caprice, or mere chance, brings to our desires, in perfect coincidence, the same words, the same actions as if we were really loved." (327)

VOLUME 2

Volume II of *Cities of the Plain* (in English—for the French *Sodome et Gomorrhe* is divided into more than three volumes) begins with a comic interlude concerning the misadventures of

Nissim Bernard with twin brothers who are identical in every respect except that one of them is homosexual and the other is not. (1–2) But the major part of the action takes place in the country house which the Verdurins have rented for the summer from the Cambremers. The Verdurin drawing-room had been the first to which we were introduced in *Swann's Way*. There is marked irony in the juxtaposition of the Princesse de Guermantes's very smart salon in the previous volume and "the lower depths," socially speaking, represented by the Verdurins (who are mere millionaires without any titles or a trace of aristocratic breeding). Yet the Verdurins, too, as had been hinted before, are engaged in "a timid evolution towards fashionable ways." (22) One of the signs of this is that they now require their dinner guests to dress formally. The guests have with the years risen to estimable places in their professions. Doctor Cottard (now Professor) and his wife are still among the faithful; his taste for the most atrocious puns is still in evidence but with his increased medical reputation his snobbery has grown. He is now something like the gross Professor E., and we are told that he would willingly skip a social function at the Verdurins' for a government minister's cold but not for a workingman's stroke. (36–37) Madame Verdurin's sense of self-preservation is indicated by her desire (in spite of her own beliefs) for another anti-Dreyfusard in her salon as a companion to Brichot who holds the fort of Nationalism alone there and "as a social counterpoise to the preponderant Dreyfusism of her salon." (43–44)

The old pianist at the Verdurins', Dechambre, who used to play Vinteuil's sonata for Swann and Odette, has just died, but the Verdurins, like their betters in society and incidentally like Huck Finn too, "don't take no stock in dead people" and forget them completely from the day they are gone. M. Verdurin asks his guests not to discuss Dechambre's death in front of Madame Verdurin because she is too sensitive, sympathetic, and easily upset—exactly as the Duke of Guermantes had undertaken the task of shielding the sensibilities of the Duchess which he himself was continually outraging with his extra-marital affairs. (58) The new man who is to take Dechambre's place in the Verdurin salon is the brilliant violinist Morel, a coarse creature whose father had once been a servant to Marcel's uncle Adolphe and who is now engaged in a homosexual affair with Charlus. (66)

Madame Verdurin is still up to her old tricks of breaking up love affairs of members of her little clan when she regards these affairs as unsuitable or dangerous to their reputations. The learned historian Brichot is the latest victim of her good offices. (20) The learning of Brichot is displayed with pedantic ostentation and it would never be suffered gladly in the more sophisticated circles of the Duchess of Guermantes. A good deal of his talk in this book is given over to a critical etymology of the names of places and people (47, 115–116) and of these endless Latin derivations it may be said perhaps, as Kenneth Burke once said of the inventories in Whitman's poetry, that the reader may profitably run his eyes down them as one runs one's eyes down a column of names in a telephone directory.

The social ineptness of the bourgeois Verdurins is demonstrated by their treatment of Charlus who enters their drawing room as a friend of Morel (just as Swann earlier had entered it as a friend of Odette). They are ignorant of the proper usages befitting the grand place which the Baron holds in high society and they treat him fatuously as if he were below the rank of their landlords, the Cambremers, who are inferior provincial nobility. When M. Verdurin explains condescendingly why he has not given Charlus the place of honor at the dinner table, the haughty Baron replies sharply: "That is not the slightest importance, *here*!" (121) His irony is lost on Verdurin who seriously explains that a Marquis like Cambremer outranks Charlus who is "only a Baron." "Pardon me," M. de Charlus replied with an arrogant air to the astonished Verdurin, "I am also Duc de Brabant, Damoiseau de Montargis, Prince d'Oléron, de Carency, de Viareggio and des Dunes. However, it is not of the slightest importance. Please do not distress yourself," he concluded, resuming his subtle smile which spread itself over these final words, "I could see at a glance that you were not accustomed to society." (122) One is certain that the Verdurins will repay Charlus with interest for his scorn when the proper moment presents itself, but that is not to be for still another volume. Meanwhile, they are satisfied with his mock deference to them, adopted cunningly since they provide a comfortable setting for his affair with Morel. (136) We are given samples of the brutal conversation between Charlus and Morel, by which they rouse each other's sensual fury. (210–212)

Passages on such subjects as Sleep and Time, Habit and Memory provide the ordinary cement which the narrator uses to bind the disparate materials and forms of his story together. (174 ff) The familiar leitmotif of a "horizon of waves" in connection with Albertine also makes its expected appearance as she comes on the scene once more. (228) Marcel's mother's objection to his increasingly obsessive concern with this girl has the adverse effect on her rebellious son of tying him more closely than ever to Albertine. (226) In general, the emphasis in this section is again upon change, flux in all things of this world, from new inventions such as the airplane, which makes its first appearance here and frightens the narrator's horse, to the continual alterations which occur in the relations between people.

Yet it appears at times that he shares the feeling of Ecclesiastes that all this sound and fury does not really signify, that "there is nothing new under the sun," and that underneath all of the surface variety there are a few basic, unchangeable patterns and a profound unity in human experience. In this vein, the affair between Charlus and Morel is compared by Marcel to that between Saint-Loup and Rachel (284), for in affairs of the heart the sex of the participants makes little if any difference. Normal and abnormal are not as far apart from each other as we have thought, and one can easily be transposed into terms of the other (as those critics suspected who have thought that Gilberte and Albertine, unusual names for women in French but extremely common in their masculine form, disguise the true sexual identity of the persons Marcel loves). It is not who or what one loves that is important, as Charlus observes at one point, but the fact of loving itself. The philosophically subjective and idealistic assumption behind this statement is also that of the author. Jealousy, torment, the unceasing seesaw of affections are as much the rule in homosexual as in more normal heterosexual relationships. Morel is a bisexual brute who is ready in a moment to crush anyone who stands in his way. (241) Charlus's attitude to him is compared to that of a doting father forgiving the coldness and rudeness of a beloved child. (286) In addition to other causes of irritation inseparable from all amorous relations, there is a rude class-conflict on the most primitive level between the Baron and his protégé. Reminding Morel unwittingly one day of his father's humble status as a serving-man, the Baron attempts to placate him by saying: "There was a time when my ancestors were proud of the title of groom, of butler to the King." "There was also a time," Morel replies with characteristic brutality, "when my ancestors cut off your ancestors' heads!" (287) Some of the wildest, most hysterically funny passages in Proust, put into the mouth of the Molièresque Charlus (298, 303–304), are to be found here. They seem literally to beg for extensive quotation had we room enough to include them. The incident involving the Prince de Guermantes, Morel and Charlus in a brothel, where Charlus has gone to spy on his beloved boy and has the tables unexpectedly turned on him to his complete discomfiture and overthrow is great humor worthy almost of Rabelais or Cervantes, which only the dourest, most strait-laced readers will fail to enjoy, in spite of the Neronian corruption of its subject matter. The unclean underside of society deserves its expert depicters as well as the more respectable and familiar one. And art is neutral as between the subject matter of Watteau and that of the makers of the frescoes at Pompeii. Proust on occasion resembles both.

Towards the end of *Cities II*, Marcel reaches a condition of ennui in his affair with Albertine where he decides to do as his mother has long advised him—break off with her. (337) The idea which had once crossed his mind of marrying Albertine appears to him in this new mood of sobriety to be sheer madness. (357) "I was only waiting for an opportunity for a final rupture." He tells his mother that he has at last "decided not to marry Albertine and would soon stop seeing her." (359) But his reckoning proves faulty, for, happening by chance one day to mention to her that he intends to ask Madame Verdurin to tell him what she knows about the publication of other works by Vinteuil in addition to the well-known sonata, Albertine turns out to be amazingly well-informed on the subject for the reason that one of her own best friends years ago is "the dearest and most intimate friend of your Vinteuil's daughter, and I know Vinteuil's daughter almost as well as I know her. I always call them my two big sisters." (361–362)

Being completely unaware of that unforgettable scene between Mlle. Vinteuil and her perverse friend which Marcel witnessed accidentally long ago at Montjouvain, Albertine cannot gauge the explosive effect which this revelation has upon his mind. It plunges him into an unbelievable hell of jealousy as if through a trapdoor. (362) All of his own feelings of guilt immediately come to the fore. He regards the blow which her information has struck his self-confidence "as a punishment, as a retribution (who can tell?) for my having allowed my grandmother to die perhaps; rising up suddenly from the black night in which it seemed forever buried, and striking, like an Avenger, in order to inaugurate for me a novel, terrible, and merited existence, perhaps also to make dazzlingly clear to my eyes the fatal consequences which evil actions indefinitely engender, not only for those who have committed them, but for those who have done no more, have thought that they were doing no more than look on at a curious and entertaining spectacle, like myself, alas, on that afternoon long ago at Montjouvain, concealed behind a bush where (as when I complacently listened to an account of Swann's love affairs) I had perilously allowed to expand within myself the fatal road, destined to cause me suffering, of Knowledge." (362) The figures in this passage are suggestive of the Bible and of biblical morality. At one stroke, Marcel appears to have grasped the entire Indian notion of Karma—that system of divine bookkeeping which insists on balanced accounts with the ineluctable rigor of the second law of thermodynamics or that force in the ethical universe which his youthful favorite Emerson preferred to call Compensation. He is completely broken up by Albertine's words and reduced to tears of helpless frustration. (364)

The metamorphosis in Marcel brought about by this unpredictable mishap is so radical that it has the effect of changing Albertine's familiar leitmotif, or rather it introduces another, older motive into his mind as he thinks of her: "Behind Albertine I no longer saw the blue mountains of the sea, but the room at Montjouvain where she was falling into the arms of Mlle. Vinteuil with that laugh in which she gave utterance to the strange sound of her enjoyment." (365) He invents some fantastic cock-and-bull story with which to explain the agony he is going through to Albertine, because his greater experience and maturity have taught him to be less candid than he once was; he cannot now afford to be "guilty of the imprudence that (he) should have committed in Gilberte's time of telling her that it was she (Albertine) whom (he) loved." (373) Instead of breaking with her as he had intended, he invites her to come and stay at his house in Paris where he can keep jealous watch over her to see that she does not renew her youthful, vicious associations. She quite properly objects that staying at his house with him might look exceedingly odd to the world. (374-375) The comparison of the kiss he gives Albertine and his mother's goodnight kiss at Combray returns as an exceedingly familiar theme by this time: "I kissed her as purely as if I had been kissing my mother to charm away a childish grief which as a child I did not believe that I would ever be able to eradicate from my heart." (375) Once again Marcel enlarges upon the theme of the subjective nature of love in language which is reminiscent, at least to my own ear, of that which Nietzsche uses in the part of *Zarathustra* in which he speaks of the love-relationship as the mutual recognition of two pagan deities in disguise. (379) In a touching scene with his mother, she invites him to look at the sunrise over the sea but all that he is able to see in his mind's eye is that agonizingly obsessive image of Albertine in the room of Mlle. Vinteuil at Montjouvain. (382) Besides, for him, or at least for the clarity of his mind, the sun is already setting, not rising. He is in the grip of a compulsion so far as his thoughts and actions are concerned. "Why this is hell, nor am I ever out of it," says Mephistopheles in Marlowe's *Dr. Faustus*. Marcel could echo these words. The world around him has changed its import into something so unrecognizable because of an eruption of irrational jealousy that he seems to experience a mental breakdown. On the last page of *Cities of the Plain*, Marcel suddenly reverses all that he has said to his mother about breaking off with Albertine. He tells her with an infinite number of tergiversations and apologies, conscious only that he is in the grip of feelings too powerful for him to control, no longer master of himself: "It is absolutely necessary that I marry Albertine." (384) The stage is now set for the spectacle of a man transformed into passion's slave, which unfolds in the following volume.

6. The Captive

THIS VOLUME AND THE FOLLOWING ONE ARE LARGELY CONCERNED WITH THE RELATIONSHIP BETWEEN MARCEL AND ALBERTINE. SINCE together, *The Captive* and *Sweet Cheat Gone* contain almost a thousand pages—that is to say a little less than one fourth the length of *Remembrance*—it is evident that more space is devoted to this story than to any other Proustian love affair. But what it gains over the much briefer account of the affair between Swann and Odette in elaboration it loses in concentration and relentless dramatic continuity. It may be said that it treats love epically, while the earlier volume treats it tragically, and it has long been noted that the severity, the logic, and the condensation into a limited compass which are characteristic of tragedy make it more aesthetically satisfactory, on the whole and when it is well-done by a master craftsman, than the looser and more digressive form of the epic. One reason that has been given for its relative inferiority is that it is part of the work that Proust had still not seen through to publication at the time of his death in 1922. It is not unfinished, of course, in the sense of having any of its parts missing or incomplete; it *is* unfinished in that Proust was not able to give it the same attentive modification (in the stage of galley proofs) which he gave to his other work and which was aimed at achieving a high degree of polish. It is hard to see, however, how any amount of polishing could have removed the kind of objections that are made by critics to this section of his work.

Edmund Wilson in *Axel's Castle* makes a representative criticism of *The Captive* and its sequel: "The episode with Albertine, upon which Proust put so much labor and which he intended for the climax of his book, has not been one of the most popular sections, and it is certainly one of the most trying to read. Albertine is seen in so many varying moods, made the subject of so many ideas, dissociated into so many different images, and her lover describes at such unconscionable length the writings of his own sensibility, that we sometimes feel ourselves going under in the gray horizonless ocean of analysis and lose sight of the basic situation, of Proust's unwavering objective grasp of the characters of both lovers which make the catastrophe inevitable. Furthermore, the episode of Albertine does not supply us with any of the things which we ordinarily expect from love affairs in novels: it is quite without tenderness, glamour or romance—the relation between Albertine and her lover seems to involve neither idealism nor enjoyment. But this is also its peculiar strength: it is one of the most original studies of love in fiction and, in spite of the highly special conditions under which it is made to take place, we recognize in it an inescapable truth. And it ends by moving us in a curious way. . . ."

Fortunately for the interest of *Remembrance*, *The Captive* is diversified with other subject matter than the relationship of Marcel and Albertine, or rather with the endless cerebrations of Marcel on his relationship with Albertine. It contains the account of the death of the novelist Bergotte (243–251) which is so fine an example of Proust's style and of his vision that it has been chosen perhaps more often by anthologists in search of a short specimen of his work than any other passage, though it is not as distinguished as any of the great parties which are described with a strange combination of loving detail and irony. One of the best presented of these parties, in fact, is a section of *The Captive* which shows the Baron de Charlus "bringing out" his protégé Morel before the choicest society of the Faubourg Saint-Germain in a concert given at the house of the Verdurins. This concert is immediately followed by Morel's brutal quarrel with Charlus (which is instigated by the Verdurins, outraged by the insolence of the Baron and his friends). This is one of the most cleverly managed narratives in Proust and must be discussed in more detail later.

Nowhere is the influence of the philosopher Schopenhauer upon Proust's vision of the world clearer than in the delineation of the particular stage of Marcel's relationship with Albertine chronicled in *The Captive*. All the love affairs of *Remembrance*, whether heterosexual or homosexual, bear a family resemblance to each other, but the situation of the narrator and Albertine as it is portrayed in this book is without exact parallel elsewhere. For here, the woman is not only poorer than the man and for that reason financially dependent upon him either completely or in large part (as Odette was upon Swann, Rachel upon Robert de Saint-Loup, and Morel upon Charlus) but she is living in his house under the watchful care of himself, his servant Françoise, his chauffeur, and even her friend Andrée with whom Marcel is in league. The problem Proust poses for himself in this book is to find out what would happen if a man possessed the means virtually to isolate his loved one from the corruptions of the world and not only to keep her but to keep her "prisoner." Marriage in Proust's pages, as I have had occasion to remark before, is strictly separated from love. Swann marries Odette only after he is no longer in love with her; Robert de Saint-Loup marries Gilberte Swann only in order to lay hold of her considerable fortune. Proust is interested in seeing what happens when one human being holds another "captive" not with the bonds of law or of social convention but despite and almost in the teeth of such things. Some readers have complained that the situation portrayed is, from a realistic point of view, impossible and they have felt that the reason must be that Proust himself, being admittedly homosexual in his tastes, has transposed the character of the woman from an original male model, whom they easily identify. But there is no weakness, as I see it, in this transposition; the author has the fictional skill to carry it off successfully. Proust was not a *realist* in the programmatic sense of the term and the objections to the lack of verisimilitude in this story would have seemed a small objection to him; nevertheless, I shall indicate that even on fairly rigid realistic grounds his story in *The Captive* is not so weak as is sometimes made out.

No, the weakness if it has one stems from another source and that is the fact that the affair with Albertine supports in almost dogmatic, doctrinaire fashion a pessimistic philosophical view of the world which insists that humanity is condemned from the outset to a pitiless alternation of pain and boredom in all of its experiences and more particularly in the development of its sentiments and passions. Perhaps the same moral may be read from the other love experiences narrated by Marcel, but nowhere else does he insist on interpreting that meaning for us so completely. It is this perhaps that results in the impression of a somewhat dry mathematical demonstration which the story has made upon some readers.

The key to the feeling Marcel would impress upon us in this narrative is contained in one of the final pages of the book which deserves, in fact needs, to be quoted entire: "I felt that my life with Albertine was, on the one hand, when I was not jealous, mere boredom, and on the other hand, when I was jealous, constant suffering. Supposing that there was any happiness in it, it could not last. I possessed the same spirit of wisdom which had inspired me at Balbec, when, on the evening when we had been happy together after Madame de Cambremer's call, I determined to give her up, because I knew that by prolonging our intimacy I should gain nothing. Only, even now, I imagined that the memory which I should preserve of her would be like a sort of vibration prolonged by a pedal from the last moment of our parting. And so I intended to choose a pleasant moment, so that it might be it which would continue to vibrate in me. It must not be too difficult, I must not wait too long, I must be prudent. And yet, having waited so long, it would be madness not to wait a few days longer, until an acceptable moment should offer itself, rather than risk seeing her depart with that same sense of revolt which I had felt in the past when Mamma left my bedside without bidding me good night, or when she said good-bye to me at the station." (537–538)

The tone, the rhythm, even the vocabulary of the initial sentence in this passage is straight out of *The World as Will and Idea*. As for the reasoning in the latter half of the passage it reminds me of nothing so much as of Hamlet's when he is busy convincing himself, as he comes upon the king kneeling in prayer, that this is not a propitious moment for him to exact his revenge. Marcel is no less a procrastinator than the Prince and no less ingenious in the variety of the rationalizations with which he hides this characteristic from himself. The passage contains the essence of what happens in the story of Albertine's captivity. Everything is here, even the comparison with his mother's goodnight kiss at Combray, which is a leitmotif lacing itself through *Remembrance* from beginning to end. Nowhere else does he labor so singlemindedly to expose the vanity of love and possibly of life itself.

Human beings, in this vision, are walled off from each other "like so many houses" (the phrase is from Céline's *Journey to the End of the Night* but accurately expresses Proust's feeling too). A premonition of this is already present in the opening pages of *The Captive*, which are concerned with the happier aspects of the experience. Marcel speaks of his delight in "the double privacy" of washing himself in a dressing room separated from Albertine's by a thin partition. (4) To be sure, the intention which is realized here is to convey a feeling of sensual intimacy, and yet the theme of separation (no matter by what thin partitions) of Albertine from himself is unmistakably sounded. Like the woman in T. S. Eliot's *Waste Land*, Marcel's torture is that he never knows the answers to the questions: "What are you thinking of? What thinking? What? / I never know what you are thinking." But the dispiriting conclusion of Marcel is that there is nothing unusual in this. The feeling is not simply due to neurosis or eccentricity but is the result of the ordinary, normal condition of humanity—a condition which we never become aware of so painfully as when we are in love.

Albertine's presence, from the beginning, represented for Marcel (again in language reminiscent of Schopenhauer's) "a release from suffering rather than a positive joy." (5) When his suffering which is caused by jealousy of Albertine is quieted and seemingly disappears for a time, so correspondingly does Marcel's love for her disappear. (17) But this does not often happen, for the city of Paris, like the rest of the world, is swarming with desires, lust, evil, assignations, and deceit. (19) The particular facet of this universal observation which interests Marcel is that the original Gomorrah, which represented according to his imagination the concentration of all feminine lusts into one spot, has been "dispersed to the ends of the earth." (20) As an object in herself, Albertine seems daily less attractive to Marcel who observes that it is only the desires she arouses in others and feels for others that succeed in tying him ever more closely to her: "Pain she was capable of causing me; joy, never. . . . Pain alone kept my tedious attachment alive." (27)

One noticeable feature of this affair with Albertine is the frequency with which Marcel describes her appearance when asleep. (e.g. 84 ff, 147, etc.) These are among the most lyrical and, despite Wilson's denial of the quality, the most tender passages of the story. When she is awake, the relationship is characterized only too often by hostility, suspicion, and conflict. It is when she is "animated . . . only by the unconscious life of vegetation, of trees" that Marcel can be wholeheartedly fond of her. He dramatizes the saying of old-fashioned parents that a child is good only when he or she is asleep. At other times, she is in flight from him in the direction of her own dreams and desires, and she stubbornly resists his attempts to encroach any further upon her imaginative domain than she is prepared to let him. Love is difficult indeed between intensely subjective human beings; it is difficult to the point of being impossible between complete solipsists. One is not sure to which category Marcel belongs and one is not certain too if he is saying that everybody else in the world, in spite of pretences to the contrary, belongs to the same category as himself.

Love in Proust is an exercise in futility when it is not the most painful of punishments. The reason for this is that "generally speaking, love has not as its object a human body, except when an emotion, the fear of losing it, the uncertainty of finding it again have been infused into it. This sort of anxiety has a great affinity for bodies. It adds to them a quality which surpasses beauty even; which is one of the reasons why we see men who are indifferent to the most beautiful women fall passionately in love with others who appear to us ugly. To these people, these fugitives, their own nature, our anxiety fastens wings. And even when they are in our company the look in their eyes seems to warn us that they are about to take flight. The proof of this beauty, surpassing the beauty added by the wings, is that very often the same person is, in our eyes, alternately wingless and winged. Afraid of losing her, we forget all the others whom at once we prefer to her. And as these emotions and these uncertainties may vary from week to week, a person may one week see sacrificed to her everything that gave her pleasure, in the following week be sacrificed herself, and so for weeks and months on end."

The universe of Marcel is a Heraclitean universe in which, to use the bitter expression of Aristophanes, Whirl is King. Neither people nor things ever remain really stationary for very long. "The stability of nature which we ascribe to (anything) is purely fictitious and a convenience of speech." (78) All human activities and ambitions turn out to be "striving after wind."

All persons and institutions are transitory, ephemeral, ultimately unreal. Marcel writes despairingly: "I am brought up against the difficulty of presenting a permanent image as well of a character as of societies and passions. For it changes no less than they, and if we wish to portray what is relatively unchanging in it, we see it present in succession different aspects (implying that it cannot remain still but keeps moving) to the disconcerted artist." (444) To depict a Bergsonian world in which life is defined as "a perpetual gushing forth of novelties," the artist is in need of something like the futuristic painting technique of the Italian Marinetti which produced the famous picture of a running dog with a dozen fanned-out legs (in a desperate effort to catch that feeling of movement which is central to the vision of such artists). The style of the Futurist Manifesto of 1911 is inferior to Proust's, but the feeling which inspired it is similar to the one in the passage I have just quoted from him, and *The Captive* at times reads as if it were designed as an illustration of its theory. The Futurists wrote: "The simultaneousness of states of the soul at a given moment is the basis and end of our art."

Here, for instance, is one of the descriptions of the uncapturable essence of Albertine: "It was incredible how spasmodic her life was, how fugitive her strongest desires. She would be mad about a person whom, three days later, she would refuse to see. She could not wait an hour while I sent out for canvas and colors, for she wished to start painting again. For two whole days she was impatient, almost shed the tears, quickly dried, of an infant that has just been weaned from its nurse. And this instability of her feelings with regard to people, things, occupations, arts, places, was in fact so universal that, if she did love money, which I do not believe, she cannot have loved it for longer than anything else." (556)

Change and chance divide the rule of such a world between them. And all change is in the direction of disappearance and annihilation. The way Marcel puts it, with a twinge of pathos in his voice, is this: "All love, and everything else, evolves rapidly towards a farewell." (483) Hemingway has said the same thing in a somewhat more muscular fashion: "All stories, if continued far enough, end in death, and he is no true story-teller who would keep that from you." And speaking of Hemingway reminds me that Proust is streaked with a nihilism that is not surprising in an admirer of Schopenhauer and that never comes out so clearly as when he speaks of death. In *The Captive*, it is the death of the writer Bergotte that gives him the occasion to express some feelings of the bleakest pessimism. At the beginning of the following passage, it is into the mouth of Bergotte that such sentiments are put, but at the end it is clear that they are those of Marcel too. In fact, the dying Bergotte bears a marked resemblance to descriptions of Proust himself in his last days: "Bergotte never went out of doors, and when he got out of bed for an hour in his room, he would be smothered in shawls, plaids, all the things with which a person covers himself before exposing himself to intense cold or getting into a railway train. He would apologize to the few friends whom he allowed to penetrate to his sanctuary, and, pointing to his tartan plaids, his travelling-rugs, would say merrily: 'After all, my dear fellow, life, as Anaxagoras has said, is a journey.' Thus he went on growing steadily colder, a tiny planet that offered a prophetic image of the greater, when gradually heat will withdraw from the earth, then life itself. Then the resurrection will have come to an end, for if, among future generations, the works of men are to shine, there must first of all be men. If certain kinds of animals hold out longer against the invading chill, when there are no longer any men, and if we suppose Bergotte's fame to have lasted so long, suddenly it will be extinguished for all time. It will not be the last animals that will read him, for it is scarcely probable that, like the Apostles on the Day of Pentecost, they will be able to understand the speech of the various races of mankind without having learned it." (245–246)

The character of Bergotte is modeled, in addition to Proust himself, upon Anatole France and John Ruskin, and it is the first of these that the style and mocking scepticism in the tone of the passage above bring to mind. There is a passage in Anatole France's *La vie littéraire* which seems to me not at all distant from it in content or in manner: "Our planet will be very old and will approach the term of its destiny. The sun whose spots, not without reason, trouble us even now, will in those days turn to the earth a face of sombre and fuliginous red, half covered by opaque scoriae, and the last men, taking refuge in the depths of mines, will be less anxious to dispute on the essence of the beautiful than to burn their last fragments of coal before plunging into the eternal ice."

But struggling against this nihilistic scepticism in Proust and in contradiction to it is another element which probably came to him from the teachings of Plato or of Kant. For Proust possessed a powerful will to believe in the redemptive quality of art itself (redemption by means of art may be said to be the most important theme of his work as a whole) and in order to be able to do so he had to postulate a world of ideas or a noumenal world above the evanescent world of passing phenomena. The pressure of this contradiction drives him some pages later in the section on Bergotte's death to speculate that the appearances which have led him into despair may be deceptive and that the truth is possibly very different and more hopeful. It is not the dogmas of religion which reassure Marcel but the devotion of the artist (or indeed of any man) to the task he has set for himself: "All that we can say is that everything is arranged in this life as though we entered it carrying the burden of obligations contracted in a former life; there is no reason inherent in the conditions of life on this earth that can make us consider ourselves obliged to do good, to be fastidious, to be polite even, nor make the talented artist consider himself obliged to begin over again a score of times a piece of work the admiration aroused by which will matter little to his body devoured by worms, like a patch of yellow wall painted with so much knowledge and skill by an artist who must forever remain unknown and is barely identified under the name Vermeer. All these obligations which have not their sanction in our present life seem to belong to a different world, founded upon kindness, scrupulosity, self-sacrifice, a world entirely different from this, which we leave in order to be born into this one, before returning perhaps to the other to live once again beneath the sway of those unknown laws which we have obeyed because we bore their precepts in our hearts, knowing not whose hand had traced them there—those laws to which every profound work of the intellect brings us nearer and which are invisible only—and still—to fools. So that the idea that Bergotte was not wholly and permanently dead is by no means improbable." (250–251)

The feeling expressed here is not to be found in Hemingway

or in Anatole France or in any of our modern existentialists, but is peculiar to Proust himself and is a residue of an older philosophical idealism which he drew upon in striving to make of Art a substitute for the religion which was no longer meaningful to him. The mention of Vermeer's patch of yellow wall relates to the precise manner of Bergotte's death, for the writer had gone to an exhibition of the painter's works because of a critical article he had read which had drawn attention to an exquisitely painted little patch of yellow wall in a famous picture by Vermeer, which he did not clearly remember. It is at this exhibition that he is felled by the stroke that kills him, but before he dies he has time to savor the perfection with which that little patch of yellow wall is done and to regret that his work has never been so completely finished. He says to himself looking at Vermeer's painting: "That is how I ought to have written. My last books are too dry. I ought to have gone over them with several coats of paint, made my language exquisite in itself, like this little patch of yellow wall." (249) And there appears before his mind a pair of "celestial" scales with life, his life, in one, and art, Vermeer's art, in the other. He vainly regrets the surrender of one for the other—that is, as I interpret it, he regrets having wanted so much to live that he has left his art, the only justification of his life, unfinished. Art to him is something higher than life and can be produced only by the continual sacrifice of life. (250)

Chapter 2 of *The Captive* (259 ff.) is concerned with the monumental quarrel between the Verdurins and Charlus. This surpasses in venom even the quarrel between Swann and the Verdurins narrated in the first volume of *Remembrance*. The causes of both quarrels, however, is the same; it is the constancy in the character of the Verdurins' jealousy of their position of dominance in their "little clan" and their ferocity when they feel that their position is in any way threatened. Their partiality to members of their "clan" is attended with the condition that these members must owe their first loyalty to the Verdurins rather than to each other. Consequently, a too intimate relation between any two of the "faithful" and more particularly a love affair between them represents a grave danger from the Verdurin point of view. In the past, they had broken up amorous relationships of Swann and of Brichot; now they undertake to do the same thing in the case of the homosexual affair between Charlus and Morel. In a sense, the sexual invert is in a more exposed position to those wishing to assault him than is the man whose tastes are within the normal fold, and yet Charlus, because of his noble lineage, the haughtiness of his temper, and his general unpredictability, offers a more difficult problem to the Verdurins than either Swann or the timid pedant Brichot ever did.

The quarrel had been brewing for a long time, as I have indicated earlier. The occasion is provided by the concert arranged by the Baron for Morel's presentation to society in the house of the Verdurins. The narrative of this episode seems to me on the highest level of story-telling technique, and I should like to indicate the essential steps of the development. If any proof were still needed that Proust is *professional* in the best sense, it would be here. He does not miss a trick in scoring his effects, which are all calculated and are made to seem spontaneous, so that at least two readings are necessary to lay bare and appreciate the mechanism of his contrivance.

To prepare for the role reserved for Morel in the climactic scene, he lays in his preparations in advance by showing the violinist behaving brutally to his fiancée, the niece of the tailor Jupien (the matchmaker is Charlus, who takes his substitute avuncular role very seriously; Morel is evidently lustful with regard to both sexes!) (216–217) A little while later, the narrator comes across Morel crying bitterly with regret for the hurt he has done the gentle girl whom he loves. (260–261) It is important to Proust to establish the range of his characters' possibilities. The sentiment of regret shown by Morel indicates to Marcel that the brute whom he had seen earlier that day is on his way from being an animal (specifically he is compared to an orang-outang) to becoming a human being, (261) but the point has been made that he can, if provoked, behave with merciless brutality. The next hint that is dropped is that Charlus has entered a new and degrading phase in the development of his vice, where he has become the helpless target of numerous blackmailers "by whom this powerful monster was, evidently against his will, invariably escorted, although at a certain distance, as is the shark by its pilot, in short contrasting so markedly with the haughty stranger of my first visit to Balbec, with his stern aspect, his affectation of virility, that I seemed to be discovering, accompanied by its satellite, a planet at a wholly different period of its revolution, when one begins to see it full, or a sick man now devoured by the malady which a few years ago was but a tiny spot which was easily concealed and the gravity of which was never suspected." (274–275)

With these advance preparations, the action proper of the scene can begin to unfold. The concert at the Verdurins serves to introduce Morel to society, but it also serves to introduce a new work by Vinteuil, a septet, which is a later and profounder work than the sonata of which we have heard so much in earlier volumes. This work was deciphered by the daughter of the composer and her perverse friend, whom Marcel saw many years ago at Montjouvain spitting upon the old man's picture. Her beneficent action in bringing to light a new, unknown masterpiece by Vinteuil gives the narrator the opportunity to reflect on the many-sidedness of the human personality and on the connection of homosexuality (and Lesbianism) with a heightened aesthetic sensitivity often absent in normal people.

The basic motivation of the Verdurins in their plot to embroil Charlus with Morel is his insulting attitude toward them, his contempt which he makes them feel at every moment, but the boredom of their lives also has a part in making them wish to create trouble: "Assiduous attendance at their Wednesdays aroused in the Verdurins . . . the desire to quarrel, to hold aloof. It had been strengthened, had almost been wrought to a frenzy during the months spent at la Raspelière, where they were together morning, noon and night. M. Verdurin went out of his way to prove one of his guests in the wrong, to spin webs in which he might hand over to his comrade spider some innocent fly. Failing a grievance, he would invent an absurdity. As soon as one of the faithful had been out of the house for half an hour, they would make fun of him in front of the others, would feign surprise that their guests had not noticed how his teeth were never clean, or how on the contrary he had a mania for brushing them twenty times a day." (309–310)

The boredom of such idle people combines with their resentments as social parvenus to create mischief. In making plans for the great party, M. de Charlus has wounded Madame Verdurin's susceptibilities a hundred times by the kind of criticism he made of her social sense and sophistication. The examples furnished by Marcel of the Baron's demands and the mimicry of the scathing tone which he uses to Madame Verdurin are so ingenious and convincing that the reader feels that if she were gifted with the hide of a rhinoceros, her sensibilities must still have been wounded. Material is being accumulated for an explosion, which occurs before the evening is over. Even better is the description of the really inimitable insolence of Charlus's smart guests from the Faubourg Saint-Germain, all of whom (with one exception) are so oblivious to the presence of Madame Verdurin—treating Charlus as their host of the evening—that they make rude and insulting remarks about her in her very presence. (331) The exception to the rule (and this has a surprising function in the narrative) is the most eminent guest of all, the Queen of Naples, who does not think it is beneath her to speak kindly to Madame Verdurin as well as to the Baron de Charlus. (333) This does something to mollify Madame Verdurin's feelings but not enough and other causes of offence follow. It is bad enough that Charlus bids goodbye to his aristocratic friends without asking them to express their appreciation to Madame Verdurin in whose house, after all, they are guests. (359) But when he goes to the length of telling her that the Duchesse de Duras, who was "enchanted" by the concert, has engaged Morel to play in her house and that he is "even thinking of asking her for an invitation for M. Verdurin" (375) he is either seeking the punishment which swiftly descends upon him or else in his narcissism he is completely oblivious to the fact that "this civility to the husband alone was . . . the most wounding outrage to the wife."

While Charlus is exulting in the success of his venture both socially and artistically, M. and Madame Verdurin conspire against him by drawing Morel aside and convincing him that the gossip which is rife about him and M. de Charlus is going to be the ruin of his career. (420–421) This part of the narrative is treated with great adroitness and particularly with regard to the lie that convinces Morel beyond a doubt that they are telling him the truth. This careerist who places his reputation as a musician above every other consideration is sufficiently alarmed by the information that the world seems to be in on the secret of his unnatural relationship to Charlus, but still he cannot resist the feeling that such an event as the one this evening has done much to enhance his name with an important segment of the public. The coup de grâce is struck when Madame Verdurin, perhaps sensing his hesitation, is inspired to tell him that she has heard Charlus refer to Morel as "my servant" (425) and to reveal what he has been at such pains throughout to conceal—namely, that his father had been a valet to Marcel's uncle. From this point on, Morel's mind is made up; he is as filled with bestial fury as he was on that afternoon when he had given his gentle fiancée so brutal a tonguelashing. He rebuffs Charlus abruptly and so publicly (428) that the latter is completely thunderstruck and fails, as the narrator knowing his character had expected him to do, to pulverize his ungrateful protégé with Jupiterian scorn. It is at this point that the Queen of Naples returns to the scene. Something had been said earlier about a fan she had forgotten when she left. Coming back unobserved into the room, she witnesses the humiliation of her kinsman Charlus, understands its cause in an instant, and unhesitatingly goes to his support. She snubs Madame Verdurin, whom she had earlier been polite to, rebuffs Morel's effort to be presented to her, gives her arm to the degraded Baron to help him out of this drawing room which had witnessed his scintillating social triumph and abysmal personal defeat in so short a span of time. (434)

Now this, if you prefer, is a melodrama and caricature which seem fit for a low-class stage (in spite of the elevated status of its participants) and yet there is some magic in Marcel's narration which makes the story serious rather than merely droll or ridiculous. He is able to carry at least this reader with him (and I suspect many another too) when he says concerning his reaction to the spectacle of wanton cruelty he has presented: "The sense of justice was so far lacking in me as to amount to an entire want of moral sense. I was in my heart of hearts entirely won over to the side of the weaker party, and of anyone who was in trouble." (394) By this excuse, he means to say, I suppose, that the moment that the Baron becomes the victim of a conspiracy, his own aberrant sexual behavior and his insolence and malice are forgotten and he lays claim to the universal sympathy extended to the underdog. In several places in this volume, Marcel indicates that he is self-conscious that the unusual nature of his characters seems to require some apology or explanation to the reader: "Art extracted from the most familiar reality does indeed exist and its domain is perhaps the largest of any. But it is not less true that a strong interest, not to say beauty, may be found in actions inspired by a cast of mind so remote from anything that we feel, from anything that we believe, that we cannot ever succeed in understanding them, that they are displayed before our eyes like a spectacle without rhyme or reason. What could be more poetic than Xerxes, son of Darius, ordering the sea to be scourged with rods for having engulfed his fleet?" (54)

Even more direct is the self-justification in the following passage: "The poet is to be pitied, who must, with no Virgil to guide him, pass through the circles of an inferno of sulphur and brimstone to cast himself into the fire that falls from heaven, in order to rescue a few of the inhabitants of Sodom! No charm in his work; the same severity in his life as in those of unfrocked priests who follow the strictest rule of celibacy so that no one may be able to ascribe to anything but loss of faith their discarding of the cassock." (281) Well, he needn't have worried that the reader would leave him in the lurch because of his eccentric characters, for somehow he has been able (like Dostoyevsky and Shakespeare in this respect) to endow his eccentrics with so much humanity that it is impossible for the reader (except through general aesthetic insensitivity) to fail to identify himself with them or to have compassion for them. He may think concerning them occasionally what one of the characters of Fitzgerald's novel says of the murdered Gatsby: "The poor son of a bitch!" but it will not be intended as a distant, cold, uncharitable judgment.

One more note on the aftermath of this party. It is significant that directly in the wake of showing the Verdurins attacking their prey with tooth and claw, Marcel tells how he learned later on of their secret benefaction to their relative Saniette, whom they have so often persecuted and made fun of, but whom they aided (without his knowledge) in his time of dire financial need. (440) The purpose of introducing this moral whitewash into the picture at this point appears to be to soften the harsh black of the characters he has drawn into a softer gray, which has a greater fidelity to the facts of human nature, the discontinuity of character, as these appear through Proust's eyes.

If even the deepest dyed of Proustian villains, like Morel and the Verdurins, show spasmodic impulses in the direction of human kindness, more important characters like Albertine are even more ambiguous and Janus-faced. It is never really certain, for example, that Albertine is "by nature" a liar as Marcel calls her at one point. (125) To be sure, she is caught lying on a number of occasions—for example, when she had unwittingly claimed a visit to Bergotte at a time when subsequent newspaper reports indicate that he was already dead! (252) Or when Madame Bontemps, her aunt, visiting Marcel, casually reveals that Albertine had been lying when she denied having visited Buttes-Chaumont. (531) When Marcel says at one point: "Albertine, can you swear you never lied to me?" she replies, "Yes, that is to say no. . . ." and immediately confesses having taken a three-week trip with a girl whom she had that very morning denied ever meeting! (479) But Marcel admits to lies which he himself uttered to Albertine in a cunning attempt to make her love him and do his bidding; he says candidly, "My words, therefore, did not in the least reflect my sentiments." (475) And he clearly recognizes the possibility that his jealousy of Albertine (and consequently his entire response to her and his evaluation of her character and motives) may be merely a projection caused by his own unfaithfulness to her: "As we have no personal knowledge, one might almost say that we can feel no jealousy save of ourself." (526) This kind of subjectivism is surely close to the edge of complete solipsism.

One possible explanation for the shifts and evasions so characteristic of Marcel's affair with Albertine may lie in the commonplace comparison made between war and love, which is developed here to epic length so that it becomes anything but commonplace. (494–495) Every tactical device is fairly used in both situations. Marcel recognizes that the relationship he depicts is basically one of hostility: "I here give the name of love to a mutual torment." (142) And again: "We love only what we do not wholly possess." (138) Physical "possession" is a mockery in which "we possess nothing," because the soul, more delicate and subtle than a perfume, penetrates through the thickest walls and frustrates every stratagem to imprison it.

In Schopenhauer, the ultimate reality behind which human intellect cannot go is the restlessly striving Will, and similarly in Proustian love there is something endless, impersonal and compulsive: "Amorous curiosity . . . forever disappointed . . . revives and remains forever insatiable." (188) A man may think that he is in love with a particular person who is irreplaceable for him; this necessary illusion is the cause of much of the suffering which love brings with it. Actually a man's love is simply "an ardent and painful devotion . . . to the youth and beauty of Woman." (94) It is not voluntary at all but purely involuntary and instinctive. The philosophical approach and the search for general psychological laws which are characteristic of *The Captive* result in that aphoristic, abstract quality of the work which are complained of by those who find too little verisimilitude or realism in its treatment of the concrete situation within it. How is it conceivable, they ask, that an unmarried young girl like Albertine would permit herself to get into a situation where she was living in the Parisian apartment of Marcel? How is it possible that the respectable, bourgeois Madame Bontemps, her aunt and guardian, would permit such a thing? These rhetorical questions having no satisfactory answer to them, such critics go on to surmise that the situation is really homosexual and that Albertine is a thinly disguised male character.

But it seems to me that the author has anticipated such objections and has dealt with them adequately. The fundamental premise of the situation is that Albertine is a wild, impulsive, self-humoring, unconventional creature who acts to please herself and is not too concerned with appearances or what people will think or say. As for the complaisance of Madame Bontemps, the first one to be shocked by it is not the ultra-critical reader but Marcel's mother. (8) The narrator explains his mother's own permissiveness in what might be regarded as a scandalous arrangement by indicating that he has so far succeeded in taming her through illness and self-indulgence that she no longer dares reproach him for "my nervous instability, laziness" (7) or presumably anything else. Marcel also realizes that Madame Bontemps, as a tight-fisted French bourgeoise, is delighted not to be spending anything to support Albertine, is hoping to marry her off to Marcel, and even eventually to get back what she had already spent upon her before marriage. (259) Albertine herself is obviously hoping that the situation will be resolved by marriage, though she says that she is "too poor" for Marcel to marry her. (12) There is no formal promise of marriage on his part, but he mentions the subject from time to time and evidently dangles the prospect before her as an inducement to stay on with him. This is so true that his mother, who knows him very well, is finally forced with the aid of an appropriate quotation from Madame de Sévigné to tell him that he must desist from his course and stop disturbing the mind of a girl whom he has no intention of marrying. "This letter from my mother brought me back to earth." (496)

It is clear, then, that Marcel is intended to be up in the clouds during the greater part of this phase of the affair, and he himself remarks on the improbability of Albertine's living with him as she is doing. (55) Aristotle pointed out paradoxically in *The Poetics* long ago that it is probable that many things happen contrary to probability. He warned the dramatist against utilizing merely possible contingencies in the action of his play. But Proust is not a classicist in his principles, and he avails himself of the romantic, adventurous possibilities in life as a subject for his art. Granted that the given facts which are axiomatic in this story of Albertine and Marcel are somewhat implausible, cannot the same objection be made to all the romances of the world: Balzac's *Droll Stories*, Boccaccio's *Decameron*, or Marcel's own favorite *Thousand and One Nights?*

As for the transposition of the sex of the heroine, that may have been necessitated by the nature of Proust's own experience, but as I have indicated earlier he should have had to be a negligible author to have left any telltale seams after the change. Certainly, he has the power of evoking the purely feminine charm of Albertine, (98) and the single most original and vivid touch of the affair, the description of the effect of the linked shadows of himself and Albertine upon Marcel's sensibilities, delineates the figure of a woman: "At our feet, our parallel shadows, where they approached and joined, traced an exquisite pattern. No doubt it already seemed to me a marvellous thing at home that Albertine should be living with me, that it should be she that came and lay down on my bed. But it was so to speak the transportation of that marvel out of doors, into the heart of nature, that by the shore of that lake in the Bois, of which I was so fond, beneath the trees, it should be her and none but her shadow, the pure and simplified shadow of her leg, of her bust, that the sun had to depict in monochrome by the side of mine upon the gravel of the path. And I found a charm that was more immaterial doubtless, but no less intimate, than in the drawing together, the fusion of our bodies, in that of our shadows." (232)

One of the successful effects of Proust is to demonstrate that the psychological laws governing human interrelationships are constant and govern unconventional as well as conventional affairs, but that is not to say that one can see the original man behind his ostensible women or vice versa. The end of Albertine's stay in Marcel's house is foreshadowed by narrative devices which are at the same time painstakingly realistic and intentionally symbolic. Such are the incidents when Marcel's jealousy having broken all reasonable bounds, Albertine is angry with him and turns aside *three* times from him when he wishes to kiss her goodnight (543) leading him into a state of anxiety such as he had not experienced since his mother's refusal to appease his nervousness at Combray. (547) This leitmotif returns, among all the others which serve to bind the narrative of *Remembrance* together. An excellent touch (which combines realism and symbolism) is Marcel's description of his feeling of alarm upon hearing Albertine throwing open violently the window of her room as if she were trying to say in sign language: "This life is stifling me; . . . I must have air!" (547) All this helps to prepare the final, surprising irony of her departure without his permission just at the moment when he had at last made up his mind to break with her and set off on a long-delayed and much dreamed-about trip to Venice. (563) And the result of this abrupt break with him, which was precisely what he thought that he himself desired (so little does he know himself or what he really wants), is that he immediately finds himself short of breath and is beaten down by an asthmatic attack which obviously has originated in anxiety. And upon this suspension, *The Captive* comes to an end.

Aside from the narratives of the Marcel-Albertine affair, the quarrel between Morel and Charlus engineered by the Verdurins the death of Bergotte, *The Captive* is notable, too, for the number and quality of its criticisms and reflections upon the nature of art. The subject of art is absorbing to Proust at all times, and each of the volumes of *Remembrance* has some memorable things to say about it, but it is significant that as the whole work is nearing its final stages, the theme of art should emerge with a degree of prominence it had not enjoyed before. The Proustian method of being delivered from the tyranny of time and chance is adumbrated in the contrast plainly drawn between the incalculable value of Art and the "nullity" of all pleasure and even love. (355) In the grip of their passions and Will, men and women are depersonalized into compulsive mechanisms indistinguishable from each other, while "in art (there is) a profound reality in which our true personality finds an expression that is not afforded it by the activities of life. Every great artist seems different from all the rest and gives us that sensation of individuality we miss in everyday existence." (209) Marcel plays many different variations upon this basic underlying theme. He tells us that "Art . . . (renders) externally visible in the colors of the spectrum the intimate composition of those worlds we call individual persons and which, without the aid of art, we should never know." (348) We get to know and to share the feelings of a Bergotte or of a Vinteuil through their works, even though they themselves are long dead, as we do not get to know the innermost sentiments of those around us who have not achieved artistic expression. (344)

Interspersing the longueurs of his affair with Albertine and inspired by the discovery of a new and profound work by the composer Vinteuil, Marcel launches upon sizable little essays which attempt to define the kind of unity which one senses in the works of Wagner (209 ff), in Thomas Hardy, Vermeer, Dostoyevsky. (514–515) The value of comparative criticism is questioned here (just as in *Contre Sainte-Beuve*, the biographical and social approach has been refuted). Comparisons of Dostoyevsky to Gogol or to Paul de Kock, such as are stock-in-trade of criticism, are worse than useless according to Marcel, for they ignore the author's unique and novel and secret beauty. (516) Only appreciations which point to this special quality of vision are useful and worthwhile, and he illustrates his meaning with some sensitive remarks on Mme. de Sévigné which serve incidentally as a summary of his own narrative method. (516)

There is an amusing *jeu d'espirit* on the changing epithets that have been applied to the moon by poets down the centuries that serves to remind us among other things of the great facts of subjectivity and the transitoriness of fashions. The moon in itself presumably remains the same forever, but the eyes through which it is glimpsed and the sensibilities by which it is described are never quite the same. (557) As is true for most romantics, music to Marcel is the queen of the arts. (510–511) Precisely because it is the least pretentious in an intellectual (or rather an ideological) way, it proves most satisfactory to his taste. Literature and the other arts, according to him, aspire to the purity of music "in which the sounds seem to assume the inflexion of the thing itself." (510) The phrasing here is reminiscent of Schopenhauer's remarks about music, which he too placed at the apex of the hierarchy of the arts. Literature goes about its tasks more indirectly, by analysis, but it is firmly based only when it recognizes its own root in instinctive feeling of the kind which is more directly grasped by music. Marcel concludes that "nothing resembled more closely than some such phrase of Vinteuil the peculiar pleasure which I had felt at certain moments in my life, when gazing, for instance, at the steeples of Martinville, or at certain trees along a road near Balbec, or, more simply, in the first part of this book, when I tasted a certain cup of tea." (511)

Art in general is for him the realm of order, calm, and peace. That is to say it is in complete contrast to the hectic emotional and social life which is described in *The Captive*. It is not idle, as we can see, for Marcel to speak of the inferno of the passions, particularly the aberrant ones, nor to seek respite and escape from the endless, tormenting, vicious round which love and society came to represent for him in the peace and clarity of great works of art. He is not yet quite ready to create one of his own, but his course is set in that direction.

7. Sweet Cheat Gone

Sweet Cheat Gone IS DIVIDED INTO FOUR PARTS. MORE THAN HALF IS DEVOTED TO THE STORY OF WHAT HAPPENED TO THE NARRATOR after Albertine left him. Smaller sections describe a meeting between him and his first sweetheart, Gilberte, a trip to Venice in the company of his mother, and the marriage of his friend Robert de Saint-Loup at the very time that the latter's affective life indicates that he is following in the footsteps of his uncle, Charlus.

The story of the first half of the volume, in its general outlines, is not hard to follow. Its trajectory takes Marcel from a suicidal intensity of anguish over the departure (and later the death) of his beloved through the gradual setting-in of indifference to complete forgetfulness. Just how complete the process is can be seen from the postcript to the affair when Marcel, through an implausibly erroneous telegram, is led to believe that Albertine is not dead and is willing to rejoin him and, instead of reacting with joy to the announcement, pretends that he has not received the news.

It is a curious and fortunate fact that though this section is so largely concerned with a penetrating and minute introspective analysis of the sensibilities of Marcel, it is also diversified with a good deal of outward action from the shocking news of the accident which kills Albertine (brought to the narrator, like the fateful and bloody turns in Greek tragedy, from offstage by a messenger) to the mediating efforts of Saint-Loup and the detective work undertaken by the headwaiter Aimé at the narrator's request to bring to light the malefactions of Albertine in the distant past as well as the more recent one. The curiosity of Marcel concerning the betrayal he has suffered is as fraught with danger and as hard to satisfy with anything short of the complete truth as that of Oedipus. The reader watches him with horror proceed relentlessly in a direction which can seemingly lead only to harakiri (in fact, Marcel speaks at one point explicitly though somewhat ironically of disemboweling himself in front of Albertine's house). Long after a less masochistic character should have desisted from a quest leading to consequences only too apparent to the objective and the neutral, he goes on torturing himself with the accumulation of additional proofs. Concerning M. Bovary after Emma's suicide when he adroitly evades the most direct proof of her infidelity, Flaubert remarks that the doctor was without the courage to explore to the bottom the painful truth. But Marcel seems to be gifted with only too much of such "courage" which, pushed to this extent, becomes somewhat psychopathological.

The theme of the book is Greek and Socratic in character. It is sounded on the very opening page: "How ignorant we are of ourselves!" (1) Marcel had thought he wanted nothing better than separation from Albertine, and yet when Françoise brings him the news that she has packed her boxes that morning and left suddenly he finds himself short of breath and goes through such hell that he can seriously say "This calamity was the greatest I had experienced in my life." (12) He is not left in the dark for very long after his education is taken in hand by *suffering*, which "alone is our real teacher." (2) Albertine, in her farewell note, had written: "I leave you with the best part of myself"; Marcel does not believe a word of it and thinks it only another stratagem to shock him into doing what she wishes. (4)

What Marcel learns about himself under the tutelage of pain must itself be divided into two parts: first, what he learns about himself immediately and second, what he learns about himself in retrospect. It is from the second division that the reader in turn may learn something important even more than from the first. The first lesson is that even to men of great imagination like Marcel the effect of coming events cannot really be visualized. We think of ourselves as active, controlling participants and planners of the future, but actually we are more like passive spectators of whatever it is that happens to us and sometimes overwhelms us. A crisis, an unexpected twist of events reveals us to ourselves as bottomless gulfs of contradiction, incomprehensibly profound. In retrospect, we also become aware that what we call our thinking is really directed by instinct. For in a real sense the meaning of these opening pages is that when the truth becomes too painful to bear, the wish is father to the thought.

He does not want to believe that she has had the nerve to walk out on him without warning, and so he doesn't believe it. He tells himself and tries to make his servant believe that it is all a mistake or pretence and that she is bound to return to him promptly. But another part of him (and one consequence of her action is that he has been divided against himself) does not believe this comforting fiction at all. He is prepared now that it is too late to grant complete security and complete autonomy to Albertine. (5) Reasoning by forced analogy, he convinces himself that (as was the case at a certain stage in the love affair between Swann and Odette which he has heard about) all that Albertine now desires is to compel him to make up his mind to marry her. And he says to himself that "marrying her is what I ought to have done long ago." (6)

At every turn, he is faced with the failure of intellectual imagination: "Of her departure . . . I might have gone on thinking for years on end, and all my thoughts . . . would not have been comparable for an instant . . . with the unimaginable hell the curtain of which Françoise had raised for me when she said, 'Mlle. Albertine has gone.'" (8) The cause of his intense suffering is what he calls 'the immense force of Habit" which riveted him to Albertine and which had been absent from the relationship with Gilberte, who caused him suffering, it is true, but with whom he had never lived. (16) The suffering at first is so great that it will not permit him to face reality. His rationalizing faculty produces the hypothesis that Albertine is only fooling, that her action is a mere "feint" and her real intention very different from what it appears to be, and "the hypothesis of a feint became all the more necessary to me the more improbable it was, and gained in strength what it lost in probability." (23) This seems to be the very definition of wishful thinking.

His fantasy evolves various futile, double-dealing plans for coping with the intolerable situation. Above all, he is conscious that he must not let Albertine guess the true state of his feeling and the true depth of his need for her. He deviously plans, for example, to write a letter to Albertine in which he pretends to accept her departure as final, while at the same time getting his friend Saint-Loup to bring to bear upon her aunt, Mme. Bontemps, "the most brutal pressure to make Albertine return as soon as possible." (25) Through Robert, Marcel offers Mme. Bontemps 30,000 francs to help with her politician husband's election expenses, and he also informs her that he is "engaged to marry" Albertine. (33) Looking back, this approach is not only futile but foolish, and yet by keeping hope alive in Marcel it serves its purpose perhaps of keeping his sanity intact. One cannot live through such times without a measure of self-deception, since "it is in reality our anticipation, our hope of happy events that fills us with joy which we ascribe to other causes and which ceases, letting us relapse into misery, if we are no longer so assured that what we desire will come to pass. It is always this invisible belief that sustains the edifice of our world of sensation, deprived of which it rocks from its foundations." (39)

Underneath the pleasant surface of his wish-fulfillment, however, Marcel tastes the bitter dregs of pessimism which assures him that in this world of ours at all times "three events out of four are unfortunate." (38) Albertine's departure has rocked his world to its foundations and completely opposite and contradictory thoughts and desires with regard to her succeed each other with great rapidity. (41–42) He simply hasn't the strength necessary to utter the word "Never" in connection with Albertine's name. (44) The most salutary philosophy for him in this situation, when he has to some extent regained his equanimity, is to recognize that in spite of the illusions which flatter us with the thought that it may be otherwise, "we exist alone." (47) Happiness is no more than freedom from suffering, and the key to contentment is not the fulfillment of insatiable desire but resignation. (48–49) And little by little, other elements than rending grief enter into the mental economy of Marcel. Calm and forgetfulness, the great enemies of grief and love, make their first tentative appearances. (42–43) And a little later, they come again and the first faint seeds of oblivion have been sown. (48)

He receives a letter from Albertine reproaching him with the crudity of Saint-Loup's intervention, for which he is compelled to deny responsibility. (50) He replies in a long rambling letter which rings false and actually is false from beginning to end, though the ear of the lover is completely off key and does not perceive the flatness of the notes he strikes. He borrows his hackneyed formulae from the opera and the melodramatic stage: "Life has driven us apart," (52) and he tells her that by an ironic coincidence his mother had consented to their marriage the very day Albertine chose to leave him but that it is now too late to think of returning to their old relationship. Living as he does in what he himself calls "the psychopathic universe" of the jealous lover, he miscalculates entirely the possible effects which his words might have. (56–58) A comparison of his feelings with those expressed in the classic *Phèdre* serves only to deepen and universalize what is happening to him without relieving the pain of it. (58–59)

At last, after exhausting every device and indirection to attain his object without seeming to aim at it, Marcel breaks down completely and sends a despairing telegram to Albertine asking her to return to him with no conditions attached. (82) And at the very moment he dispatches this unconditional surrender to her, news reaches him from Mme. Bontemps that Albertine has been killed in an accidental fall from a horse. (82) And so at last he is forced by death to utter the dread word "Never!" in connection with Albertine; the manner in which he does so results in one of the most beautiful pages in this book. (83) Two letters from Albertine (mailed just before her death) reach him at this moment, almost unhinging his reason. They reveal her in the throes of just such contradictions as are tearing her lover apart, too. In the first letter, she still pretended to go along with his idea that the break between them be allowed to become permanent, but in the second she frankly revealed the same desire for a reconciliation which had inspired his own final telegram to her—the one that never reached her. (83–84) We are aware of the author tightening every possible screw of coincidence and irony in an effect to wring the maximum possible pathos out of the situation.

The different situations, seasons, associations that serve to bring Albertine's image back to his mind involuntarily are now accompanied by a much greater freight of emotion than before. Even previously, the feeling of nostalgic regrets for what had been in actuality a joyless situation had set in: "I put my feet to the ground; I stepped across the room with endless precautions, took up a position from which I could not see Albertine's chair, the pianola upon the pedals of which she used to press her golden slippers, nor a single one of the things which she had used and all of which in the secret language that my memory had imparted to them, seemed to be seeking to give me a fresh translation, a new version, to announce to me for the second time the news of her departure." (17) Her death heightens and accentuates these sensitivities: "Bound up as it was with each of the seasons, in order for me to discard the memory of Albertine I should have first to forget them all, prepared to begin again to learn to know them, as an old man after a stroke of paralysis learns again to read; I should have had first to forego the entire universe." (94)

These prose passages remind me somehow of a stanza from Stephen Spender's poem, *The Double Shame*, which also speaks of the anguish of separation between a man and a woman:

> Solid and usual objects are ghosts—
> The furniture carries great cargoes of memory,
> The staircase has corners which remember
> As fire blows most red in gusty embers,
> And each empty dress cuts out an image
> In fur and evening and summer and gold
> Of her who was different in each.

The evocative passages are among the best in the book and, in view of the doubts raised by some critics as to the sexual identity of Albertine, it is interesting to note the emphasis upon her purely feminine charm: "How could she have seemed dead to me when now, in order to think of her, I had at my disposal only those same images one or other of which I used to recall when she was alive, each one being associated with a particular moment? Rapid and bowed above the mystic wheel of her bicycle, tightly strapped upon rainy days in the amazonian corslet of her waterproof which made her breasts protrude, while serpents writhed in her turbaned hair, she scattered terror in the streets of Balbec; on the evening on which we had taken champagne with us to the woods of Chantepie, her voice provoking, altered, she showed on her face that pallid warmth coloring only over her cheekbones, so that, barely able to make her out in the carriage, I drew her face into the moonlight in order to see her better, and which I tried now in vain to recapture, to see again in a darkness that would never end." (99–100)

It is after Albertine's death that Marcel goes to work in earnest to obtain proofs as to her character and conduct both while she was living under his roof and earlier. He is devoured by a macabre form of jealous curiosity to establish definitely what her tastes really were. The ultimate purpose of this destructive investigation is hard to fathom; it may be the product of what is something like moral masochism—a perversion of spirit which leads him into such paradoxical aphorisms as the one in which he tells us that "a woman is of greater service to our life if she is in it, instead of being an element of happiness, an instrument of sorrow, and there is not a woman in the world the possession of whom is as precious as that of the truths she reveals to us by making us suffer." (111)

The chief collaborator in this phase of his jealousy is the head-waiter of the Balbec Hotel, Aimé, who has impressed him with a certain dogged fidelity, earthiness and absence of squeamishness. Aimé's initial investigation in some of the bathing establishments in the neighborhood of Balbec yields circumstantial evidence of Albertine's Lesbianism which is definite enough to satisfy a district attorney. (137–138) Its striking verisimilitude of detail plunges Marcel more effectively and deeply into the Hell of jealousy than anything he had thus far experienced. (141–142) But then his scrupulousness or his wish-fulfillments again raise doubts as he remembers that his grandmother once said of the bathwoman, who had been quoted by Aimé as his chief informant: "She must suffer from a disease of mendacity." (144) The convincing details may after all be the product of an inventive fancy, and so he's still not absolutely certain of Albertine's guilt.

The point is that the certainty Marcel seeks (in the absence of direct ocular proof such as he had had at Montjouvain with regard to Mlle. Vinteuil and in the courtyard of the Guermantes with regard to Charlus and Jupien) is unobtainable. After completing his tour of duty at Balbec, Aimé is dispatched by Marcel into Touraine to see what he can find out in the country around Madame Bontemps' home. Taking infinite pains, which finally lead him to go to bed with a laundress he suspects of having had carnal relations with Albertine, Aimé's second letter to his employer is filled with such vivid details that he should have had to be gifted with the imagination of a creative writer to have invented them. (150–151) Yet after his initial shock has worn off, Marcel manages to find grounds on which to question his emissary's truthfulness or accuracy. He "reasons" that Aimé is so good a servant, so conscientious, that he must feel the need to come back with some tangible results of his detective work to justify to himself the wage he is being paid by Marcel. Wishful thinking is the most tenacious and invulnerable of all. Marcel does not want to believe in Albertine's deceptions and betrayals in the very act of gathering evidence to prove them. He believes and yet does not believe. In spite of his infinitely greater courage, intellectual perseverance and scepticism, he shares in the universal human weakness delineated by Flaubert in the character of Charles after Emma's death when "he shrank from the proofs." Wish-fulfillments are in fact the strongest and most insuperable of all human sentiments. (157–158)

Yet in spite of all his weakness of stomach and revulsion of taste, Marcel unlike Charles Bovary keeps probing his own wound. He is not simply lost in an "immensity of woe" but follows the train of associations of words, thoughts and ideas in his own mind which in due course lay bare other lies that Albertine has told him in addition to those which he already knows. (175) He also initiates a direct investigation of his own by questioning Andrée about her relations with Albertine. She readily admits her own transgressions (which make her an inhabitant of "Gomorrah") but vehemently denies those of Albertine. (182) Being pressed, however, by the narrator who uses Aimé's technique of making love to her, she supplies him with some additional proof of Albertine's perversity, including her betrayals of him with Morel, with girls who had been corrupted and turned over to her by Morel, and finally with Andrée herself under Marcel's own roof. She clears up the meaning of one particularly puzzling incident which he did not know how to interpret. She tells him that Albertine regarded her own lust as "a sort of criminal lunacy" which filled her with such contrition and shame that Andrée finds it possible to believe she may have killed herself. (252–253) Albertine's Lesbianism, her perfidy to Marcel—these things are confirmed from multiple sources which could not have all been in collusion with each other and are as certain as anything in this world is ever likely to be. And yet . . . And yet Marcel does not feel satisfied in his own mind, nor can he bring himself to doubt either. He began this story by complaining in Socratic fashion about how ignorant human beings are of themselves, but his progress has been in the direction of showing that they are just as ignorant of each other. All certainty tends to dissolve under the scrutiny of a sceptical intelligence. And in this hopeless morass of ignorance, tired by his search and sickened by what he has found, Marcel feels more and more the force of oblivion which had shown itself so tentatively long ago and which now slowly erases and weakens the hold which Albertine's memory has over him. (194) Human problems are less often solved than forgotten.

The first of the three smaller episodes which follow in the second half of *Sweet Cheat Gone* has to do with a chance meeting between Marcel and his first sweetheart Gilberte, whom comically he does not recognize at the beginning and, through a series of wishful errors, identifies as a certain Mlle. d'Eporcheville, a girl whom Saint-Loup described encountering in a brothel! In answer to an inquiry, a telegram arrives from his friend telling him that the name of the other girl is de l'Orgeville (207), and immediately thereafter Marcel encounters the girl herself in the drawing room of the Duchesse de Guermantes, where he learns that her name is really de Forcheville (216), in other words the title of Odette's second husband after the death of Swann. It is, then, none other than Gilberte herself who seems a stranger to him after so many years of not seeing her.

We now learn that after the death of Swann, which surprisingly enough in view of his wife's superficiality caused her "profound, prolonged, and sincere" grief, Odette married her old friend Forcheville who condescended to bestow his title upon her in consideration of the money she brought him. (218) There is poignant irony in the meeting which time, whim, altered circumstances have all helped to arrange between Odette and her daughter on the one hand and the Duke and Duchess on the other. (219–223) This meeting had been Swann's dream and dearest hope when he had married, but we have seen earlier how his friend the Duchess frowned upon his sentimentality. After his death, however, she thinks it proper to relent in her decree of exclusion of his widow and daughter, who furthermore are now respectably connected with the minor nobility. We witness once again how badly the bourgeois is treated by the Faubourg Saint-Germain even when he is not merely a climber, not only during his lifetime but after his death, as we listen to the Duke and Duchess indulge in some of their snobbery at the expense of their old friend Swann. (226–227) All his efforts to assimilate himself to their standards have evidently gone for nothing. Yet who can blame them when even his daughter Gilberte who has inherited some of his "exquisite tact combined with intellectual charm" (229) shows herself to be ashamed of her father's Jewish name and his Jewish friends? (233–234) It was only another instance of pathetic vanity on Swann's part to hope that he might be remembered in the world through his daughter, who has adopted her foster-father's name, suppressed the name Swann to the initial S. in her signature, and actively resents every allusion no matter how innocent to her real father. (243–244)

Marcel himself feels the lash of aristocratic scorn on this occasion. For having published his first article in the newspaper *Figaro* (207–209) and inquiring timidly of the Duke and Duchess (who are both readers of that newspaper) what they have thought of it, he finds to his chagrin that neither of them has noticed it. (231) The Duchess is completely uninterested in the news of his publication, while the Duke, sitting down at once to read it has only unfavorable comments to make on it and the sole compliment he chooses to pay Marcel is on the score of the occupation he has found to fill out his leisure time. The trouble with journalism, Marcel feels, and the trouble with even the greatest journalists, like Sainte-Beuve, is that their aim is merely to provoke a response from the audience and not to practice, as the real artist does, a self-contained, self-sufficing, and, to use T. S. Eliot's fine word for it, *autotelic* activity. (211–212) One gathers, for instance, that the creation of these speaking likenesses drawn from the Faubourg Saint-Germain was for the author so completely satisfying a pursuit that he should not really have been interested very much in what the Duke or Duchess or anyone else thought of his performance. He had risen far above the level of ephemeral journalism with its trivial motivations of being pleasing or agreeable (or else that particularly modern variation of being displeasing and disagreeable).

Venice (286 ff)

This forty-page section describes the realization of a lifelong dream of Marcel's, which is not altogether a disappointment, since just as he had once pictured the experience to himself he now finds himself wandering in "an enchanted city" like a character from the *Arabian Nights*. (315) It is in Venice that he has his first premonition of the destructive effect of age upon human beings, which is the subject that will occupy a great part of the succeeding volume, *The Past Recaptured*. The warning comes in the form of a scene (beautifully rendered and much admired in Proustian criticism) involving the diplomat Norpois, his mistress of long standing the Marquise de Villeparisis, and one of the neighbors of Marcel's family in Combray, Madame Sazerat. The years have not been kind to the former Ambassador and the Marquise, who are now reduced to mere caricatures of themselves. Her face is covered by "a sort of eczema, a red leprosy" while age has weakened his voice and given "to his language, formerly so reserved, a positive intemperance." (294) Madame Sazerat has been compelled to live in the country most of the year because her father had compromised his financial position many years before through an infatuation with Mme. de Villeparisis, whose maiden name was Mlle. de Bouillon and who was, according to Mme. Sazerat's emotionally colored language, "beautiful as an angel, wicked as a demon, who drove my father out of his senses, ruined him and then forsook him immediately." (299) The poor woman's consolation is to think that her father showed good taste and was in love with one reputed to be "the most beautiful woman of his generation." But even of this comfort she is to be robbed when she asks Marcel to point out the Marquise in the restaurant where they are dining. She cannot believe her eyes: "We can't be counting from the same point. At what I call the second table there are only two people, an old gentleman and a little hunchbacked, red-faced woman, quite hideous." Marcel replies: "That is she!" (299)

Such is the first half of this anecdote, and it is the part that is usually singled out for notice, but there is a second half which is just as important to the total meaning of the episode. For if the horrible, mutilating effect of age is so graphically illustrated in the first half, the moral of the second half appears to be that in their inner Will, which gives shape to their characters, people (or at least some especially stubborn people like Norpois) remain essentially unchanged no matter how much time passes. The story of Norpois's "famous" and lucky intervention in domestic Italian politics to the dismay of the official French ambassador to that country and to the delight of the rest of the diplomatic corps for twenty years afterwards is distinguished by a witty flavor quite worthy of the great master of the genre, Stendhal himself. (301 ff): "As I say, Prince Foggi had mentioned more than twenty names to the diplomat who remained as motionless and mute as though he were stone deaf when M. de Norpois raised his head slightly, and, in the form that had been assumed by those of his diplomatic interventions which had had the most far-reaching consequences, albeit this time with greater audacity and less brevity, asked shrewdly: 'And has no one mentioned the name of Signor Giolitti?' At these words the scales fell from Prince Foggi's eyes; he could hear a celestial murmur. Then at once M. de Norpois began to speak about one thing and another, no longer afraid to make a sound, as, when the last note of a sublime aria by Bach has been played, the audience are no longer afraid to talk aloud, to call for their hats and coats in the cloakroom. . . ."

The section on Venice is a flawed gem. Its brightest facet is the episode I have just spoken of, which has a controlled irony worthy of the best social scenes in *Remembrance:* the ones which take place in the drawing-room of the Verdurins, at the Marquise de Saint Euverte's or at the Princesse de Guermantes's. More faulty is the incident involving the telegram supposedly sent by Albertine (310) which turns out to have been not indeed a hoax but due to the telegrapher's error in reading the affected, courtly signature of Gilberte. (325) On a second or third reading of *Remembrance,* one realizes with some astonishment that the author had evidently planned this stroke some thousands of pages earlier in the first volume of *Within a Budding Grove* where, having occasion to describe the appearance of the first letter Gilberte ever sent him, Marcel adds: "Françoise declined to recognize Gilberte's name, because the elaborate capital 'G' leaning against the undotted 'i' looked more like an 'A', while the final syllable was indefinitely prolonged by a waving flourish.

. . ." (W.B.G.I, 104) The painstaking preparation for this surprising development so long before is one more indication of the solidity of Proust's architectural blueprint, of the fact that nothing can be conceived of that is less improvisatory, less haphazard, or more unified than the development of his narrative, and yet the incident seems somewhat forced, wooden, and cerebral (offered as it is as the clinching intellectual proof of his complete indifference to Albertine whom he had lately loved to the point of distraction). Perhaps this failure is due simply to the fact that the author did not have the opportunity unfortunately of making some final revisions in this section of his work.

Fresh Light on Saint-Loup (327 ff)

The new development in the story of Saint-Loup had been foreshadowed by a strange scene earlier (74–75) in which the narrator, in one of those eavesdropping or frankly voyeuristic situations which made Edith Wharton complain that Marcel was no gentleman but which also constitute one of the necessary conventions to explain some important developments in the story, overhears his old friend "playing Satan" and hatching a diabolical plot to get rid of one of the servants of his aunt, the Duchess of Guermantes. This instance of melodramatic villainy is worthy of the obnoxious violinist Morel, who had engineered a similar conspiracy earlier against the coachman of the Verdurins whom he had wished to see discharged so that a friend of his might get the job, and it is quite unlike anything that Marcel should have found it possible to believe or suspect about Saint-Loup from all that he has known of him. The explanation is that Saint-Loup is no longer the same man he was before. Time, acting upon the sympathetic secret ink latent in his character, has brought out in him his uncle Charlus's vice (and its accompanying sadism) and he is now the lover of the vicious Morel, who turns up in the latter part of *Remembrance* whenever some particularly dirty piece of business is to be performed. This section, too, contains accounts of two surprising marriages, brought to the narrator first by his mother who finds their mixture of classes flabbergasting from the "Hindu caste point of view" characteristic of Combray. They are designed in the text to demonstrate the kaleidoscopic nature of all social relationships. The first is that of Robert de Saint-Loup himself to Gilberte. Marriage is an act of social convenience for an aristocrat, completely independent of love or even, as in this case, of the sexual taste of the partners. The death of a distant relative of Swann's, who had no direct descendants, had resulted in making Gilberte one of the wealthiest girls in France, and a most desirable match for those families in the Faubourg Saint-Germain in need of replenishing their finances. (335) The maneuvers of several personages from these families (including Saint-Loup's mother, Mme. de Marsantes) are chronicled by Marcel with an urbane irony which mercilessly exposes all the hypocrisies and insincerities implicit in the process.

The second unexpected marriage is that between Jupien's niece, ennobled by Charlus with the title Mlle. d'Oloron, and Leonor de Cambremer, the son of Legrandin's snobbish daughter. There are multiple ironies in the very idea of such a union which underscore the "vanity of human wishes." Was it worthwhile for the engineer-poet of Combray, who now styles himself after some tentative moves in this direction with the usurped and pretentious title of Comte de Méséglise, to have strained and striven with every nerve and sinew of his being in the direction of the aristocracy in order that his grandson, possessing legitimately the provincial title of Cambremer, might ally himself to the house of a humble tradesman, Jupien the tailor, whose claim to fame is that he panders to the sexual needs of the Baron de Charlus? If it is of such stuff that nobility can be manufactured, what is this "nobility" really worth? Looking at it from the other side of the equation, the satisfaction which Jupien must have derived from the ennoblement and honorable marriage of his niece (whom Morel had once coveted and insulted) is extremely shortlived, for soon afterwards death carries off the unhappy girl.

Legrandin's personal life also undergoes an ironic development. No sooner has he attained his social objective of mingling freely with the highest aristocracy whose doors have been opened to him by his literary talent and by his family connections than he renounces respectable society almost altogether. A similar reversal takes place in the character and outlook of Bloch in the latter half of the next volume. The meaning of such overturns can probably best be summed up in the words of Ecclesiastes: "Vanity of vanities, all is vanity and striving after wind."

Finally, there is the progression in the experiences of Marcel himself in the direction of disillusion. This is the darkest part of the night before the dawn of the consciousness of his own artistic vocation, which is to be the subject of *The Past Recaptured*. No longer in love with Gilberte, he finds no difficulty in becoming once more an intimate friend of hers (355) as he had earlier become a friend of the Duchess after losing interest in her as a woman. And going back to the Tansonville estate in the country (formerly the residence of Swann, now the residence of the Saint-Loups), Marcel takes walks in all the old haunts of Combray that he had known as a child. What a disappointment they are! His beloved stream, the Vivonne, turns out to be nothing more than "a meager, ugly rivulet" (372) and the whole town is something reduced and skimpy in comparison with his memory and imagination of it. Not yet having received his almost mystical summons to the higher vocation of being an artist, Marcel finds that the recovery of the past by visiting physically the places where we have once lived is a barren, self-defeating enterprise. At the end of *Sweet Cheat Gone* it is still some time before Combray will spring like magic out of a little cup of tea, the feat brought about by the accidental co-incidence between a sensory perception of the present and one in the distant past which alone is capable of stimulating the "creative unconscious," the involuntary memory of Marcel into activity.

8. The Past Recaptured

THE LAST VOLUME OF *Remembrance* OPENS ON THE TANSONVILLE
ESTATE OF GILBERTE DE SAINT-LOUP WHERE THE NARRATOR MARCEL
is a guest. The idea of Marcel, who had suffered such boyhood
agonies over Gilberte, being an indifferent guest in her country
house, and the idea of Gilberte, born of Swann's disgraceful
marriage with Odette in a segment of society far below that of
the fabulous Faubourg Saint-Germain, being married now to one
of the adornments of the aristocratic house of Guermantes, are
enough to indicate how much time has passed since the beginning of the story and how many radical, seemingly impossible
changes the passage of time has brought with it. Robert with
increasing age grows slimmer and more handsomely military
in his bearing as a result of the same vice that has had the effect
of making Charlus corpulent. (2–3) Gilberte is unhappy with
him (6) because he belongs to that division of sexual inverts who,
to distract public attention from their real tastes, make their
wives fearfully jealous by being flagrantly unfaithful to them
with other women. (9) Gilberte, who had once been annoyed
by Marcel's excessive devotion and jealousy, now goes through a
similar experience with Robert, because the pattern of Proustian
love always remains basically the same. Experience, Marcel tells
us, is of no avail whatever in love, which he compares to being
"under an evil spell." (13)

But the most important of the contents of the first thirty
pages of *The Past Recaptured* consists of a Proustian pastiche of
some pages from the Goncourt Journal, which Marcel amuses
himself by reading at Tansonville and which describe a visit to
M. and Mme. Verdurin and their "little clan" in their house in
Paris. Marcel is idly reading the Goncourt Journal when he comes
across the Verdurin passage. (14–23) How amusing this turns out
to be, from the reader's if not from the narrator's point of view!
What a perfect illustration of the truth of the narrator's observa-

tion that the world was not created once and for all but is created anew every time an original pair of eyes looks at it. Or, one is tempted to add after reading the pastiche, even an *un*original pair of eyes. For what a *different* Verdurin salon emerges out of these "Goncourt" pages from the one we are thoroughly familiar with. In the Goncourt Journal the Verdurins are not the vulgar bourgeois social climbers we know so well but romantic aesthetes. Their "clan" does not consist largely of pedants and boors but of charming and cultivated men of the world. Brichot and Cottard appear to be learned and polite gentlemen whom it is a joy to listen to. And the abode of the Verdurins, their furniture, decorations, dress and even dishes have aesthetic attractions for the journalist which we have never fully realized.

Marcel, on reading the passage, is astonished. These are *not* the Verdurins, Brichot, Cottard that he has known so much better than Goncourt who was a guest in the house (which Marcel visited every day for extensive periods) exactly once. He has a desire to go and see all these "wonderful" people once again and reflects on the magical, alchemistic powers of literature when it sets to work on commonplace reality. And he feels more discouraged than ever by his own lack of literary talent, for he could never have observed the social milieu or listened to people with such minute attention and care as the writers of this journal evidently did in order to describe them so attractively. And at the same time, he is aware of how grossly the journal has falsified the actual truth, and his respect for the fidelity of the art of literature correspondingly diminishes.

We must remember that at the time he is supposed to have read this Journal entry, Marcel has not yet found himself as a writer. He has *experienced* the Verdurins and their "clan" but he has not yet re-created that experience in literature, since the span of the narrative of *Remembrance* takes him only up to the time when he sets himself seriously to work upon it. André Malraux has speculated in his *Psychology of Art* on the origin of art in the artist's impulse to imitate other art that he admires. The significant relation, according to this theory (which is not altogether incompatible perhaps with that found in Aristotle's *Poetics*), is not that which exists between art and nature (perceived naively and directly, as the Romantics would have us believe) but between art and nature perceived indirectly through the medium of art. This would explain why there is a history and a classic tradition of art, considered as a virtually autonomous activity rather than in relation to the general history of other human activities. There is no doubt that this point of view is helpful to our understanding; to see Proust's work in relation to the *Arabian Nights* and the *Memoirs of Saint-Simon* and the novels of Balzac proves to be at least as illuminating as to see him in the context of his contemporary social history. But the artist's relation to other art is both positive and negative—if he is attracted by certain stylizations of reality, he is also repelled by others, and he may be just as inspired to undertake his own work by his antipathies as by his affections. The history of the novel in general always seems to begin (or at least to be refreshed and continued) because of such antipathies—whether it is Petronius's reaction against the falsifications of life by academic Roman rhetoric, or Cervantes' rejection of the romances and epics of chivalry, or Fielding's outrage at the maudlin pieties and sentimentalism of Samuel Richardson's *Pamela, Or Virtue Rewarded*.

There is, in other words, not merely the impulse to "go and do likewise" operating on the artist's mind but the impulse "to set the record straight" in the face of a fashionable or successful "school of falsification." One such "school of falsification" in Proust's eyes was that of the most literal realism or "naturalism" represented, among others, by the Goncourts. One of the forms of art that he most vehemently rejects in this volume later on is a kind of realism which he calls "a miserable listing of lines and surfaces." (218) The trouble with the Goncourts is that they were too superficial; they took the Verdurins and their "little clan" too much at face value. They saw reality, to use Blake's expression, *with* their eyes instead of *through* them. And so what emerged from their camera was a lie so far as the deeper truth about their subjects was concerned. They completely lack what Marcel takes the liberty of referring to as his own "x-ray" vision. (25) Yet at the same time that he realizes this, he is astounded by the vivifying power of literature; he appreciates the Goncourts as far as they go, but he is critical of their limitations, their "naturalism," their materialism, their insensitivity, and to say it all in one word their *blindness*. (24) When he rehearses the well-known mirror theory of art that we find from Shakespeare to Stendhal and tells us that a writer is great only insofar as he has the ability "to reflect his life, however mediocre" (29), we must understand him to mean a reflection in depth, a reflection of the truth of life which lies hidden below the surface and is unavailable to the photographic and stenographic apparatus and method used by the naturalistic school, which included Zola and the Goncourts and which idealized the objectivity of "experimental" science in its approach to reality.

At the end of this opening section, the narrator makes one of a succession of withdrawals from society to a sanitarium (30), presumably in an attempt to cure himself of the asthma that he has complained of periodically since the beginning of the story. He returns to Paris in 1916 in the midst of the first World War when the institution to which he had committed himself can no longer afford to keep its medical staff. (30) This withdrawal and return, followed by a later withdrawal and a second return, enable him to see the effect upon his familiar world of war, suffering, and time. He is able to see it more clearly and to separate what remains constant in it from what is subject to breakdown and change.

At the beginning of Chapter 2 of *The Past Recaptured* (pp. 31 ff) Marcel gives us a potent satire on the continuing search for pleasure and luxury which he found in Paris in 1916, particularly among women, in the midst of the most bloody and bitter war in human history up to that time. (31–33) Politics had undergone a change, symbolized by the fact that "Dreyfusism had now been given its place in a whole category of respectable and accustomed things." (35) Nobody in the fashionable Faubourg Saint-Germain now seems to remember the Dreyfusism of the war minister, M. Bontemps, since "society folk are absent-minded and forgetful" and also "a long time had passed since then." (36) The social kaleidoscope had received several violent shakes and rearranged its configurations. But those who "create for themselves an enveloping inner life" pay little atention to such outward changes. Marcel reflects upon the insignificance of even the greatest and most startling political changes (the French Revolution, the Napoleonic Empire) when compared with the literature of Chateaubriand which was being created at the time and will enjoy for all time "an infinitely greater value." (36)

The war has been a means of boosting Madame Verdurin on

the social scale (39) for she enjoys a number of inside contacts with the government and consequently finds various aristocratic personages (in their eagerness to learn the latest news and gossip) making overtures to her. (38) The crisis exposes people in various lights. Morel, for instance, is a deserter (39) until he is caught and, instead of being shot, is sent to the front where he acquits himself so creditably that he is decorated for valor and is regarded, later on after the war, as an exemplary character. What had saved Morel was his friendship with Saint-Loup, who is among those killed in the war. The unpretentious bravery of Saint-Loup (who has at last the opportunity of showing that danger is his native element and lives up to the noble ideals of his warlike ancestors) is contrasted sharply with the behavior of Bloch, "a braggart and miserable coward" (50) who makes a show of patriotic sentiments as long as he feels sure of being deferred from military duty because of his poor eyesight. Saint-Loup, on the other hand, filled with "hidden generosity and unexpressed heroism" (50), had made a show of timorousness while moving heaven and earth to have his application for re-enlistment accepted. (48) To the astonishment of the nationalists, the socialists whom they had called "men without a country" at the time of Dreyfus demonstrate the same qualities of bravery and patriotism in the war as their bitter foes, the "aristos" (aristocrats), do. (52–53)

Marcel observes the lack of relation between moral qualities and aesthetic powers. Heroes of mediocre, commonplace intelligence continue writing poor, hackneyed poems about the war, which they have experienced but lack the ability to re-create and communicate to others. (60) Charlus, who is compelled to have an original view of everything (we recall his singular and startling interpretation of the Dreyfus Case!) turns out to be a defeatist during the war. (69) He is too conscious of the German blood mixed with the French in his aristocratic veins (his mother was a Bavarian duchess—p. 85) to be able to share his countrymen's vindictive attitude toward the Kaiser and the "Boches." (84) Marcel does not share these ideas, and yet he too cannot help regretting the tragedy of "earth . . . on which (men) are insane enough to continue their own revolutions and their vain and useless wars, like the one that was at that moment drenching France in blood."(71)

Character is fate, and life for many who feel irresponsible goes on during the war much as it had during peacetime. Madame Verdurin continues with her social receptions and Charlus continues at an ever wilder pace to indulge his homosexual appetites "as if nothing had changed." (80–81) Of course, Charlus is far more intelligent than most of his patriotic opponents whose emotional arguments get on his nerves. His detachment and calm give him an insuperable advantage over them, since "the logic of passion, even in the most righteous cause, can always be refuted by a man who remains dispassionate." (85) Charlus aims satiric shafts and sarcasm in all directions—at language, people, etc. (91–92) His analysis of society has a vitriolic, an almost Célinean quality of bitterness and insight: "People see everything through the eyes of their favorite newspaper." (96) "The surprising thing is that this public which judges men and war questions only through its newspapers is convinced that it is doing its own thinking." (99) He very cleverly exposes the numerous self-contradictions on the part of the dominant nationalists and militarists: "I fully expect one of these days to find myself seated at table below a Russian revolutionist or even below one of our generals who are now carrying on war because of their horror of war and in order to punish a people for cultivating an ideal which they themselves, fifteen years ago, esteemed to be the only invigorating one. Only a few months ago the poor Czar was being praised for having called together the Hague Peace Conference. But now that they hail liberated Russia, they forget the thing for which they used to glorify her. So turns the wheel of the world! Yet Germany uses so exactly the same expressions as France that it would almost make you think she was quoting verbatim. She does not tire of declaring that she is 'fighting for her very existence.' When I read, 'We shall continue to struggle against our cruel and implacable enemy until we have secured a peace that shall guarantee us against aggression for all time to come and in order that the blood of our brave soldiers shall not have been shed in vain,' or 'He who is not with us is against us,' I do not know whether the remark comes from Emperor William or M. Poincaré, for each of them has used it, with slight variations, a score of times—although, to be frank, I have to admit that, in this instance, the Emperor is imitating the President of the Republic. Perhaps France would not have been so anxious to prolong the war if she had been the weaker party; but even more probably, Germany would not have been so eager to end it if she had not ceased to be the stronger. Not that she is not still strong, as you shall see." (111–112)

The cynicism could be straight out of Céline's *Journey to the End of the Night* and more particularly from that first chapter on the terrasse which shows two anarchist students conversing on the eve of the outbreak of war and running down M. Poincaré and all the institutions of republican France with an equal enthusiasm. It is interesting that these anarchist underdogs are not more alienated from their French contemporaries than Proust's sexual pariah who is a great nobleman by birth, the adornment of the most fashionable of Parisian Faubourgs, the Baron de Charlus.

One of the journalistic bellwethers of the war period is, surprisingly enough, the Sorbonne pedant, Brichot, who is able to turn his historical learning to account by becoming a newspaper columnist and "expert." (101–102) He has fallen out with Madame Verdurin, who now launches a campaign among her faithful designed to turn his belated fame into ridicule. (103) Less popular than Brichot's column but more impressive (and possibly prophetic) are the jeremiads launched by Charlus, as he foresees the same fate for modern Paris as had overwhelmed (thousands of years ago) the cities of Pompeii and Herculaneum, with the bombs dropped from modern Zeppelins as the counterpart of the ancient volcanic eruptions. (120–121) Pompeii, he reveals with a flash of his odd learning, had also feared a fate similar to that which had overtaken the Biblical cities of Sodom and Gomorrah. Apparently all these cities destroyed by fire from heaven or rising out of the bowels of the earth had been tainted by the vice which is the Baron's.

Charlus's vice, in a new stage of debasement, occupies a good deal of this section of *The Past Recaptured*. The blacked-out streets of wartime Paris became as mysterious as those of Bagdad in *The Arabian Nights* (124), and the narrator Marcel stumbles by accident one evening on a mysterious house located in a sinister side street which is the scene of a bustle of activity that leads him at first to surmise that he has discovered a nest of spies. (125 ff) Only gradually does the truth transpire that this house is something even more rare and unlikely—what Marcel calls (in the original) a Temple de l'Impudeur, which is rendered into

English feebly as the Temple of Dishonor (Scott Moncrieff who had made a much admired translation of the earlier volumes had died before completing his task, and this last volume is the work of Frederick Blossom). The French word *impudeur* may be translated variously as immodesty, indecency, shamelessness— even I suppose dishonor. This "Temple" is the scene of Charlus's orgies, which provide him with sensual satisfaction through the most cruel masochism. Jupien is the manager of this hotel, and in a voyeuristic scene comparable to those at Montjouvain and in the courtyard of the Guermantes described in the beginning of *Cities of The Plain*, Marcel watches the Baron being tied (at his own command) to an iron bed with chains and beaten mercilessly with a whip studded with nails by a young Parisian tough. (131) Even while he is crying out with pain, Charlus complains that the young man is not brutal enough to satisfy his depraved taste for punishment. (133) After witnessing the horrible spectacle which is almost a tableau out of a picture-book of medieval tortures, the fires set by the "volcanic thunder" of the German bombs seem to Marcel appropriately symbolic of the doom of Sodom, (154) and some of his fellow-citizens (for Charlus is far from being alone in his shameless hotel which is the rendezvous of some prominent politicians, a Deputy, aristocrats, army officers) assume the appearance in his eyes of "Pompeians on whom fire from heaven was already raining down." (155)

The end of the war brings little respite to the process of degeneration so far as the narrator's observation goes. The flower of young France (among others, his friend Saint-Loup) has perished in the holocaust. What is left on the political scene are the old hacks and pushing young new men who trade on their military service and supposed heroism as a way of getting political preferment. The faults of democracy become increasingly writ large, though all the alternatives to it (as Winston Churchill once remarked) seem to be even worse. In a sentence distinguished by multiple ironies, Marcel reflects bitterly, after thinking that had Saint-Loup survived the war he might have been able with his brilliant military record to win election to the Chamber of Deputies, that "perhaps Robert was too sincerely attached to the people to succeed in winning their support, although they would doubtless have forgiven him his democratic ideas in view of his noble lineage." (175) One who commands the confidence of the masses proves to be a habitué of Jupien's parlors—"that deputy of *l'Action Libérale* who was elected without opposition. He continued to wear his uniform of territorial troops, although the war had been over for a long time. His election was hailed with joy by all the newspapers that had joined the coalition in support of his candidacy and by the rich noblewomen, who now dressed in old rags, through a feeling for the proprieties and also through fear of taxes, while the men on the Stock Exchange bought diamonds uninterruptedly, not for their wives, but because they had lost confidence in the credit of any country and therefore took refuge in this tangible form of wealth. This made De Beers stock go up a thousand francs. All this stupidity was somewhat exasperating, but one was less vexed with the *Bloc National* when one suddenly saw the victims of bolshevism, Grand Duchesses in rags and tatters, whose husbands and then their sons, had been assassinated, the husbands in wheelbarrows and the sons stoned to death, after first having been left without food, then forced to walk amid hoots and jeers and finally thrown into wells and stoned because it was believed they had the plague and might infect others. Those who succeeded in escaping turned up in Paris all of a sudden and added new and terrifying details to this picture of horror." (175-176)

CHAPTER 3 (177 FF)

After another stay of unspecified duration in a sanitarium, Marcel returns to postwar Paris in a dejected mood. He has given up all hope of accomplishing anything memorable in the field of literature: "If there once was a time when I was able to believe myself a poet, I now know that I am not." (177) In spite of his long absence he has not been forgotten by society, and he finds two invitations waiting for him—one from the Princesse de Guermantes and one from the famous actress Berma. (178-179) He decides, along with the rest of fashionable Paris, that the prospect of the Guermantes reception is the more attractive, leaving the great tragedienne Berma (whom he had seen play Phèdre on his first visit to the theater as a young man) with an empty drawing room. (339 ff) The story of how the old actress finds herself deserted by everyone including her only child, a daughter, and her son-in-law who go off to the Guermantes reception and beg Rachel, now a famous actress and the triumphant rival over Berma, to have them admitted is melodrama in the most sentimental tradition. (361)

Another melodramatic stroke (an even more daring one) is essayed by Proust when he has Marcel reveal, after a long period of silence and misdirection of the reader's attention, that the Princesse de Guermantes, who is giving this reception, is not identical with the lady long familiar to us under that awe-inspiring title but another woman, even better known to the narrator and the reader, old Madame Verdurin. (293) Time, the greatest of all destroyers and transformers (even more so than a Dreyfus Case or a World War, which it readily includes in its repertory) had given the social kaleidoscope its most violent shake of all, at least during the lifetime of Marcel. In his long absence, both M. Verdurin and the Princesse de Guermantes had died. Madame Verdurin had first married a penniless cousin of the Prince, and after her second husband had died, the Prince himself, his financial position very much shaken by the long-drawn-out war with Germany, had asked for her hand. So here she is presiding over a fashionable society to which she had not even belonged at the beginning. Yet the character of Madame Verdurin has not changed a bit, and when she opens her mouth to say: "That's it! We'll get up a little clan! How I like these intelligent young people who take part in everything. Ah, what a muzhishian you are!" (324), her voice is immediately recognizable not only to the ear of Marcel but to the ear of the reader as well—and there are all sorts of odd ironic echoes around it.

So many things have changed that Marcel experiences the sensation of being at a costume ball. What a trick it is simply to recognize perfectly familiar people, who have grown white beards, have wrinkles plastered all over the stiff skin of their faces, and are silver-haired and supported on trembling limbs! The frightening apparition of the aged Charlus, who had recently suffered a stroke, is compared by the narrator to that of King Lear. (182) In his broken-down state, he bows obsequiously to Madame de Saint-Euverte whom he had once so brutally snubbed, (183) causing Marcel to reflect on the subject of "how perishable is the love of earthly grandeur and even human pride itself. . . . A child indeed he had become but without a child's natural pride." (184) Only one thing had not left the Baron, and that was what he could very well have done without—his vice. Jupien tells Marcel that he has found his master dishonoring a child "not ten years old." (188) Charlus, in his old age, has plunged into the same abyss of shamelessness as Dostoyevsky's Stavrogin had penetrated in his early youth.

Nor is Marcel himself left long with the comfortable illusion that he himself has not changed as much as the others. Young men defer to him with the sort of respect that he himself had once shown to older men. The Duchess of Guermantes (now consorting with actresses whom she once would not have admitted to her drawing room and humbling herself before Rachel, whom she had once insulted as callously as her brother-in-law Charlus had insulted Madame de Saint-Euverte) refers to Marcel to his astonishment as her "oldest friend." (261) His friend Bloch has also at last, through his many books which create a simulacrum of wisdom, managed to gain free admittance to this charmed circle of the aristocracy, and he seems in the process to have lost a good deal of his familiar vulgarity. He no longer boasts of the invitations he has received; in fact, he has attained "a sort of social age." (312) Marcel considers the curious and unexpected development that Swann, Legrandin, Bloch, and himself, all starting out from the middle-class basin of Combray, have, by independent roads, found their way into the milieu of the exclusive aristocracy of the Faubourg Saint-Germain.

And what a change here in the Faubourg itself! Madame Verdurin's rise is only the most phenomenal example of what has become a rule: "The persons who, according to the old social code, should not have been here were, to my great astonishment, on terms of close friendship with others of excellent family who had been willing to come and be bored at the Princesse de Guermantes only for the sake of meeting their new friends. For the distinguishing characteristic of this social set was its prodigious aptitude at wiping out social classifications. . . . Whether relaxed or broken, the springs of the protective apparatus no longer functioned and much foreign matter was getting in and destroying the homogeneousness and distinctive appearance of the group. Like a senile old dowager, the Faubourg Saint-Germain replied only with timid smiles to insolent servants who invaded its drawing room, drank its orangeade and introduced its mistresses to it." (297–298)

Much has been made of this passage by influential critics of the Marxist Thirties—much more, I am sure, than is really intended or actually present in it. Proust was supposed in that doctrinaire decade to have become a sociologist or social historian who had depicted the fusion between the class of the big bourgeoisie and that of the old aristocracy of France. But Marcel indicates clearly enough in the pages that follow this famous passage (which were conveniently ignored or forgotten by those propounding the evolutionary thesis) that what he was describing was no new social phenomenon. The interpenetration of the bourgeoisie and the aristocracy had been going on for centuries, and the entry of the bourgeois Colberts upon the fashionable scene long ago had probably been as shocking to other observers as the eruption of Madame Verdurin was to himself. What he is interested in portraying is not so much a change in the objective world as in the narrator's vision of that external world. Long experience had made Marcel critical of the pretensions of those continually being admitted and absorbed by smart society; but when he himself had been a young man who had just gained admittance, others older and more experienced than he had probably been just as critical of himself, just as shocked by his ignorance of social usage and unconscious lapses of taste.

In other words, the change depicted by Proust has less in common with that postulated by such social scientists as Marx than it has with that vision of the instability of all things earthly which belongs to the pessimistic philosophers and the Biblical Ecclesiastes. This should be clear from the following sentence which is his last word on the subject of the personal and group vicissitudes he has witnessed: "Thus does the form of the things of this world change; thus the center of empires, the cadastre of private fortunes and the chart of social positions, all that seemed definitively fixed, is being continually made over and the eyes of a man can during his lifetime contemplate the most complete change in the very quarters where it had seemed to him the most impossible." (368)

We are left with the image of the kaleidoscope once more! Try to make sense—let alone science—out of the succession of its patterns before you try to understand or explain society. In the midst of this sea of change, certain characters, of course, stand out like impregnable rocks. Thus, the Duke of Guermantes is still engaged in pursuing women and his latest mistress turns out to be Odette (364) who has managed to "freeze" her style of beauty at a certain age so that almost miraculously she looks younger than her own daughter.

But all of the social observations play a decreasingly important role in the coda of *Remembrance*, the first notes of which are struck at the moment when Marcel is on his way to the Princesse de Guermantes (alias Madame Verdurin). Some strange things begin to happen to him this fateful day. He steps from one flagstone to another along an unevenly paved street and finds himself instantly transported in imagination as if by a magic carpet to Venice where he had once experienced a similar sensation as he stood "on two uneven flagstones in the baptistry of Saint Mark's." (192) Later in the afternoon the accidental striking of a spoon against a plate by an awkward waiter (192) and the touch of the texture of a napkin suddenly resurrect other segments of his dead past. Now these experiences are certainly strange, but they are not unprecedented for Marcel. They had been prefigured by that extraordinary change wrought in his consciousness by the taste of the madeleine soaked in tea which is described in *Swann's Way*. Marcel himself compares the effect of these fresh sensations to that produced by the taste of that madeleine and tea. (191) What is unusual is only the number of these sensations that occur in a limited period of time and the ease with which he deciphers their significance (as compared to the inexpressible difficulty he had encountered in connecting the madeleine and tea to Aunt Léonie and his own childhood at Combray).

He is forcibly struck by these repeated revelations of his past through the medium of an identical sensory perception uniting the present moment and the past, and no longer does he feel so completely hopeless about his lack of artistic ability or of an intellectual, philosophical message to deliver to the world. He becomes increasingly aware that the miracle of liberation from the bondage of time, which is the object of art, is not something that can be accomplished by the conscious intelligence or by the voluntary memory. (196–197) Rather, he sees that it comes as a kind of gift from without, as something which arises from the unconscious and is the product of involuntary memory. It is revelations of this kind, he concludes, that give art its true distinction, and make of art something so great and important that other supposedly important things and values in life—society, friendship, love—pale into insignificance beside it. (201–202) Writers who occupy themselves with outward social activities (the Dreyfus Case, the World War) are really attempting to escape from their primary obligation to interpret the inner significance of their own impressions. This interpretation is extremely difficult; it is much easier to lose oneself in outer, socially significant activity than to find oneself in the more subjective, personal exploration which is the sole solid basis upon which art is constructed. The commandment to "Know thyself," which is that of both the Delphic Oracle and of Socrates seems to Proust, in the special imaginative interpretation which he puts upon it, the hardest of all to fulfill.

Practitioners of so-called realistic, "naturalistic," "socially conscious" art seem to him to evade the difficulty completely and consequently to produce things which are utterly ephemeral and basically worthless. Their productions are even less valuable than a newspaper which is meant only to last for a day and serves it sufficiently, whereas it is the object of the artist to create an object that will "brave time," that will last for a century, sometimes for many centuries. "I realized," writes Marcel, "that I would not have to trouble myself about the various literary theories that had disturbed me for a time, more especially those the critics developed at the time of the Dreyfus Case and revived during the war, which sought to 'make the artist come out of his ivory tower,' scorn frivolous or sentimental subjects, depict great working-class movements and, if not huge crowds, at any rate no more insignificant idlers ('I confess that the portrayal of these useless persons is of no particular interest to me,' Bloch said) but highminded intellectuals or heroes." (208)

It is ironic that in Albert Thibaudet's article on Proust in the Encyclopaedia Britannica, exactly such "social-minded" objections as are here waggishly attributed to Bloch are seriously advanced against his own work. Thibaudet speaks of "the idle life and ultimate nothingness of the people of his world, their lack of all interests other than those of social life (he means by this snobbish and fashionable society) and the indifference that the ordinary reader must always feel to their fate."

If by the ordinary reader is meant one who is insensitive to high accomplishment in art, then it is no wonder if we find him indifferent to *Remembrance*. But Proust insists that the important thing in art is not its subject-matter but the manner in which this subject is handled. The *how* of art is more important than the what. An artist is defined as the one who can make something out of nothing and, if necessary, a silk purse out of a sow's ear: "Perhaps it is more by the quality of the language used than by the aesthetic principles observed that one can determine to what level an intellectual or moral effort has been carried." (209) He points out that just as the laws of anatomy may be studied and demonstrated on the body of an imbecile on that of a genius, so (if there is such a thing as human nature) the great moral and psychological laws which govern humanity may be demonstrated as well from the lives of those people who are sterile and unproductive as from those who belong to the working, struggling, productive mass of humanity. In fact, for certain purposes, the aristocratic and wealthy groups he has chosen to dissect and analyze are even more suitable than others; he had indicated as much earlier when he quoted Balzac to the effect that only among people who enjoyed complete leisure did love unfold in its untrammeled form. Since so much of Marcel's narrative is concerned with love and its shadow, jealousy, the leisure-class which serves him as a subject would seem ideally adapted to his purpose.

The naturalistic novel he calls "a cinematographic parade" (210) and he has nothing but contempt for it. In its superficiality, it fails entirely to convey the quality of life as we ourselves know it from experience. Memory has taught him that every hour of our lives is "a vase filled with perfumes, sounds, and colors"—a truth which one would never realize from the drab, objective, colorless representations made by the "naturalists." (212–213) Those who think that naturalism is best suited to the taste of the popular masses are insulting their intelligence and sensitivity; from his experience, Marcel says, he knows that the real illiterates in society are to be found in the fashionable Jockey Club rather than in the General Confederation of Labor. (216) As for subject matter, what makes the critics think that people are necessarily overjoyed to read only about others in their own circumstances and their own social condition; perhaps the poor are as delighted by the romantic escape of reading about the rich as the rich often are by the romantic escape of reading about the poor? Proust is obviously still hoping to reach a wide, popular audience, and he does not agree with Thibaudet that he is necessarily handicapped by his choice of leisure-class subjects. T. S. Eliot indicates in one of his essays that an author might sensibly prefer to an audience of the half-educated an audience of the completely illiterate which should at least not be burdened with prejudices against his novel procedures. Proust has a similar thought when he contrasts "sophisticated" critics with the general public to the advantage of the latter: "Whereas the real essence of talent is a gift, an attribute of cosmic character, the presence of which should first be sought for underneath the surface fashions of thought and style, it is by these latter qualities that the critics classify an author. Because of his peremptory tone and his ostentatious scorn of the school that preceded him, they put the mantle of prophecy on a writer who has no new message to deliver. This constant aberration of the critics is such that a writer should almost prefer to be judged by the public at large (if the latter were not incapable even of understanding what an artist has attempted in a line of effort unfamiliar to it). For the talent of a great writer—which, after all, is merely an instinct religiously hearkened to (while silence is imposed on everything else), perfected and understood—has more in common with the instinctive life of the people than with the superficial verbiage and fluctuating standards of the conventionally recognized judges." (222–223)

There is nothing spontaneous about the so-called popular taste, especially in troubled times. It seems to him dictated by ideologists, theoreticians, and doctrinaires, and he finds it ironic and poetic justice that artists of the old Régime in the eighteenth century in France like Watteau and La Tour should now seem greater in stature than all the artists of the Revolution. (217) For the truth to him is that, contrary to evolutionary theories, there is no visible "progress in the arts" and there are writers in the 17th century who had no acquaintance with modern ideas and who are nevertheless superior to the best that the 19th and 20th centuries have to offer. (349) In this section of literary theory, too, he warns the reader to beware of critically worthless biographical studies which attempt to pin down the precise models used for chapters in books. (239) It is an idea he had already advanced in his then-unpublished *Contre Sainte-Beuve.* He seems to have foreseen with resentment that his own *Remembrance* should become in time the happy hunting ground for biographers who treat it as a *roman à clef* and thus evade the more difficult problems of understanding and analyzing it on its own terms. The shape of *Remembrance* as a whole grows clearer to Marcel on that afternoon at the Guermantes reception, and he cites a number of literary precedents which occurred to him to fortify his conception of the role played by the involuntary memory in the genesis of art drawn from the works of Chateaubriand, Gerard de Nerval, and Baudelaire. (252–253)

There comes back to Marcel's mind the thought of that night long ago at Combray when he had been so unhappy and disturbed because of his mother's failure to kiss him goodnight, so that eventually she had to spend the night reading to him in his room. That night, which Marcel calls "the sweetest and saddest night of my life" (214–215) because it marked the beginning of the abdication of parental authority in his life and the resulting decline of his own will-power, is implicitly contrasted with this happiest of all the afternoons of his life when he firmly grasps for the first time the form that his literary vocation, which he had been in search of for so many years, was finally going to take. From this day on, his literary labor would become the most important thing in the world to Marcel. (330) How trivial, vain, and provokingly foolish now appear to him that fashionable life and those social conquests by which he had once set so much store. What judgment sufficiently harsh could be passed upon the younger snobbish set he now sees around him which remembers the noble Swann as an adventurer and regards the adventuress Odette as the paragon of nobility in her family?

(299) At best, what did the Faubourg Saint-Germain have to offer a man for the loss of his own youth? Bloch, after endless efforts and failures, has at last attained to his heart's desire and succeeded in gaining acceptance in the most exclusive aristocratic circles, but he now twenty years nearer to death: "So what good did that do him?" (309) Only the writing of a good book such as invites us to a vision of immortality in a timeless realm of Platonic ideas, seems ultimately worthwhile to the disillusioned Marcel. (330) As for the rest, it is, no matter how imposing its façades, as Eliot says in *The Waste Land*, "unreal."

The conclusion of such an enormously long work as *Remembrance* (like the coda of a lengthy symphony) has necessarily to be proportionate to it. Some twenty pages from the end of *The Past Recaptured*, Marcel summarizes in outline much of the plot of the whole of *Remembrance*—this summary is occasioned by his meeting with the daughter of Gilberte. (380) Unfortunately, he now feels that his own death may be near and he can only hope to be spared long enough to complete his book. (395–396) It is going to be a very long work, he feels—perhaps the work of a thousand days and a thousand nights, like his favorite Arabian romance, though its subject matter is more likely to resemble that of Saint-Simon's *Memoirs*.

He now welcomes the illness which he had previously tried in vain to cure himself of, because it serves effectively to detach him from that meretricious world of society which had kept him from launching himself seriously upon the work which is the result of a true, higher vocation and may be compared, as Kafka did in his own case, to *prayer* rather than to that ordinary condition of involuntary servitude which we are all familiar with and to which we give the name of work. He feels that only by dying to the pleasures and enjoyments of the world with which he is familiar can he hope to rise again in the transfigured world of art which is the repository now of all his eternal hopes; to explain his meaning he makes use of that Biblical quotation which was the favorite one of André Gide, who took from it the title of his autobiography—"for an the grain of wheat die not after it hath been sown, it will abide alone; but if it die, it will bear much fruit . . ." (399) Marcel is now ready either for death or for that shadowy condition resembling death (it may be called death-in-life) which is the price that apparently must always be paid in undertaking a great, creative work (it was the feeling that Proust somehow belongs to this nebulous intermediary sphere of shades that must have inspired Céline to refer to him in *Journey to the End of the Night* as *mi-revenant* ("half a ghost").

As the last page nears, he recalls with wonder the sound of the little bell at Combray as Swann rang it on that ever-memorable evening which had been described in the introductory passages of *Remembrance*. He sees that men occupy in the dimension of time a much more formidable place than that which they occupy in the world of space. When this dimension is added to them by our imagination, men appear to be very different from what they are in the eyes of a superficial realist—they become almost monstrous, mythical creatures "perched on giant stilts, sometimes taller than church spires, constantly growing and finally rendering their progress so difficult and perilous that they suddenly fall." (401–402) So it is no wonder to Marcel, as he looks over at the Duc de Guermantes and sees him tottering along on trembling limbs "as he made his way along the difficult summit of his eighty-three years." (401)

The final pages of *Remembrance* I find very moving, and I think most readers will share my feeling. They are tremulous with compassion for the condition of humanity which is born to experience such suffering in life with nothing to look forward to at the end (at least on the physical level) save a miserable death. Even the Duke, with all his callousness and self-centeredness, excites pity in our hearts, since he too is bound to share in our common fate. But if there is death, we must remember that for Marcel there is transfiguration also. In the rest that is silence after the last words have been written and read, one can still hear, as an overtone, the conclusion of the account of the death of the novelist Bergotte that had been given in *The Captive:* "They buried him, but all through that night of mourning, in the lighted windows, his books arranged three by three kept watch like angels with outspread wings and seemed, for him who was no more, the symbol of his resurrection."

These are the last words which tradition says that Proust himself composed before his own death. Their appropriateness as a full tonic close for his work is as evident as is that of the poetic passage from Shakespeare's last play, *The Tempest:*

> We are such stuff
> As dreams are made on and our little life
> Is rounded with a sleep.

which the playwright himself inserted into the middle of his work but which, in many modern productions, I have seen lifted out of its context and used as an epilogue, which seems to the audience very fitting indeed.

9. Minor Works

Pleasures and Days

THE FIRST BOOK PUBLISHED BY PROUST IN 1896 AT THE AGE OF
TWENTY-FIVE, WITH A PERCEPTIVE PREFACE BY ANATOLE FRANCE,
is a collection of prose and verse (the English translation retains
the prose but drops the half dozen pages of verse "portraits of
painters and musicians" which the French text includes). This
excision, except perhaps from a scholarly point of view, seems to
me to have been advisable, not only because it is difficult to carry
over the quality and felicities of even the greatest poetry from
one language to another but because Proust's gift was definitely
not for verse. To convince ourselves of this fact, we have only to
compare the fifteen line verse tribute to Chopin with the beautiful passage which he devoted to that composer in *Swann's Way*
(429).

But the prose is another matter. The dichotomy between the
two gifts is a matter of repeated observation in literary history.
When John Dryden, according to tradition, said to Jonathan
Swift: "Cousin Swift, you will never be a poet!" he was right
in the technical sense, if we identify poetry and verse as people
were inclined to do in England at the time, but he was wrong
if we use the word poet in its larger Aristotelian sense as a
maker of plots and creator of characters. Swift, though indifferent as a versifier, became the greatest prose writer in his
language. In our own time in America, Dreiser, Hemingway,
and Fitzgerald all tried their hands at poetry in the narrower
sense and published the results, which are not very interesting
except in the documentary or biographical sense. Like Melville,
whose poetry is to be found mainly in *Moby Dick* rather than in
his voluminous verse, Proust incorporated his poetry into *Remembrance*.

This earliest collection of his sketches, stories, satires, verses is by no means a negligible production. In the authentic sense of a much abused and frequently undeserved term of praise, it is promising. Of course it does not promise so much as Proust was to perform, for whereas it is characteristic of facile and clever talents to promise more than they are able to redeem, it is characteristic of something far higher than talent sometimes to promise less. Anatole France (or, according to malicious legend, his mistress), who had the advantage of knowing the young writer personally and was consequently better able to gauge the depth of meaning in his words, caught the hint of "things to come" completely. His oft-quoted descriptive phrase about Proust as "a depraved Bernardin de Saint-Pierre and an ingenuous Petronius" is possibly more applicable to *Remembrance*, which was many years away, than to the slim volume to which it is affixed.

André Gide, after changing his mind for the better about *Swann's Way*, went back to this earlier book of Proust's and did penance by confessing that he had not done justice to it on first reading and that viewing it retrospectively it turns out to have many of the themes and qualities which later went into its author's masterpiece. Edmund Wilson, who did not have to change his mind because he came to Proust's work when it had long been famous, has also done a good job of tracing the connections of subject and manner of treatment evident between *Les plaisirs et les jours* and *Remembrance*. Without attempting to deny the validity of the insights of such gifted creators and critics, which are only too easy to document satisfactorily with quotations, it must be admitted, I think, that this book of Proust's is by no means as ripe an artistic production as, for example, Joyce's *Dubliners* is. Had Joyce died before he wrote *Portrait of the Artist, Ulysses, Finnegan's Wake* (not to mention *Chamber Music* or *Exiles*) his first precocious publication should have survived and been rediscovered in time. The same, I am afraid, cannot be said of *Les Plaisirs et les Jours*, which owes its continuing interest and preservation solely to its author's later work.

The resemblances in some details to *Remembrance* are not difficult to discover. In the story "A Young Girl's Confession," which deals with a familiar Proustian theme: the profanation of the parental image and the intolerable burden of guilt this brings with it, we come across a clear reminder of the incident involving the mother's goodnight kiss in the opening section of *Swann's Way*. (*Pleasures and Days*, p. 80). And two pages later on, there is an aphorism which is an abbreviation of the same theme that in its most complete development appears in the volume *Sweet Cheat Gone:* "Absence taught me other and still more bitter lessons, that one grows accustomed to absence, that the greatest diminution of oneself, the most humiliating suffering is to feel that one no longer suffers." (82)

The protagonist of this story, though of a different sex, obviously has the same basic character (or maybe the more appropriate word is characterlessness) as the narrator of *Remembrance*, and her mother is just as concerned about it as his is: "What grieved my mother was my lack of will. I did everything on the impulse of the moment." (83–84)

When he speaks of the benefits we derive from suffering and of those who cause us to suffer (women, "cruel friends") as benefactors, we are reminded of how much his vision of life has in common with that of Schopenhauer. Proust adds to the fundamental pessimism of this philosopher a masochistic twist of his own which occasionally has the effect of giving to it an air of affectation or preciosity. The theme of the vanity of snobbery and ambition could come from the same source or be traceable all the way back to Ecclesiastes, and yet there is a Proustian grace in the phrasing, a sense of style that is personal to himself and is the initial gift he brought with him to the art of writing. This stylistic grace is evident when he speaks, for example, of "the universal scandal of human lives, not excepting his own, that walked toward death backward with eyes turned toward life." (10)

In the story "Violante, or Worldly Vanities," there is an evocation of the torrid, lustful atmosphere of Gomorrah (32–33) which is significant in the light of the importance of this theme later on and at the same time makes more understandable Anatole France's mention of the name of Petronius in connection with that of Proust, though I do not see his reason for qualifying with the adjective "ingenuous" the name of the Roman satirist, unless the adjective indicates (aside from adding a characteristic spice of paradox) that the old author was loathe to believe that his young friend was as sophisticated about corruption in sexual mores as certain passages in this book seemed to suggest. But

Proust was certainly not ingenuous, and if his work reminds one of the satire of the Roman decadence it may be because he was so well acquainted with the seamier side of contemporary manners and morals.

But Petronius is not the only Latin satirist whom Proust brings to mind. In "Fragments from Italian Comedy," in addition to its titular models, the reader is reminded of a range of satire from the relative good-nature of Horace to the bitter sarcasm of Martial's epigrams. Here is one of the characters whom he rather mildly makes fun of: "Myrto, witty, pretty, and kind, but something of a social climber, prefers, to all her other friends, Parthénis who is a duchess and smarter than herself; yet she enjoys the companionship of Lalagé whose social standing is exactly equal to her own, and she is also by no means indifferent to the attractions of Cléanthis who is obscure and has no pretensions to brilliant rank. But the friend Myrto cannot endure is Doris. Doris's worldly situation is a little below that of Myrto, and she seeks out Myrto, as Myrto does Parthénis, because she is more fashionable." (36)

The eccentric Oranthe is delineated in a more incisive, epigrammatic manner. In this character, foibles and vices are almost indistinguishable from each other: "So you didn't go to bed last night? You haven't washed this morning? But why proclaim it from the housetops, Oranthe? Brilliantly gifted as you are, isn't that enough to distinguish you from common mortals? Must you insist upon acting such a pitiful role besides? You are hounded by creditors, your infidelities drive your wife to despair . . . You know how to make yourself very agreeable, and your wit, without your long hair, would be enough to make people notice you . . . The trouble with you is that to the soul of an artist you have added all the prejudices of a bourgeois, only showing the reverse side and without deceiving us." (43)

The character Olivian, though he is described in more than a page, is really *caught* with a single sentence: "Olivian, you are truly unfortunate. Because, almost before you were a man, you were already a man of letters." (51)

But if he is clearly indebted to ancient models (beginning with the very title of his book, which is an ironic echo of Hesiod's *Works and Days*) he has learned from the standard authors in his own culture as well. A maxim such as the following is a recognizable variation upon a well-known theme by La Roche-foucauld: "A libertine's need of virginity is another form of the eternal homage love pays to innocence." (45) And a passage such as the following derives not only from observation but even more obviously from *Madame Bovary:* "There are women in the provinces, it would seem, little shopkeepers whose brains are tiny cages imprisoning longings for Society as fierce as wild animals. The postman brings them the *Gaulois.* The society page is gobbled up in a flash. The ravenous provincial ladies are satisfied. And for the next hour their eyes, whose pupils are inordinately dilated by veneration and delight, will shine with an expression of perfect serenity." (41)

At least one other literary debt of Proust's deserves mention—the one he owes to Tolstoy. The last story in the book entitled "The End of Jealousy" and particularly its concluding pages read in parts (152–153, 161–162) almost like involuntary pastiches of the Russian master's great story *The Kreutzer Sonata* and the scene at the death-bed of Prince Andrey Bolkonsky in *War and Peace.* Tolstoy is explicitly mentioned by Proust on a number of occasions, and it is certain that his work was one of the most lasting admirations in Proust's life.

Pastiches et Mélanges

In an essay on Flaubert reprinted in the volume *Chroniques,* Proust speaks of the therapeutic function of writing conscious imitations or pastiches of famous authors. His idea is that the styles of the masters are so infectious to the sensitive beginner that if he does not get them out of his system somehow, he will continue in involuntary servitude to them all of his life *without knowing it.* To exorcise them and neutralize their gravitational pull upon himself, he must consciously imitate them (to the degree of parody) instead of unconsciously doing so.

This may have been a rationalization of his own delight in mimicry (of the mannerisms of his friends as well as those of celebrated stylists in literature). In any case, he succeeds in these pastiches in being both amusing and instructive. (Especially excellent, I think, is his take-off on a typical *Lundi* article by Sainte-Beuve. (24 ff) Here, in a few lively pages, he has condensed the essence of his hundreds of expository pages directed against Sainte-Beuve in his then unpublished work of that name, and furthermore he has made his serious point in a delightfully entertaining way. Presumably criticizing a mythical novel by Flaubert (a portion of which served for the previous pastiche), Sainte-Beuve displays a positive aversion to the prospect of coming to grips with the work he is supposed to be criticizing. He escapes from his duty as a critic somewhat in the manner of Stephen Leacock's celebrated horseman who galloped rapidly off in all directions. The "article" consists of an endless series of irrelevancies: digressions about Flaubert's father, digressions about the lack of complete realism in his portrayal of a scene in a law court (Sainte-Beuve's authority is an eminent lawyer of his acquaintance), pedantic allusions—a la Brichot—to Martial, to Napoleon, to Villemain and to whatever and whomever else the critic's capacious memory can dredge up. At the end, we realize (if we are reflective—but how many newspaper readers *reflect* on what they have read?) that we have been titillated, interested, and informed on every possible subject but the one that the critic is ostensibly concerned with and ought to have dealt with—namely, the work of art by Flaubert. And we realize, through the distortion of caricature, that this parody has exposed the journalistic technique of Sainte-Beuve, which is never so completely awry from its critical purpose as Proust pretends here but is so only at its weakest points which the parodist has mercilessly seized upon.

And we realize the cardinal sin of journalism—which according to Proust means writing to please others, in distinction from "true" writing which is more subjective in its motivation (to the point of being self-centered) and derives its possible importance from this central characteristic. In another connection, later in this book, he writes: "When one works to please others, one cannot succeed, but the things one has done to please oneself always have a chance of interesting someone else." (102–103) The sentence refers to Ruskin whose analysis and appreciations of the Gothic Cathedrals of France are the subjects of the greater part of this volume. Ruskin for Proust was "one of the greatest writers of all times and of all countries." (187) So great was his feeling for the English master, some of whose works he translated and annotated meticulously, that at the latter's death in 1900 Proust describes a pilgrimage he made to the Cathedral at Rouen in search of an obscure, small bit of sculpture there which Ruskin had discovered and spoken of with infectious enthusiasm. (174) This is one of the more striking passages in Proust himself and invites comparison with the passage in *The Captive* describing the death of Bergotte which happened during an art exhibition where, as we recall, he had gone in search of a painting by Vermeer in which a sensitive critic had brought to light a hitherto unnoticed little patch of yellow wall, exquisitely done. It is enthusiasm rightly directed that for Proust is the touchstone of the quality of aesthetic criticism: "Great literary beauties correspond to something, and it is perhaps enthusiasm in art which is the criterion of truth." (178) He applies to Ruskin himself the words which that great enthusiast spoke at the death of his favorite contemporary English painter, Turner: "It is with these eyes, closed forever at the bottom of the tomb, that generations yet unborn will look at nature." (180)

But Proust points out that while Ruskin himself recommended reverence as the proper attitude to assume towards great art and great artists, he rejected what can only be labelled as blind infatuation and dared to find fault even with sacred scripture since there is no form of writing which does not contain an admixture of error. (188) This authority is used to justify his finding some fault with Ruskin. In light of the fact that Proust himself has been subjected to the same criticism by religiously oriented crtics, it is especially interesting that he should accuse Ruskin of what he calls the "idolatry of art." (181) Briefly, he believes, that Ruskin was so sensitive to beauty that, *without knowing it,* he elevated aesthetics above every other consideration, including ethics, and he cites passages from *The Stones of Venice* which are impressively eloquent and lovely prose without ringing really true or sincere. (183–185) In other words, he thinks that excessive devotion to art forms led this most consciously moral of men (who carried sincerity to the point of giving away his private fortune and of recommending to his readers that before allowing themselves to enjoy the beauties of a Cathedral like Amiens they should give alms to the beggars at the door!) into unconscious prevarications by which (through the process of what Freud was to call rationalization) he disguised from himself the luxurious sensuality of his own basic motivations. Proust plays with the curious notion that immoral ideas (or amoral ones? Nietzsche, for example?) sincerely expressed may be less dangerous to integrity of spirit than moral ideas insincerely expressed. (182) Such a notion complicates the problem of evaluative judgment almost beyond belief, and Proust may (from what we know of the problems of his personal life as well as those he faced in choosing his artistic subjects) have been pleading his own case; yet the distinction he insists on appears to be valid. The greatest of all aesthetic as well as ethical virtues for him is to be sincere, which is another way of saying that it is tremendously difficult to know when one is being really honest with oneself! He criticizes Ruskin, too, (and perhaps this technical fault which he discovers grows out of the substantive one just discussed) for emphasizing overmuch the ideas or literary equivalents of painting. For Proust (and his point of view was to gain increasing currency with artists and critics later in the twentieth century) painting can hope to rival literature only when it realizes that its peculiar genius is not at all literary! (157)

Yet in spite of such criticisms which establish his independence, his overwhelmingly favorable reaction to Ruskin is allowed to stand. He quotes pages and pages of Ruskin's text and accompanies each quotation with learned footnotes which cite parallel passages from Ruskin's other works. He is himself evidently steeped in Ruskin's works and invites the reader to immerse himself in it as well. He warns of the danger of trying to get to know an author through selections, anthologies, or even a complete book: "To read but one book by an author," he tells us, "is to enjoy merely a passing acquaintance with him" (107) His own knowledge of Ruskin is clearly not superficial but thorough, broad and deep. To give us a sample of the richness his master's work contains, he composes a detailed guide to Ruskin's *Bible of Amiens*, which is itself a guide to that Cathedral. (131 ff) Though the following words are not meant to be applied directly to him, Ruskin in Proust's estimation was undoubtedly one of those who realized and is capable of making us realize that "the supreme effort of the writer as of the artist is partially to lift the veil of ugliness and insignificance which leaves us without curiosity about the world." (250)

A strange thing to find in the volume is the evidence of what can only be called, in a predominantly romantic setting of materials and ideas, elements of a classical point of view concerning art (which may help to explain how it came about—biographers have offered some *ad hominem* explanations of the phenomenon —that one of the most favorable criticisms of Proust's first book was written by the reactionary classicist, Charles Maurras, a fact which Proust remembered with gratitude all his life). In true romantic vein he speaks of "the man of genius" but notice that the romantic man of genius in the following passage is engaged in a seemingly classical activity: "The man of genius cannot give birth to undying works save by creating them not in the image of the mortal being that he is, but in the image of the representative example of humanity that he bears within him." (148) And he notes the paradox that while the most intelligent public tends to be romantic in its taste today, "the masters (even the so-called romantic masters preferred by the romantic public) are classical!" (267) To compound the ambiguity, he claims that the romantics have always made the best commentators on classics, like *Phèdre*.

Part of the greatness of Ruskin for him consists of the fact that he was so enamored of the past and turns our thoughts towards it with understanding, love, and humility. Writing against an anti-clerical bill introduced into the Chamber of Deputies by Briand in the wake of the Dreyfus Case—a bill that would have ended the state subvention of services in the great Cathedrals of France—Proust foresees with trepidation the ultimate result, so dear to the heart of all progressive thinkers, that "the dead (that "great silent democracy" as Proust called it in a phrase resembling one of Chesterton's) will no longer govern the living. And the oblivious living will cease to fulfill the vows of the dead." (209) Passages such as this one help us to understand better why, though some Catholics have been among the most outspoken critics of Proust, other Catholic writers like Mauriac have by and large found it possible, with some reservations, to defend his work strongly.

But the most interesting selection in *Pastiches et Mélanges* to my mind is the one most frequently translated and reprinted entitled "Filial Sentiments of a Parricide." (211–225) The story in brief has to do with a man, Henri van Blarenberghe, whom Proust knew very casually over a long period but with whom, due to circumstances relating to the death of both their fathers, he was in touch by letter shortly before van Blarenberghe was involved in a family tragedy so macabre that it supplied the subject of a horrifying item in the press of the day, the kind of sensational story we glance at briefly, read with indifference, and immediately pass over. The newspaper item was headed with the words "Drama of a Lunatic" and it told how van Blarenberghe, a wealthy, sensitive man (his sensitive nature has been established by Proust previously through quoting from a couple of the letters he had received from him over the years) had in a fit of rage killed his mother suddenly and then, when he realized what he had done, shot himself so awkwardly in the head that he died a tortured, lingering death, with a police inspector at his elbow badgering him in his final moments in search of some clue which might help to unravel the motives of the catastrophe.

Proust's idea in his little piece is to go back of the bare journalistic facts reported in the paper, not by analyzing the psychology of the participants in the action (he didn't know any of them well enough to do so) but to point out how various of the incidents reported by the press serve to remind the reader who is in some way sympathetically attuned to the people involved, of moments in the highest classical drama of Greece and novels of the modern world—of *Ajax* by Sophocles and of *Oedipus*, of Shakespeare's *King Lear*, of Dostoyevsky's *Brothers Karamazov* and of Cervantes' *Don Quixote*. Proust's object is to show that this journalistic sensation is not just cheap melodrama but has within it the stuff of great tragedy. To use his own words: "I want to bring into the room of the crime something of the breath of heaven, to show that what this newspaper paragraph recorded was precisely one of those Greek dramas, the performance of which was almost a sacred ceremony; that the poor parricide was no criminal brute, no moral leper beyond the pale of humanity, but a noble example, a tender and a loving son whom an ineluctable fate—or, let us say, pathological, and so speak the language of today—had driven to crime, and to its expiation, in a manner that should be forever illustrious." (In other words, Proust's theme has something in common with that of Kafka's story *The Hunger Artist*, in which the author tries to indicate that the ethic of asceticism, which once gave rise to so many illustrious religious martyrdoms, is today regarded as merely ridiculous, meaningless, or diseased; martyrs are thus robbed of the attention which was once theirs, without ceasing to suffer or to be less worthy of fame and celebration than their great predecessors—the saints over whom so many tears have been shed and for whom so many prayers have been intoned. It is humanity that is fickle and from time to time changes its style in heroes or refuses to recognize the existence of the hero altogether, as at the present time).

But there is another idea that Proust develops at the end— that such a newspaper melodrama, like the high tragedies of the Greeks and Elizabethans, merely carries to an extreme of crudity, impulses and actions that are far from uncommon, and his conclusion is that every man and woman in this world is to some degree guilty of parricide (and matricide) though the means used are not usually revolver and dagger but only words, hateful looks, etc. "Filial Sentiments of a Parricide" is an extraordinarily powerful piece of literature which, appearing years ago in English translation in one of our more fashionable literary periodicals, so completely dwarfed and put into the shadow the articles and stories which the editors had to print side by side with it that there was no sense of competition or comparison between them. Proust is able to breathe life and imagination into the classical myth while using it to give a higher meaning to an otherwise sordid contemporary scandal. His handling of his materials has something so masterful about it that it brings to my mind the story about Cezanne, who, after rebelling successfully against a lifeless academicism in painting, proposed that modern artists measure their art against the solidity characteristic of the classics displayed in the museums. Cezanne proposed to be modern and alive and exciting (unlike the academic painters) without ceasing to be monumental and permanent in his intentions. If anything by Proust aside from *Remembrance* deserves the attention of the conscientious, careful or merely curious reader, I suggest that it is the pages entitled "Filial Sentiments of a Parricide."

Chroniques

This is a miscellaneous collection of pieces by Proust in various newspapers and magazines up to a year before his death in 1922. It was made by his brother Robert in collaboration with the publisher Gallimard, and it contains a good many things of interest to the Proustian reader. For example, an anecdote about the Prince Edmond de Polignac reveals that this personage "sat" for a moment to supply at least one touch in the portrait of the writer Bergotte (whose more important models are Anatole France and John Ruskin) in *Remembrance*. In *The Captive*, the ailing Bergotte in his last years always feels chilly, wears his plaids and travelling clothes, and apologetically quotes to his friends a Greek sage to justify his change of habits: "Anaxagoras has said: Life is a journey!" Well, Polignac is evidently the personage from real life about whom this story was told. In fact, a good many of the incidents in *Remembrance* have sources traceable in contemporary history, sometimes in the journalistic writings of Proust himself, and this is the reason undoubtedly that he referred to the form of his greatest work as a cross between fiction and the memoir.

Among the most interesting of the selections are those modified excerpts from *Swann's Way* which Proust chose to publish in the newspaper *Figaro* from 1912 to March 1913, just before the first installment of *Remembrance* went into print. (92–122) The striking thing about all these selections is their distinction of style, and if one were to do a pastiche of Proust himself one would have to capture in particular his habitual use of what I have elsewhere called "the Art-Simile"—that is to say, the simile in which nature is compared to a work of art, rather than vice versa, as is usually the case in romantic art. The Art-Simile seems to me the most important Proustian innovation in imagery, and the number and quality of such images in these selections indicate that the author himself was conscious of how characteristic they were of his vision of the world, which elevated art to a pinnacle of importance in a hierarchy of values previously occupied for Rousseau and the Romantic poets by nature unretouched.

A ray of sunlight on the balcony breaking through the clouds on a day which had started out to be gloomy is strikingly compared to the crescendo in an orchestral overture in which a single note is artfully led through all sorts of intermediary stages until it reaches the utmost degree of sound in a fortissimo. (103) Street noises become for the writer's ear: "a thousand popular themes finely written for different instruments . . . orchestrating lightly the morning air." (106) A childhood reminiscence that he has evoked becomes "something fantastic, melancholy and caressing, like a phrase of Schumann." (105)

. Proust's feeling for just comparisons which form the bases of similes and metaphors gives substance to Aristotle's observation in *The Poetics* that the quality of metaphor constitutes the hallmark of poetic genius, and it is interesting to note that in a discriminating essay on Flaubert's style reprinted in this book in which Proust praises Flaubert's originality in the way he employs certain tenses (past definite, past indefinite, present participle) as well as his use of certain pronouns and prepositions, he also takes occasion to criticize the flat commonplaceness of that prose master's metaphors. (193 ff) It is clear, on the other hand, that the originality and freshness and unexpectedness of Proust's own metaphors are among the chief beauties of his poetic style.

The essay on Flaubert is one of Proust's attempts to confirm his thesis that "we no longer know how to read." (206) Lack of careful discrimination and failure of sensibility alone could account, so far as he is concerned, for recent harsh criticisms that had been leveled at Flaubert (without doing justice to his genuine originality) and flattering notices directed once more towards the criticism of Sainte-Beuve. In 1920, as more than a decade earlier, the difference between a Sainte-Beuve and a Flaubert appeared to him to be the difference between very good paste and slightly-flawed pearl. He protests vehemently against the injustices and perversities in which the world, under the dictates of fashion and in its restless, frantic search for novelties, indulges itself in the course of time. He detects, for example, a tendency among musicians and the public in the wake of the First World War to depreciate the compositions of Wagner, just as certain avant-garde Wagnerians a generation earlier had depreciated the music of Chopin. (218) The reaction against Wagner appeared to him to be connected with an absurd cultural nationalism aimed against all things German. He tells us of a recent so-called History of Philosophy which somehow managed to exclude the names of Leibniz, Kant, and Hegel! (218–219) To the excessively refined aesthetes and intellectuals, whose thirst for novelty and the bizarre accounts for many of the idiocies in contemporary judgments, he makes the plea (rather unusual for an avant-garde writer!) that "we must read the masters with more simplicity." (209)

Yet even in the act of admiring and imitating them, he cannot help noting the fact that "all the 'sages' of our time have been

more or less mad—from Auguste Comte to Nietzsche." (147)
Even the lucid Tolstoy was "singular" and Proust tells us that he
has heard that his great master Ruskin in his last years appears to
have suffered from a mental illness. From these observations,
however, he does not draw Irving Babbitt's conclusion that there
is something radically unsound about the romanticism of the
nineteenth century and that we had better begin searching for
wisdom in a new, a more traditional direction. However much
Proust loved the classics, he was conscious of the importance of
being sensitive to the literary situation of one's own time. To
write as well as Voltaire he tells us (since this had become a common critical compliment of late) would involve writing not at all
like Voltaire now but very differently from him. Only tone-
deaf academicians could think otherwise; empty formalism repels
him.

He makes one remark which seems to suggest an adequate
criterion by which his own accomplishment will ultimately be
measured as well as the accomplishments of other significant
writers ("more or less mad") of the time in which he lived.
"Posterity," he says, "cares about quality of work; it does not
judge quantity." If Proust's work contained no more quality than
that of some of his prolific contemporaries, then indeed quantity
even much greater than the 4,000 pages of *Remembrance* should
not be sufficient to protect his name against oblivion.

One thing above all seems to me to promise well for the permanence of Proust at his best: It is the clarity and radiance
of his work, the absence in it of those difficulties, obscurities, and
(let us admit it) outright impossibilities which too often dis-
figure the work of even the more gifted among his contemporaries. This being so, I find it interesting that one of the best
articles in this book should be entitled *Contre l'Obscurité* written
when Proust was no more than twenty-five years old and directed
against the affectation and lack of clarity which he found in some
of the "ideas and images" fashionable among the young Symbolists of his day. Taking a conservative point of view, which he
himself recognizes is unusual at his age and therefore "all the
more meritorious in the mouth of a young man," he cautions his
contemporaries that "talent is in effect more than originality of
temperament. . . . It is the power of reducing an original temperament to the general laws of art, to the permanent genius of the

language." (138) It is because he never forgets this, never pretends to be more profound than he is, that Proust's work seems to some of us more than the merely "mammoth" production which is, even according to its harsher critics, one of the wonders of modern world literature.

10. Jean Santeuil

after his death. Some of the material of this earlier work was
transformed, some retouched, and much incorporated in altered
shapes in his later work. Though artistically imperfect and unfinished, it seems to me a fascinating work both in its own right
and because of its connection with *Remembrance of Things Past.*
We should consider, to begin with, the size of the work, its sheer
bulk. In the French original, it is very nearly a thousand pages
long, and even in the English translation it numbers over 740
large pages of closely serried type. In other words, this composition, which was apparently completed in the years between 1896
and 1900, is somewhat less than one fourth the length of its
famous successor.

In undertaking a work of such scope as *Jean Santeuil* Proust
was being very ambitious indeed. He was twenty-five years old
at the time and his previous work had consisted of the relatively
limited sketches, stories and poems of *Les plaisirs et les jours.*
Now suddenly he attempted to make the leap to a work of
enormous length which should be (to use the title of the final
chapter which he wrote for it) "the history of a generation."

It was not an altogether successful attempt, of course, as Proust
himself must have known, since he did not publish the book.
Jean Santeuil has style, beautiful pages of verbal texture, interesting thoughts, situations, and characters; what it lacks is the
conviction of a truly organic form that should hold its scattered
though individually admirable qualities together. What it lacks,
in a word, is the sense of construction which was to distinguish
Proust's mature work.

It is not that he did not attempt to give it form of a kind. The
form he chose was the time-honored one in romance of ex-
plaining in the first person singular how he had come into posses-

196

sion of a certain manuscript which formed the substance of the work. It is a convention worn threadbare with use, yet it might serve as a satisfactory framework for holding a narrative together, as Hawthorne sufficiently proves in *The Scarlet Letter*.

As for the material of the main body of the book itself, it is a story of its hero's development from childhood to manhood, a type of narrative that hesitates between an account of the education, formal and informal, of a young man and a chronicle of the principal public events of his time—the Panama Scandal and the Dreyfus Case. The plan is simple but it could have been effective. The fundamental idea of *Remembrance*, too, is the essence of simplicity, and still it manages to be very effective. There is no failure of intelligent planning (or perhaps it might better be called intellectual patterning) in *Jean Santeuil*. The feelings are present on the individual page, in the individual episode, the individual character, but they absent themselves from the "plot" when it is considered as a whole. The end result is a collection of striking and talented but unbound fragments; the single sticks are there and they are carved prettily enough but the hoop to hold them together collectively is lacking and so the strength of the episodes is lessened and they do not, as in a unified composition, add up to something more than the sum of its parts. The whole here is weaker than its parts which prove to be sensitive and delicate but somewhat short-winded and therefore ephemeral in our memory. It gives the impression of a series of interim reports. The book deals with growth, yet there is no growth in it of the kind familiar to readers of Proust's later work.

The epigraph which Proust affixed to *Jean Santeuil* reads: "Should I call this book a novel? It is something less, perhaps, and yet much more, the very essence of my life, with nothing extraneous added, as it developed through a long period of wretchedness. This book of mine has not been manufactured: it has been garnered." In speaking of the book as less than a novel, the author seems to admit, possibly with the hope of disarming criticism, that it lacks artistic unity. He expresses the thought, however, that whatever he may lose because of this deficiency will be compensated for by the gain he makes in spontaneity and sincerity. Finally, he tells us that his work has not been "manufactured" (the word casts aspersions on artificiality in literature, though it is difficult to dissociate this objectionable quality from legitimate and even necessary artifice). The claim that it has been "garnered" leads us to suspect that many of the parts had been written without a view of their being incorporated into a larger work. In fact, a good deal of the contents of this "novel" are indistinguishable from a miscellaneous collection such as we have in his first published work.

All in all, the theory back of this epigraph is the familiar romantic one that the highest reach of art is to compete with natural phenomena rather than with man-made constructions. *Jean Santeuil* may be compared to a quarry containing precious materials that might later be used for an impressive architectural labor. F. Scott Fitzgerald's first novel *This Side of Paradise* was waggishly nicknamed *The Collected Works of F. Scott Fitzgerald* by some of his Princeton classmates. Even more justifiably *Jean Santeuil* might be called The Collected Works of Marcel Proust Between the Ages of Twenty-five and Twenty-nine.

The narrator of the introductory chapter, while on vacation with a friend, makes the acquaintance of a man they regard as the greatest writer of his generation—"the novelist C." The latter, flattered by the admiration of the young men, reads them a part of the book he is working on, and when they go back to Paris he gives them a copy of it to take along. Some years later, but not before he has sent for them to bid them an affectionate farewell, the novelist dies; when nothing is said in the press about the new book he had been working on, they decide that they are bound to give it to the world themselves.

It is to be noted that the character of the novelist C. is portrayed very critically, in spite of his stature as an artist (the same contrast between character and talent may be observed in *Remembrance* in the case of the writer Bergotte). He is malicious, egocentric, and inconsiderate.

C. is described as "a man of thought" who finds that the company of simple people is far more favorable to intellectual activity than fashionable society. He tells his young admirers that he should have enjoyed a pleasant existence teaching philosophy in "some small provincial town." C. enjoys playing cards and drinking beer with his unintellectual neighbors and he does not miss Paris at all. Cities, he thinks, are good for those in need of intellectual stimulation, theaters, etc. But the important thing for the writer is "the world within" and the superficial feelings inseparable from life in a highly sophisticated society merely get in the way of his real work. Such social stimulations produce in him "a mood of sterile excitement."

Another thing to notice about C. is that though he confesses the lack of "the gift of invention and could write only of what he had himself experienced," he is never able to say of any of his acquaintances, "You're in my book." The reason for this is that "he knew well enough that they, as persons or objects, counted for nothing in those moments of vision which had so often come to him in their presence." These "moments of vision," these epiphanies set his work apart from simple realism and the copying of surfaces (the phrase reminds us of the "x-ray vision" which the narrator of *Remembrance* claims for himself).

The story told in the manuscript of the novelist C. begins with a scene that will seem familiar to readers of *Remembrance*. Madame Santeuil says goodnight for the third time to her son Jean while entertaining company—a doctor to whom she explains that till this evening she has never failed to say goodnight to her son after he is in bed. The scene is essentially the same as the one in the introductory section of *Remembrance* with Professor Surlande playing the role here that Charles Swann plays in the later book. Madame Santeuil and M. Santeuil express the wish that their "impressionable" son might grow into a "manly little fellow" and that he should not be spoiled. Their ambition for him is that he should study law or enter the foreign service. They do not approve of the arts (music or poetry) as a possible career for him. All children, says his mother, have a little bit of talent and if too much is made of it they grow up thinking of themselves as misunderstood geniuses.

Augustin, the manservant here playing the role enacted in *Remembrance* by Françoise, refuses to take a message from the boy to his mother. But M. Santeuil, becoming aware of Jean's unhappiness, tells her to go up to his room. The Doctor who is their guest (a somewhat boorish fellow reminiscent of Cottard) makes light of the boy's suffering and says: "Unhappiness at his age is not a very serious matter." The author intervenes to argue with his character and comments that the bent of a personality may be produced precisely by such trivial experiences as this: "The strokes endured in those hours of childhood fell on the very metal of his heart, and the sounds they gave off might well reverberate with a fuller, a more cracked, or a deeper note as age set a harder crust upon his feelings." (3) The mother says in the presence of their servant (thus setting an official seal of recognition if not of approval upon the fact): "Jean doesn't know what is the matter with him. He is suffering from nerves."

The outline of the mother's character is continued at the beginning of the second chapter which also contains a sharply etched satiric portrait of Jean's father as, on the whole, a rather obtuse, self-important man. His wife is described as "much cleverer than he was, endowed with artistic taste, a wider ranging intelligence, tact and a lively sensibility—qualities which he almost completely lacked." (36) Jean's father and grandfather (M. Sandré, the parent of Madame Santeuil) are concerned about the possibility of his becoming a poet and a "scamp." The picture is of a middle-class household with an atmosphere hostile to art taken seriously as a vocation instead of as a pastime. In this chapter for the first time memory is referred to as "that powerful element in nature" and is compared in elemental force to light and electricity. The reference is a forecast of the important role which it is to play for Proust later on.

The admirable texture of the work in spots is indicated by the touching passage which describes Madame Santeuil's feeling for her aging father: "Her sense of pity grew as she thought that the evocation of the past, by reminding him how old he was, must be filling her father's mind with the sense of his great age and haunting him as she herself was haunted. Had it been her own death of which she was thinking she would have felt neither sorrow nor pain, but, though she knew her father to be even braver than herself and less concerned about his life, she thought with pity of this thing within his consciousness as of some pain which, if she could, she would have spared him. For it is the way of life to soften the sense of our own ills that we may better bear them. But imagination leads us to dwell upon the ills of others in all their solitary desolation but does not let us see what makes these ills to them quite insignificant and even sweet. It is on those ills, therefore, that pity makes us spend our tears while our own we do not even see." (40)

A passage such as this makes one vividly aware of Proust's powers of psychological penetration and analysis, which are at times carried to the point of affectation but which never fail to be impressive. On the whole, in this book he wavers between presenting Jean's parents with the clarity of brutal realism and surrounding their images with a romantic and slightly senti-mental haze. We note, too, that from the point of view of nar-rative almost no progress is visible in these chapters. Sketch has followed upon sketch, held together tenuously by the excuse that they relate to Jean, the hero, or to his relatives. These sketches do not seem to the reader to be informed internally with the conviction that they are being conducted purposefully towards the predetermined end. The third chapter introduces us to a boyhood sweetheart of Jean's, Marie Kossichef, a pre-liminary study of Gilberte in *Remembrance*, except that the latter's blonde beauty is replaced in the "little Russian girl" by a mass of black hair and bright mocking eyes and rosy cheeks. The year in which this takes place is identified as the one in which Jean learns Lamartine's *Le lac* and Verlaine's *Il pleure dans mon coeur* . . . At the age of ten, he thinks Verlaine's verses the most beautiful in the world—perhaps because in them he gives expression to feelings which correspond to those of his own "shadowed childhood" over which "sadness reigned in un-disputed sovereignty."

Jean's affection for Marie, like his feeling for his mother, is characterized by nervous agitation and melancholy settles over him when he becomes aware "that her kindness to him had nothing in common with his devotion to her." Changes in the weather and the corresponding chances of her coming out with her governess to play in the Champs-Élysées cause him con-tinual dread and feverish disturbance—so much so that his parents become alarmed about his "constant state of overexcitement." He has never yet been invited to Marie's house, and to make matters worse she catches a bad cold and is forbidden to go out for a long time because of the severity of the winter weather, but just as he despairs of ever seeing her again an invitation from Marie arrives asking him to come to her home for the first time. (54).

In Chapter 4, Jean's parents propose to separate him from Marie. The boy becomes violently angry with his mother and his grandfather; some of the family scenes described in this book are as ugly, as sordid, as naturalistic as the ones described in the domestic life portrayed by Clifford Odets. In this respect there is a vast gulf between *Jean Santeuil* and *Remembrance* where the family life of the narrator's early years is powdered over with a golden haze of nostalgia. There is another ironic portrait of Jean's father in this chapter: "M. Santeuil, who was peaceable enough so long as his comfort was not threatened, was the more inclined to lose his temper when it was. 'Papa, *dear* Papa,' said Jean, falling to his knees, 'they want to hurt me, mama is persecuting me—you must protect me, you *must*.' 'Nonsense! Your mother's perfectly right,' said M. Santeuil, not at all sure what he was going to say next. 'This business of you and that girl is becoming intolerable. I can tell you this, you're not going to see any more of her!'—'Not going to see any more of her?' screamed Jean. 'Brutes! that's what you are, all of you, brutes! No more of her!—We'll soon see about that!' and Jean, as his father gave him a slap and pushed him towards the gloomy study, collapsed in a violent attack of nerves." (58–59)

Chapter 6 brings us to the Lycée Henri IV. Here attention is focussed on the teacher Clodius Xelnor who has "advanced" literary tastes after Jean's own heart. To this teacher Verlaine and Leconte de Lisle are the greatest of modern authors, and their works (particularly those of Leconte de Lisle) "were more alive for him, more profound, more stimulating, than those classical works from which . . . mental unease is absent." The director of this new school agrees that Horace and Ovid are "pretty poor fish." (54)

One might think that such agreement between the tastes of teacher and pupil would be welcome to the latter, but, suddenly adopting the point of view of tradition and classicism which insist upon the salutary effect of working against the grain of a young man's native, untutored, romantic taste, the author writes that Xelnor "could not imagine that for Jean there might be a moral good superior to aesthetic pleasure or that he might attain to it by resisting the allurements of delight and doing his duty." There is in Proust occasionally something of a Puritanical attitude implanted in him by his parents, so that he is at the same time the sinner and the stern judge over the sinner. There is little in him of the rationalizer and defense counsel of transgressors that we find in André Gide, for example.

The poet Rustinlor who is the director of the Lycée resembles the obnoxious Bloch in *Remembrance*. And one of the episodes in this chapter is a schoolmate's invitation to Jean to go on a "woman-hunt" which brings him for the first time into a brothel. Bloch plays a similar role in the life of the narrator Marcel.

Part II of *Jean Santeuil* introduces us to a place called Étreuilles which is readily recognizable as the Combray of *Remembrance*. Étreuilles is the place of holidays, of innocent country pleasures. It is a pastoral idyll. In contrast to the social life and the life of love previously presented, what is represented here is a picture of almost entirely unalloyed joy. The pleasures are not violent as are those which might result from the more active affections, but they are lasting and satisfactory. Here we have descriptions of flowers, fruit trees, bees, butterflies, which rival the charm of some of the most bucolic pages in Rousseau. Even the common flies, in this aesthetic vision, contribute in making "the chamber-music of summer."

Étreuilles, like Combray, is dominated, both architecturally and spiritually by its Church, to which every eye is drawn at once and where all the festivals and pageants of the season in the little town unfold. Going to Church on Sundays is one of the memorable experiences of Jean at Étreuilles, but not so much for the religious feeling it inspires in him as because of the tranquil social atmosphere he finds there, especially after the services are over: ". . . belated greetings . . . stored-up conversations . . . adjourned good fellowship. . . ." Sunday church-going is one more item in the comfortable life of Étreuilles.

There are the pleasures of the table, too, as at Combray, and the shocking but unavoidable cruelty when the cook kills the duck which is to be so deliciously served up for lunch. There are studies in still life which remind us of Proust's lifelong admiration for the Dutch painters of domestic interiors. And, of course, there are the joys of reading in the country. Jean is at the age when Gautier's *Le Capitaine Fracasse* means everything and *Faust* or *Hamlet* nothing. The author comments that though we miss many things in our youthful enthusiasms, we respond to others far more wholeheartedly than we shall respond to anything later in life. Gautier's romance is presumably one of those things which elicit such a youthful response.

The section devoted to Étreuilles is remarkable as a paean to the loveliness and freshness of nature, but Proust's descriptions, it should be noted, are not merely designed to be ends-in-themselves. They verge on that quality of aesthetic mysticism which was to distinguish his work later on. He is already aware that "beneath the varnished green of the leaf and the satin whiteness of the flower, some especial being lives." "Our pleasure is in something deeper, all a-quiver there within, something we desire to seize and which holds an exquisite sweetness." "Each blossom and each leaf comes responsive to some longing in ourselves. Moment by moment we think with happiness—'Yes, this is it!' What smiles upon us from out these clouds of whiteness treading on one another's heels, spaced by their clusters of pink buds, is something utterly different, a life unlike what we sometimes think of as life, the thought of losing which, though we may find it needlessly intrusive, brings sadness. But then, contrariwise, our happiness is such that we have no fear of losing it, no apprehension that the fullness of its gift can be taken from us. For what in our pleasure is so ravishing is something that we feel deep down, something more than the mere passing moment for the sensation of an earlier time, when we saw just such apple-trees in bloom, is there within us." (85)

The meaning here is still somewhat murky as compared with the lucidity of meaning in the madeleine-and-tea episode of *Swann's Way* or the similar episodes in *The Past Recaptured*, but the feeling of the later passages in *Remembrance* is foreshadowed by that which is still struggling for complete and satisfactory expression in such a passage as this.

The hero of Part III is the philosophy teacher, M. Beulier, who is contrasted favorably with the modernist aesthete, Clodius Xelnor, in the first section of the book. Xelnor was affected, falsely brilliant, meretricious; Beulier is unaffected and genuinely wise. Jean, now seventeen years old, comes into the philosophy class with the comic expectation of being recognized at once as a genius. His first contacts with M. Beulier, who has been preceded by his reputation for extraordinary acumen, rudely disabuse him with regard to these illusory expectations. Jean is detained after class on the very first day for not paying proper attention to the teacher. And to make matters worse, his initial composition is mercilessly ridiculed, dissected, and criticized for something the young man who, like other young men, plumes himself upon his originality, could never have expected—namely, its banality and journalistic commonplaceness of expression. M. Beulier addresses Jean with the privileged irony of the gifted pedant. He finds in his composition "all those current clichés, those literary bad manners, which you have picked up from newspapers and magazines. It would be foolish to expect you at your age to have settled standards of taste. . . . You must learn to prune your style with infinite care of all those metaphors, of all those images, which if they were a good deal better, might appeal to a poet, but even so would be intolerable in a philosophical argument. But it is a mistake—even when the Professor of Literature is to be your audience—to raise your voice in order to utter banalities—*the scarlet flames of the setting sun,* indeed—how dare you write down such stuff! It's the kind of thing you might find in a small provincial newspaper—no, not even provincial, it would be truer to say, Colonial. Just conceivably, the editor of the *Mozambique Chronicle* might decorate one of his articles with such odds and ends of coloured glass and it is equally conceivable that the local ladies might hail him as a new Chateaubriand." (162–163)

It says much for the humility of Jean that he bears no grudge for this sudden deflation of his vain pretensions, though he cannot help regarding the man responsible for his discomfiture "with a timid and melancholy distrust." But this feeling is soon overcome when he realizes that M. Beulier has no malice whatever in him and that the reaction to his work is completely disinterested. Every young man needs his own living approximation to Socrates to bear witness to the fact that Plato's is not merely a brilliant imaginative invention. M. Beulier is the version of Socrates within the orbit of Jean's experience. He thinks it an accidental whim of fate to have granted greater renown to other members of the same generation such as Renan and Taine.

M. Beulier is more moderate and balanced in his literary tastes than was the foppish Xelnor. He appreciates romantic writers like Michelet, yet he doesn't think the classics a bore as M. Rustinlor did. He follows a reading of Michelet with a chapter from Xenophon, teaching Jean to savor the charm of its simplicity: "Antiquity is not the nineteenth century. But this stuff of Xenophon's is, in its way, just as good. No one will ever write like that again. It is all so simple yet everything is said." (230)

His New Year's gift to Jean is a volume of Joubert which he reads to him, again with the same object of chastening and purifying a youthful taste that is too impressed with romantic excess and gaudiness. Of real intellectual greatness in M. Beulier, Proust presents no evidence, but he does catch a certain charm, style, grace, good taste, and liveliness of expression. There is nothing corresponding to this portrait of a teacher in *Remembrance*, and it is certainly the poorer for it.

Some other things in this part of the book deserve notice. The portrait of Jean's friend Bertrand de Réveillon is one which is later to be developed into that of the Marquis de Saint-Loup. Like Saint-Loup, "what (Réveillon) truly desired was to be forgiven for being an aristocrat." But his intellectuality and democratic ideas do not succeed in eradicating the marks of his innate aristocracy, which for the author is apparently epitomized in a certain grace of bodily movement. The example he gives in *Jean Santeuil* is the same as that in *Remembrance;* it is the time when Bertrand, wishing to reach his friend quickly in a crowded restaurant, lightly steps on a number of the tables that separate them. Only complete unselfconsciousness and a body trained to be a perfectly pliant instrument of its possessor could have managed the quickness and daring necessary for such a feat. Proust seems to regard this as one of those "moments of vision" which reveal brilliantly but briefly the innermost essence of a personality.

In this section, too, the "leitmotif" (if we want to use a term that is more appropriate to the planned composition of *Remembrance*) of Jean's bitter quarrels with his parents continues to sound. The father particularly is singled out in a posture of extreme brutality. He tells Jean either to work or get out! And Jean, very much enraged, calls his parents mad once more and slams the door so violently behind him that he smashes the glass ornaments on it. Jean is so angry after this scene that he cannot even bring himself to concentrate on the reading which he has taken up to distract himself. Extremes of emotion succeed each other with almost startling rapidity in Jean, and he repents of his vehemence against his parents while they are still nursing their rage against him. The descriptions of the dizzying affective changes in Jean at this point are almost pathological in quality, but they are well calculated to communicate an idea of his character to the reader. The writer's "moments of vision" extend remorselessly even to his hero.

From a compositional point of view, one of the wildest and most unaccountable leaps in the section occurs (the possibility exists, of course, that this impression is created by the editing or the unfinished state of the manuscript) between Chapters 7 and 8 (pp. 218–219) when from the quarrel with his parents, we are thrust suddenly into an account of the public life of France. We meet, with no previous preparation, a parliamentary hero of Jean's, the socialist orator Couzon (who seems to resemble Jaurès). We learn with some astonishment that Jean is a sympathizer of Couzon's and very much concerned with the problem of social justice.

Part IV is another pastoral episode mainly, not at Étreuilles this time as in Part II but at the country estate of his aristocratic friends, the Réveillons. Pastoral idylls seem to alternate with social scenes in *Jean Santeuil*. But even the idyllic chapters at Étreuilles, Réveillon, or later by the sea at Begmeil in Brittany are enlivened by social situations. In his stay at Réveillon, for example, Jean meets the writer M. de Traves, a great magician of the pen, "a brilliant novelist," who resembles Proust's own first distinguished literary friend and mentor, Anatole France.

M. de Traves helps to widen Jean's mental horizon which, after his experiences in school, was completely dominated by the philosophical idealism of his teacher Beulier—so much so that he completely rejected sceptical and materialistic philosophies that he had previously studied. Now he finds that M. de Traves, whose literary work he admires so greatly, is interested in sceptics and materialists only. In addition, he finds in him an admirer of the eighteenth century literature, which had hitherto seemed to him "utterly worthless" in comparison with the romantic nineteenth century. M. de Traves in his own way counteracts the boy's prejudices and provincialism almost as effectively as

M. Beulier had done. M. de Traves also had an influence upon Jean by introducing him to the fascination of etymological investigations and the delights of antiquarianism. Jean learns from him the variety of uses to which the human intelligence may be put and also how completely different and outrightly opposed to each other may be the interests of two men, equally intelligent.

Among those he meets at Réveillon is Rustinlor, the director of the Lycée Henri Quatre. The latter announces surprisingly that he is through with poetry. His current passions are three in number: "politics, immorality, and cycling." It is Rustinlor who first brings up the subject of the Dreyfus Case when he says to Jean in his characteristically affected manner: "As to the historians and the dramatists, that fellow Tacitus, that chap called Shakespeare, or Messire Balzac, they never printed anything half so thrilling as what is happening at this moment. Go to the Palais de Justice, my dear man, go to the Chamber, take a look at Esterhazy, make a study of all that business, Lanevois, Picquart. If human nature's what you're after, take my word for it, you'll find it there, in the raw, passion in all its manifestations, and so on and so on." (252)

This depreciation of art in favor of life "in the raw" provokes Jean to formulate in his own mind the theory that "the value of a book is never in the material presented by the writer, but in the nature of the operation he performs upon it." (252) He also sounds, in passing, the theme which is to be central in *Contre Sainte-Beuve*, namely that lack of connection between the superficial social self of an artist and the qualities which give his art its real value. The reason for biographical criticism's failure to penetrate the problems of art very deeply is that art is a craft or a discipline having only a peripheral connection with the life of its creator. Its distinction is the result of some mysterious instinct or inspiration on the part of the artist, the source of which is as incomprehensible to himself as it is to his audience. In other words, as in Plato's dialogue *Ion*, it turns out that the artist is a man who doesn't really know what he's doing. He has the power to affect his hearers, but it is hopeless to try to learn from him how he does it. It is not by the assertion of his intelligence but by yielding to his mysterious aesthetic instinct that the artist moves us deeply.

Another thing deserving notice in this part of the book is the conviction that nature, however beautiful, does not interest the artist as an end-in-itself but because it offers him hints and clues with which to reclaim "the remembered beauty of the past and the primal substance of our lives." Without this dimension produced by its effect on memory "nature would be a poor sort of thing . . . a sequence of fine pictures." "If we look upon her with detachment she gives us nothing." But if we attempt to decipher the meaning of "a dismal autumn day when the sun sets unseen, a road drying after rain, or the coming of the earliest winter chills" the experience may be very valuable indeed. We shall hear more about the effect of sensory perceptions upon the involuntary memory as Proust grows older, but the essential outline of this point of view is present here.

The fifth section of *Jean Santeuil* which takes us to the middle of the book deals with two celebrated French parliamentary cases or struggles. One, the story of a politician, is a commentary on the Panama Scandal and the other is a more direct treatment of the Dreyfus Case. This section is in some ways the most interesting and original in the book. While other sections have scenes or characters which are evidently early versions of what was going eventually to become part of *Remembrance,* the interest of this portion of *Jean Santeuil* stems precisely from its differences when compared with the later work. The Panama Scandal is not treated in *Remembrance* at all, and the later use made of the Dreyfus Case is radically different from its treatment here.

The first question that suggests itself is concerning the choice of these two particular cases. They are outstanding public events witnessed by Proust in his lifetime to be sure, but there were other public events of the same or greater magnitude which might have been chosen, e.g. the rise and decline of the Boulangist Movement. The first reason for the presence of the Panama Scandal and the Dreyfus Case is doubtless that Proust aspired to the role of social historian, but even more important may be the fact that there is such a neat antithesis and balance between the two cases. In one, the accused was guilty; in the other he was innocent. This presented an opportunity for the writer to analyze the psychology of guilt and that of innocence.

The protagonist of the first part of this section is the corrupt government minister, Charles Marie, a colleague and friend of Jean's father. Jean's father, by the way, is presented very sympathetically here. When he is no longer involved in brutal quarrels with his nervous son, he appears to be an honorable, upright man with an extraordinary fidelity to his friends. He refuses to turn his back upon Charles Marie even when it becomes plain that the latter has betrayed his trust and that those who stick to him stubbornly are bound to be hurt by the blows legitimately aimed against him.

Marie is a man who, beneath the respectable exterior of his life, is engaged in some shady financial deals. For a long time, he is compelled to turn one face to the world and a different face to himself. Here is one of the fascinations which this case had for Proust, for just such a dilemma faces the homosexual in society. Proust here undertakes to do for Marie something of what Hawthorne has done for his character Arthur Dimmesdale in *The Scarlet Letter*. One of the most striking features of his portrayal of Marie is his analysis of the effect which religion has upon the unhappy man. Proust in his maturity was to be so little concerned with religion directly that François Mauriac once complained that God is *terribly absent* from his work.

Proust shows that the effect of religion and its rituals is not to disturb Marie's conscience but to pacify it. The analysis of Marie's religious consciousness has also for me some of the quality of Flaubert's description of the "conversion" of Emma Bovary which is sandwiched in between her affairs with Rodolphe and Léon.

"Alone with himself," writes Proust with both wit and insight, "and face to face with his conscience he no longer said, 'I have stolen twenty-five thousand francs,' words which he would have found it extremely disagreeable to hear, since they would have damaged him in his own eyes—but 'Oh God, I am a miserable sinner,' a statement which was productive of a rather pleasurable emotion." (297) He makes us aware of the cruelty of this self-deception and yet of its inescapable necessity for those to whom the truth is too terrible to face, as it is for Marie after his exposure and public ignominy. Thanks to self-deception, he is able to struggle through the last years of his life, serenely buoyed up by his illusory hopes of a political comeback.

The crucial difference between the way the Dreyfus Case is

presented in the pages of *Jean Santeuil* and in *Remembrance* is that in the former certain aspects of it enter directly into the story while in the later work they enter indirectly. In *Remembrance*, the Dreyfus Case is a touchstone which reveals the motivations of many of the characters; in discussing Dreyfus they unconsciously lay bare themselves. But in this book, some of the highlights of the case unfold before us directly—for example, the appearance in court of the army general Boisdeffre and the testimony of Colonel Picquart.

Both the episode revolving about the corrupt minister, Charles Marie, and the one centering on Dreyfus affect the hero's attitudes profoundly, and the effects in both cases are curiously similar. Both help to alienate Jean from politics and make him feel how difficult and discouraging it is to seek justice in the political arena. The result of M. Santeuil's decision to stand by his friend Marie is that he is viciously attacked in the socialist press. Jean, the socialist sympathizer and admirer of the orator Couzon, approaches his friend who is in a position to know the innocence of M. Santeuil in order to get him to stop these attacks. But Couzon explains how impossible it is to heed his request; political reasons for Couzon must take precedence over personal relationships. The good of his party is far more important to him than the harm which it may inflict upon an innocent individual. Jean is led to formulate an attack upon the use of evil means to accomplish a supposedly good end.

The Socialists who attack Marie's associates though they know that these men are guiltless of his wrongdoing are no different from the Nationalists who insist that the Army's verdict against Dreyfus must be upheld for reasons of state even if an innocent individual and his entire family are thereby condemned to undeserved suffering.

He becomes aware of how all-pervasive in society is the absurd superficiality which shows itself equally in "the 'slogans' of the schools, the violent dogmatisms or preferences of the literary 'sets,' political prejudices and cries of 'Long live so-and-so,' 'Down with t'other' and votes given in a somewhat irresponsible fashion. In the Chamber, as in the Academy, one will always be sure of seeing Tom, Dick or Harry who has made a point of coming to register his vote." (330) He arrives at a conclusion which can only be called genuinely humane that the urgent task continually facing us is not social-reform but self-reform. I think, more eloquently: "Votes, regular attendance at meetings or sessions, indispensable calls on possible supporters, canvassing, party cries—all these are so many refuges in which we shelter from the dread necessity of turning our eyes inwards."

Part VI takes us to Begmeil by the sea in Brittany. This corresponds to the town of Balbec in *Remembrance*. Some of the incidents are the same in both places. Jean is cruelly tortured by the breaking of his usual habits, and by the difficulty of going to sleep in strange surroundings. And there is a familiar incident of his talking to his mother on the telephone for the first time when he becomes aware of all that her tenderness and love mean to him. It is only absence and the power of imagination that enhance objects which had hitherto seemed insignificant. Proust's description of the effect of his mother's voice upon Jean (a voice as "pure as a tiny piece of ice, scarcely a voice at all") trembles upon the edge of the sentimental.

This section of the book is again something of a pastoral idyll, like Sections II and IV. Again, as at Étreuilles, there is a church "built in the purest Norman style," which, to add to its aesthetic charm, contains a number of barely known but admirable paintings by the master Moreau. There are the pleasures of reading on the beach—with the names of certain English and American authors (evidently the favorites of Jean at this time) mentioned: Stevenson, George Eliot, and Emerson. There is a description of a storm by the sea. The love of nature, in all its moods, is extraordinarily powerful in this book. "A long sloping ray of sunlight would be enough to set his mind on fire, a stream encountered on his walk to lead his imagination on. He would start to move fast, as we saw him awhile back, would lose his way, and reach home still filled with happiness, carrying more lightly than ever Atlas did, the world upon his shoulders." (398)

There is one remarkable accomplishment in Part VI that deserves to be noted. It is his treatment of the theme of "the past recaptured" which concludes the section (407–410). This could be incorporated into *Remembrance* and even a connoisseur of Proust might be puzzled to detect any difference in texture. The whole theory about the gap that exists between the qualities of voluntary and involuntary memory, the susceptibility of the latter to sensory impressions, and the resulting intrusion of eternity into the stream of time (in other words, the complete statement of his aesthetic mysticism) is present in this work composed by Proust in his twenties. These particular pages I should compare to that *little phrase* from Vinteuil's sonata of which so much is made in *Remembrance* and which seems to contain in miniature the whole force of its composer's genius:

> Could it be that beauty and joy for the poet reside in an invisible substance which may perhaps be called imagination, which cannot work on immediate reality, nor yet on past reality deliberately remembered, but hovers only over past reality caught up and enshrined in the reality now present. . . .
>
> What the poet needs is memory, or not strictly speaking memory at all, but the transmutation of memory into a reality directly felt. A smell meets me as I enter a certain house where to be sure I had not come expecting to find beauty but suddenly it is of beauty that I am conscious. The smell is that of a house where once we had spent some time at the seaside, a deplorable wooden villa. Each time I entered it I caught that special smell. It was a place where I had been sad, where there was nothing to minister to my hunger for the beautiful, but it was precisely that which had wrapped me round in the disguise of a far from pleasant odor. . . .
>
> The whole of that period of my life, with its worries, its hungers, its hours of sleep or sleeplessness, its effort to find joy in art—which ended in failure—its experiments in sensual gratification, so sharply terminated, its attempts to win the love of someone who had taken my fancy, and my subsequent and absurd disenchantment —all were caught up and made present in that smell. . . .
>
> And is it not more beautiful we wonder, that the imagination, which neither the present nor the past could put into communication with life and so save from oblivion and the misinterpretation of thought and unhappy memories, the varied, individual essences of life—trains and hotel rooms, the fragrance of roses, the taste of stewed fruit, washrooms and roads from which we can look at the sea while, as it were, travelling elegantly in a carriage—is it not more beautiful that in the sudden leap which follows on the impact between an identical past and present, the imagination should thus be freed from time? . . .
>
> So often seeking beauty in a mountain or a sky we find it again in the sound of rubber-tired wheels or the smell of a scrap of fabric, in the things which have hung about our lives, which chance has brought to hang there once again, though this time we may be better equipped to feel delight, separating their imagined past from

their present reality, wrenching ourselves free from the slavery of the *now*, letting ourselves be flooded with the feeling of life ever-lasting. . . .

Proust's point seems to be that there is absolutely no difference in provocative power between "animal" and "aesthetic" perceptions. In *Remembrance*, it is, among other things, the smell of a comfort station in the Champs-Élysées, the sound of a dinner bell at the Guermantes's, the rough texture of a table-napkin which awaken the past for him and give the narrator a pleasurable sensation of partaking in the freedom of eternity. The same point is made here in *Jean Santeuil* where the fragrance of roses, the taste of stewed fruit and the odor of washrooms are equally effective in liberating the hero from the present moment and helping him to recapture the past. It is the effect which is always necessarily beautiful, not the cause—which is often ugly and sometimes actually disgusting. Proust is an aesthete, but he is an aesthete with a strong stomach. Just as Aristotle in his *Poetics* notes that aesthetic delight may be produced *not* by the nature of the object which is represented by the artist (which in itself may be ugly and painful to behold, like the quartered carcass of an animal) but by the skill shown by the artist in the act of representation, so Proust holds that the nature of the sensory stimulus which resurrects the past and furnishes material for the artist is in itself indifferent; what is breathtakingly magnificent is the aesthetic vision which the perception liberates.

Part VII breaks the rule which had held up to this point that only every other chapter should be pastoral and idyllic; this one begins with a description of a second stay in the country at the Réveillon estate. The first visit in Part IV had taken place during the spring; this second visit takes place in the autumn. Walks through the October countryside are described, and indoor activities, parlor games and card-games, the pleasure of sitting beside the good fire while the wind moans outside.

At the end of the first chapter of this part (419–420) a curious episode takes place. When Jean goes to bed during the cold, windy autumn night, a young woman who is a guest at the Réveillons and has come to an understanding with him, slips into his room for the night. The encounter is so casual (the lady's name is never even mentioned) and the sexual play is described so directly, so frankly, and so "innocently" that critics of Proust's "erotic naturism" like the Baron Ernest de Seillière and Paul Elmer More should have judged *Jean Santeuil*, had it been available for their inspection when they wrote their criticisms of Proust, the most flagrant confirmation of their theory that for Proust love and sex are completely disengaged from moral or religious considerations. Sex is just one of the pleasant games to be indulged in as a distraction on dreary autumn nights.

Part VIII returns us to the social world—the world of dinner parties, salons, theaters, sch ols, duels. At the beginning of this part, we see Jean invited as a "fourteenth" to a dinner party given by the wealthy middle-class hostess Madame Marmet with whose son Julien he has struck up a friendship. Since Jean is as yet without "name or fame" his rather vulgar hostess (who reminds us a little of Madame Verdurin in *Remembrance*) makes slighting remarks to him at the table to indicate to her other guests that he is there only by force of exceptional circumstances.

It is at this dinner that he meets, after a long lapse of time, his boyhood sweetheart, Marie Kossichef. Breaking with her earlier had caused him unbearable anguish, but now that the break is complete he feels bored by her company and gets away as soon as he decently can. The irony implicit in this scene (495–497) is the kind of effect that is comparatively rare in *Jean Santeuil* and very frequent in the pages of *Remembrance* because of the better planning of the later book. Observing the change in himself, Jean reflects: "Why should we feel so terribly despairing because we have not got what we most desired? For as Time's wheel perpetually revolves, sooner or later those things will come to us. Circumstances change and what we once wanted we always get in the long run, but only when we no longer want them."

We observe that Jean is still in a mood of youthful rebellion against his parents, hatred and tenderness toward them (if he becomes aware that he has hurt them) alternating with frightful rapidity; the elements of emotional instability in him account for the feeling he expresses at one point that he may be "predestined to madness." His father has gone for advice concerning his son's professional future to an academician who has given him the astute advice that "if he has got a feeling for literature, then let him read law." So Jean finds himself in a school of political science where he is intensely unhappy and frustrated and a failure. But he does get a sharply satiric character-sketch out of the experience; it is of Ralph Savaie, a teacher of philosophy at the school who has written monographs with titles such as *The Sense of the Infinite on the Banks of Lake Tchad* and *The Impulse Towards The Better in the Balkan Peninsula.* (The sketch is incorporated into the conversation of Norpois in *Within a Budding Grove.*)

There are scenes in this part (506–508) in which the impulse of snobbery lands characters in situations so ridiculous that they recall the Dickensian quality of some of the humor in *Remembrance.* Particularly daring in the broadness and exaggeration of its caricature is Chapter 8 (536–541) which narrates the discomfiture of Madame Marmet when she had foolishly undertaken to snub Jean and had only succeeded in arousing the ire of his aristocratic friends who see to it that at an important "first night" at the theater Madame Marmet is left virtually alone in her box while young Santeuil is introduced to the King of Portugal and engages in an animated conversation during the intermission with him which becomes the cynosure of attention for everybody in the audience.

In desultory fashion a number of other characters are introduced. One evening, after a dinner party, Jean finds himself in a game of cards with a Monsieur Saylor, who, after losing steadily for some time, suddenly jumps up from his chair and accuses him before the assembled company of cheating. A duel is arranged; they meet on the field of honor the next morning and Saylor is slightly wounded. In the ensuing days, Jean finds that the story of his supposed cheating has spread and that wherever he goes in society, people glance at him accusingly. Though he has had satisfaction from the man who had insulted him, the insult itself apparently is still spreading its poison abroad. He is supported in this situation by the generosity of the Duchesse de Réveillon who stands by him in much the same way that the Queen of Naples supports Charlus after he has been wantonly hurt in the Verdurin drawing room (see *The Captive*).

Part IX begins with a discussion on love which brings in an incident from an affair of Jean's that is identical with one of the most vivid moments in the affair of Swann and Odette. One evening, Jean returns to the house of the woman he is in love with to see if she is entertaining another man in his absence. As soon as he reaches her street, he is shocked to see that her lights, which had been turned off when he had left her earlier, have been turned on again. As in *Swann's Way*, it turns out to be a case of mistaken identity; the house with the lights on is not that of Madame S. but the one next door. This absurdly melodramatic incident has the tang of experience unmistakably real upon it and Proust incorporates it into the story of "Swann In Love."

Many of the incidents of the Swann story are repeated in this chapter of *Jean Santeuil*. The difference in the effect which they produce must be attributed to the orderliness, composition, smoothness, narrative pace, accurate rendition of the rhythm of feeling in the later work. The same notes may be combined to form a melody forgotten as soon as it is heard and another melody that is immortal.

In this part, too, we have an idea about nature which seems very close in feeling to that of Wordsworth in his great *Ode on Intimations of Immortality*—namely, that the fundamental reason for the pleasure which we take in nature after we have reached maturity is that these impressions carry us back to our childhood when our relation to nature was much more instinctive and untroubled than it is ever afterwards to be: "He felt sad in the knowledge that things which touched us once touch us no longer . . . Of the things which charmed us once, things that we happen on again, is it not true to say that by their very presence they bring back to us, with the same, or perhaps with a still more, dream-like and quivering delight, the mysterious magic of an earlier day? . . . What are all these things if not witnesses of childhood's Springtime, fragments from the memories of our earliest emotions which Nature woke in us, which have lost nothing of their power, which suddenly open our hearts to the coming of the same delicious bliss, letting us escape from the tyranny of the years and give ourselves wholly to Nature's magic, to the mysterious transformation of the seasons which bathe the things and incidents around us in a life that is greater than them, which we recognize from having once already seen them in the long distance of past years, which is no more part of our childhood than it is of our old age, but seems, for a moment, to show us the world in which we live, not as a mediocre thing that soon for us will end, a place of human and familiar life, but a world eternal in itself, and young eternally, a place of mystery rich with incredible promises?" (607–609)

Though the end of *Jean Santeuil* is approaching in this part, that does not prevent the author from introducing new characters to us (in marked contrast to *Remembrance* where at least all the outstanding personages are introduced to us in the comparatively brief introductory section of *Swann's Way*). He is like a composer who, not having any power to develop a few themes, keeps bringing in new melodies to distract our attention. One of the new characters is the painter Bergotte and another is the society hostess, Madame Cresmeyer. The description of the Cresmeyer dinner party (Chapter 7, 630 ff) is enlivened by a number of humorous strokes. The hostess refuses to open a message delivered to her on the eve of her party because she fears that it may contain the news of the death of a sick relative, which would interfere with her social plans (the transposition of this incident in *Guermantes Way* is obvious). And Madame Cresmeyer cannot help wishing for a moment when her famous guest Bergotte complains that he is not feeling well that he might drop dead in her drawing room which might then become a sort of historical shrine! Sharply satiric and amusing also is the depiction of the rat-race in which fashionable hostesses compete with each other in their desire for newspaper space to publicize their parties, which should be considered failures if the world knew nothing of them.

Interesting, too, in the ninth part is the introduction of "the little phrase" from a sonata (659 ff) which is clearly identified as that of Saint-Saens (in *Remembrance*, the "little phrase" is from a sonata by the fictitious Vinteuil and has in it ingredients from Wagner, Schubert, Franck, Fauré, as well as Saint-Saens—all brewed into an inimitable literary mixture by Proust). The music is intimately associated in his memory with the love of a woman who once played it for him. Years after this love affair is over, the melody (accidentally overheard one day being played on a piano as Jean is passing through the Faubourg Saint-Germain) floods his consciousness with fresh feeling, lifts from his shoulders the weight of age, and brings back "in a flash" a whole forgotten period of his life. The sense impressions created in us by works of art, like those originating in nature, are evidently potent talismans to enable memory to recapture the past.

The tenth and last part of *Jean Santeuil* continues to introduce new characters to us and to narrate digressive episodes. Charlotte Clisette is a new love of Jean's and some of the episodes with her (the game of "Hunt the Ring" which they play together and her threat to sound the bell for help should he dare to try to kiss her) foreshadow episodes from the narrator's relationship with Albertine in *Remembrance*. It has been said by one of Proust's biographers, Richard Barker, that some of the scenes involving women in this book can be understood adequately only on the hypothesis that they are transpositions of originally homosexual experiences. This is certainly true of Chapter 4 in the tenth part (pp. 691 ff) entitled *The Dutch Nun* which tells the story of a dissolute girl who becomes a member of a religious order without being able to shake off her vice as long as she lives. For various reasons the whole episode seems to make much more sense to me if the girl is transformed by the imagination of the reader into a male novice.

The chapter precedes another (696 ff) which tells of the blackmail and suicide of a homosexual, the Vicomte de Lamperolles. Proust is gingerly skirting the edges of the territory of anomalous love which he was eventually to make his own in *Contre Sainte-Beuve* and the latter half of *Remembrance*.

In the closing chapters of the book, it is worth noting that Jean becomes reconciled with his parents (this reconciliation is intended to be the logical consummation of the phase of his experience narrated in the book), and that his parents age horribly and suddenly and unexpectedly. Some of the critics of *Remembrance* have felt that it is a weakness of that book to show its characters becoming old in the last volume with unnatural and terrifying speed. The incongruous effect of this has been attributed to Proust's failure to finish *Remembrance* completely before his death. But there is no reason to think, after reading

Jean Santeuil which shares the quality of having its principal characters fall into old age as if through a trap door, that he should have been able to depict people aging more slowly or gracefully. Proust's vision on this matter is evidently best communicated by startling and melodramatic contrasts—as if one were not aware of growing older or of others growing older until one day (due to some special circumstance of heightened attention) one is suddenly struck by the gruesome changes that are evident.

As for *Jean Santeuil* considered as a whole, its weaknesses of construction have been sufficiently dwelt on in the introduction to this chapter and in some of the remarks I have had to make as I went along. But I am not so sure that its redeeming virtue has been made clear. This virtue can be summed up in the words: *style, texture.* Proust himself speaks in this book (395) of novels which, once they are finished, have no further pleasure in store for us if we return to them. Such are the books which depend for their principal attraction on the elements of surprise and suspense. Once we know how their plots have been resolved they have nothing more to offer. They deposit neither memorable characters nor thoughts in our minds which we shall ever want to refer to again. They are like puzzles which lose all their interest from the moment when they have been solved.

But if Proust's work (even *Jean Santeuil,* imperfect and unsatisfactory and unintegrated as it may be) retains a perennial charm for us it is not because of its story or people or ideas but because of its lyricism and poetry. Auden once wrote: "Poetry makes nothing happen"—an observation that is especially applicable to this book by Proust which contains such large tracts of stationary idylls. No one is capable of refreshing our vision of the beauties of nature more effectively than Proust in parts of *Jean Santeuil* and in the whole Combray section of *Swann's Way* —not even the Romantic poets or Rousseau.

11. Contre Sainte-Beuve

THIS IS THE SECOND POSTHUMOUS WORK BY PROUST THAT HAS BEEN TURNED UP BY THE SCHOLARLY LABORS OF BERNARD DE FALLOIS. *Contre Sainte-Beuve* was composed at the end of 1908, almost a decade after *Jean Santeuil* had been laid aside, and it is its author's second great rehearsal for the tremendous work that was to go into the composition of *Remembrance of Things Past*. It is closer in every respect to the latter performance than *Jean Santeuil* was. *Jean Santeuil*, as we have seen, suggests, in many of its themes and characters, the developments in *Remembrance*, but it is manifestly a youthful work by comparison and in its style, as well as its episodic structure, it is closer to *Les plaisirs et les jours* than it is to the later work. In *Contre Sainte-Beuve*, however, it is not a question of resemblances merely—whole chunks and sections of the work, including much of the essay on homosexuality which opens the volume *Cities of the Plain* in *Remembrance*, have been quarried out of this earlier manuscript.

The form of *Contre Sainte-Beuve* does not suffer from the episodic desultoriness which had marred *Jean Santeuil*. It has unity of a kind, but the parts that are unified are basically so incongruous with each other that this is surely one of the strangest works in literature. A combination of criticism and creation, of essay, autobiography and narrative, *Contre Sainte-Beuve* is unique to the point of grotesqueness. It is a very centaur of art.

In the main, it appears to be a polemical work, aimed not merely at the individual named in the title but at the whole false conception of art for which he is taken to stand as a symbol. But the four chapters devoted directly to Sainte-Beuve and some of the writers who were the subject of his criticism (four chapters which add up to slightly less than one hundred pages of a work that is around two hundred and fifty pages in length) are introduced by eight chapters founded upon Proust's personal experiences which seem to be a world away from his reading of Sainte-Beuve and are followed by five chapters which again leave the central subject of the book behind. Certainly, Sainte-Beuve's name is mentioned near the beginning of the book and something is said of him again not far from the end, but that does not serve to change the incongruous proposition which I have indicated. A long, rambling series of personal essays introduce Proust's thoughts on criticism and another set of chapters follow those thoughts.

The "setting" for the precious stone of criticism is so extensive and ornate that it has the effect of overshadowing the criticism—which is exactly what Proust intended it to do no doubt. For criticism, as we shall see presently, cannot be to him more than a necessary evil. He has little respect for its value in itself. So he embeds the criticism between great blocks of narrative for the purpose of "disinfecting" it or of cushioning its shock, so to speak.

Another reason that suggests itself as a possibility to explain his approach is that he wished conscientiously to reveal to the reader the refraction in the subjective lens through which the object of his criticism was seen. The quarrel between Sainte-Beuve and Proust is explainable, in the final analysis, as a conflict between the two most important kinds of philosophical naturalists who have appeared in the world since the Renaissance. Sainte-Beuve is fundamentally a scientific naturalist; Proust is a sentimental naturalist whose aesthetic parentage is clearly traceable to Rousseau. The most effective instrument in the possession of the sentimental naturalist is obviously autobiography, and so Proust is led to enlist its aid in his struggle against the intellectualistic, i.e. scientific, critical approach of Sainte-Beuve to literature.

In Sainte-Beuve, criticism in the nineteenth century had attained the acme of its power—not only in the intellectual sense of the word but in the worldly one as well. It has been suggested that if one were seeking a latterday equivalent to Thomas Aquinas, the "Angelic Doctor" of the Catholic Church, Sainte-Beuve might be a logical candidate for the position. From being merely ancillary to creative literary activity (meaning by this the production of new poems, plays, novels, etc.), literary criticism had become the master and all-powerful arbiter over its destiny.

A man as sensitive and well-equipped to judge cultural trends as Matthew Arnold had remarked and repeated his statement that "of the literature of France and Germany, as of the intellect of Europe in general, the main effort, for now many years, has been a critical effort." And the man who to Arnold was identified more than anyone else with the practice of this influential criticism was Sainte-Beuve. Sainte-Beuve was a kind of uncrowned intellectual monarch over the writers of his country, and Proust felt that he had abused his power and committed injustices against some of the most talented poets and prose writers over whose reputations he had exercised the jurisdiction given him by the public. So he chose to examine Sainte-Beuve's relationship with such writers as, by the testimony of his own sensibility and the judgment of posterity, were among the most significant of the period.

What set him against Sainte-Beuve is a feeling related to the one that made him such a strong partisan of Dreyfus. In *Remembrance*, he compares the innocence of Dreyfus to the axioms of geometry, and I am sure that he regarded the immortality of Baudelaire, Stendhal, Gérard de Nerval, Balzac, and Flaubert as an aesthetic truth no less fixed and certain.

But the more basic reason for the antagonism to Sainte-Beuve felt by Proust (perhaps only obscurely known to himself) was that Sainte-Beuve's critical method was explicitly inimical to the sentimental side of romanticism which was the most sympathetic to Proust. Sainte-Beuve, after his extreme romantic beginnings in the company of Victor Hugo, was in full-fledged reaction against that movement as represented by his great friend. His cool, scientific, objective approach to literature had the effect of deflating many of the romantic pretensions, and this attitude was as menacing to that belated development of romanticism which we call Symbolism and to which Marcel Proust's own work belongs as it was to the earlier romanticism of Chateaubriand, Vigny, and Hugo—not to mention Stendhal, Baudelaire, Nerval and Balzac, whom Proust singles out for his special attention.

We may look upon *Contre Sainte-Beuve* as a rear-guard romantic action against a threatening "scientific" attitude to literature. As such it has a surprising number of things in common with romantic manifestos such as Wordsworth's *Preface to the*

Lyrical Ballads of 1798 and Whitman's Preface to the first edition of *Leaves of Grass* in 1855. It may be interesting to note, too, that if Proust's essays of 1908 look backward to these, they are also a part of an avant-garde movement in the twentieth century which was to result in many of the attitudes expressed in the so-called New Criticism of the 1940's. This is an interesting confirmation of the view that, after almost two hundred years, we are still in the grip of the backwash of the romantic movement and that all of the avant-gardes of the century from Proust and Joyce and Eliot down to the latest offspring of the so-called Beatniks look backward in time rather than forward.

The resemblances between Proust's ideas and those of Wordsworth, for example, are striking. In the very first sentence of *Contre Sainte-Beuve,* Proust announces his central theme: "Every day I set less store on intellect." And a little later on in the chapter, he tells us that "the truths of intellect seem scarcely real at all." What is this but a variant upon the romantic feeling so well expressed by Wordsworth that the intellect is merely "that false secondary power which multiplies distinctions." (To be sure, Proust in that same introductory chapter shows himself to be very much aware of the paradox that, as he puts it, "it is intellect we must call on to establish this inferiority . . . of the intellect which I spoke of at the beginning. . . . Because if intellect does not deserve the crown of crowns, only intellect is able to award it. And if intellect only ranks second in the hierarchy of virtues, intellect alone is able to proclaim that the first place must be given to instinct." But his awareness of the difficulties, or rather the impossibilities, inherent in such a position does not trouble him since it is but a proof of the subordinate place of the intellect that he is compelled to contradict himself because he feels that he "contains multitudes.")

Romantic, too, is his extreme reduction of the importance of the function of criticism, so that at the end of the crucial eighth chapter he comes to the point of confessing that "at times I wonder if after all Sainte-Beuve's best work is not his poetry . . . *Les Lundis,* the outward show; a little poetry, the reality. In the scales of eternity, a critic's verses outweigh all the rest of his works." (pp. 118–119 of the Sylvia Townsend Warner translation in *Marcel Proust On Art and Literature, 1896–1919,* New York: Meridian Books, 1958)

This judgment is all the more damning when we realize that Proust does not think highly of Sainte-Beuve's poetry. He looks upon him as at best an imitator—of Theocritus, of Cowper, of Racine. His verses appear to Proust to be a confession of taste rather than independent, original creations. There is nothing characteristic in them unless it is the author's lack of competence and craftsmanship: "Of his own, of what was involuntarily and profoundly his own, almost the only thing is clumsiness."

Most of all, I think, Proust's displeasure with Sainte-Beuve springs from the fact that the critical attitude of the latter seems to his mind to be aimed at reducing the value of literature to that of a social datum useful to the biographer, historian, psychologist, and social scientists in general. According to Proust, who is very much the Romanticist and Symbolist in his attitude on this point, the poet is a seer with vatic responsibilities. He is in communication with powers far higher than any mere rationalist or scientist could possibly hope to understand. The penalty for Sainte-Beuve's misapprehension concerning this was that he missed the meaning of the messages delivered by the most divinely inspired singers and story-tellers of his age.

Let us go, contrary to the order adopted by the author himself, to the heart of his work first of all. By the heart of his work, I understand, as I have already indicated, the four chapters (eight through eleven) dealing first with the method of Sainte-Beuve and then with a number of concrete applications of the method. To define Sainte-Beuve's object in criticism, Proust quotes the authoritative description by Taine who was even more vigorously systematic and scientific in his ideal of literary criticism:

M. Sainte-Beuve's method is no less valuable than his writings. In that respect, he was an innovator. He carried the method of natural history into the history of moral philosophy.

He has shown us how to set about knowing the man; he has indicated the series of circumstances which shape the individual and must be successively examined if that individual is to be understood: first, his race and his inherited traditions, which can often be made out by studying his father, his mother, his brothers and sisters; then his early upbringing, his home surroundings, the influence of family life and of all that shapes childhood and youth;

later, the earliest group of notable men among whom his gifts un-folded, the literary flock to which he belonged. Then comes the study of the man thus formed, the search for clues that lay bare his innermost being, the revulsions and attractions which reveal his dominant passion and his particular turn of mind; in short, an analysis of the man himself, pursued into all its consequences, through and despite those false appearances which literary bent or public appearances never fail to interpose between our vision and the actual countenance. . . . The practice of this sort of botani-cal analysis on the human individual is the sole means of reconciling the moral and the positive sciences, and it has only to be applied to peoples, races, and epochs for its virtues to be made manifest. (pp. 95–96)

The result of such a method was a Natural History of Intel-lectuals, and Proust begins his refutation of "theoreticians" whose "conception of reality (admits) no truth that (is) not a sci-entific truth" with the elementary observation what while sci-entists build upon the work of their predecessors in a very real sense, in art "there is no such thing as an originator, a precursor (at any rate in the scientific sense of the word)." The present-day writer has to begin all over again and is not any more ad-vanced toward his goal than Homer was.

But before going any further, Proust thinks it well to let Sainte-Beuve speak for himself to explain what it was that he was attempting to do. Sainte-Beuve differentiates between the facili-ties at our disposal for studying the ancient authors and those we possess for investigating modern writers. With regard to the ancient world, we have relatively limited data concerning the men who produced its art and philosophy. In the case of Plato, Sophocles, and Virgil, the scantiness of personal information "reduces" the critic to commenting on the works, admiring them, and more or less idealizing the men responsible for creating them. Though he does not use the comparison, he implies that the classics are somewhat like the cave-drawings of prehistoric man. The particular lives of the artists and even the culture to which they belonged are shadowy uncertainties beside the definite, aesthetic outlines and figures which they have left behind them.

But when we come to modern times, Sainte-Beuve goes on to say, we are in an altogether different condition. Here it is pos-sible to know the man who has produced artistic works "thor-oughly" and such knowledge, the critic assures us, "is an important matter not to be lightly dismissed." (p. 98) So much is known about artistic personalities in modern times that Sainte-Beuve declared himself firmly convinced that scientific knowledge concerning major family systems of the intellect will be increasingly possible. Though he deprecated his own accomplishment and said that men like himself were unfortunately still in a primitive, anecdotic stage of development far from his scientific aspirations, he had caught glimpses which might one day lead to the discovery of "the great biological divisions that correspond with the family systems of the intellect." (p. 98)

Furthermore, added Sainte-Beuve, and *this is the heart of the matter so far as Proust is concerned:* "I do not look on literature as a thing apart, or, at least, detachable from the rest of man and his nature . . . One cannot provide oneself with too many means or too many objectives if one is to know a man—by which I mean something other than a pure intelligence. So long as one has not asked an author a certain number of questions and received answers to them, though these were only whispered in confidence, one cannot be certain of having a complete grasp of him even though these questions might seem at the furthest remove from the nature of his writings. What were his religious views? How did he react to the sight of nature? How did he conduct himself with regard to women, in regard to money? Was he rich, was he poor? What governed his actions, what was his daily way of life? What was his vice, or his weakness? No answer to these questions is irrelevant in judging the author of a book, nor the book itself, short of a treatise on pure geometry, above all, if it be a literary work, that is, one into which everything enters." (pp. 98–99)

Proust, on the other hand, emphatically believes that literature is "a thing apart," detachable from the rest of the man. To him as to Plato, literature at its best is the product of a divine inspiration and is something sacred. The conditions under which it is produced are in the highest degree mysterious and not available to the observation of the social scientist. It is the result of a sort of immaculate conception which cannot be accounted for on naturalistic grounds. And so he concludes that Sainte-Beuve's celebrated method is a superficial one, and to hope for great results from such a method is vain, because "this method ignores what a very slight degree of self-acquaintance teaches us; that a book is the product of a different *self* from the self we manifest in our habits, in our social life, in our vices. If we would try to understand that particular self, it is by searching our own bosoms, and trying to understand it there, that we may arrive at it. Nothing can exempt us from this pilgrimage of the heart." (pp. 99–100) By all roads, we return to the Platonic problem of problems—that of knowing ourselves. Our approach to the understanding of art, argues Proust, must be subjective rather than objective first of all. It must begin with our feelings rather than with the dry light of our intellect. Sainte-Beuve's method to him is largely an evasion of the really difficult tasks of criticism.

The first case-history which Proust examines of the application of Sainte-Beuve's celebrated method by the master himself is that of his evaluation of Stendhal. Sainte-Beuve was impelled to reevaluate Stendhal by the admiration which that writer inspired in several gifted members of the younger generation. But he was contemptuous of these new critics. He preferred "in framing a clear estimate of this somewhat complex mind" to rely on the impressions and recollections of Stendhal's *person* on the part of those men who had known him—Sainte-Beuve himself first of all, and then M. Mérimée and M. Ampère.

But, asks Proust quite reasonably, in what way does having known Stendhal personally qualify a man to judge his work. And he goes on to point out that the conclusion of Sainte-Beuve is summed up in the sentence: "I have been re-reading, or trying to re-read, Stendhal's novels; frankly, they are detestable." (p. 100) What a mouse of insight to have come from a mountain of advantages! "Barrès," bursts out Proust, naming one of the contemporary masters who seemed to him to have the greatest natural literary discernment and sensitivity, "Barrès, with an hour's reading and no 'information,' would have made a better fist at it than you, M. Sainte-Beuve!" (p. 102) Proust might have argued that being the personal friend of a chess champion does not qualify one to understand the depth of the moves he makes. Only another chess player with a profound understanding of the game is qualified to appreciate his mastery of it. Similarly, it is only literary understanding, sensitivity, judgment and penetration that qualifies a critic to comprehend the achievement of a great poet or novelist—rubbing elbows with him otherwise is meaningless. All this now seems self-evident. In these days when we have learned from Eliot that poetry is a "superior amusement" (presumably like a complicated game) and from numerous lesser critics that art is a special discipline, there is nothing startling in Proust's point of view. But we should remember that he stated it forcefully more than fifty years ago! And we should keep in mind, too, that Proust's objection to Sainte-Beuve's method, as we have seen, is still more sweeping. A writer, according to him, possesses two selves—one is a social self neither superior nor inferior to the other social selves of his particular circle. Another is that higher spiritual self which shows itself only in solitude and which really creates his books.

It is at this point that Proust delivers a really lethal blow at Sainte-Beuve. Had all the evaluations of 19th century literature been destroyed by fire except *Les Lundis*, says Proust, we should see Stendhal ranked below Charles de Bernard, Vinet, Molé, Mme. de Verdelin, Ramond, Sénac de Meilhan, Vicq d'Azyr, and numerous others, who, though they may have cut imposing figures in the eyes of their contemporaries, have been reduced to insignificance by posterity. The genius of Stendhal is to Proust self-evident and axiomatic. He recognizes genius by an immediate intuition first of all; that this recognition is more and more shared by general opinion he looks upon as no accident, for the truth in such matters generally triumphs with time.

This sort of objection is all the more crushing to the critical pretensions of Sainte-Beuve because it condemns him by the criterion which he himself suggested—namely, that the worth of a critic must be judged primarily by the validity of his reaction to his contemporaries, which means, of course, to be able to separate those whose works are ephemeral from those who are destined to be permanent. Praising the classics, however meritorious it is (and Sainte-Beuve does it all the time), is a little like voting in an election that was decided a long time before the critic was born. It is by one's reaction to candidatures that are still in doubt that one shows depth of perception or the lack of it. The trouble, according to Proust, is always the same; what deflects the critic's judgment from the truth is the false principle which holds him in thrall: "At no time does Sainte-Beuve seem to have understood that there is something special about creative writing and that this makes it different in kind from what busies

other men, and, at other times, busies writers." Creative writing
he defines later in the same essay as "the secretion of one's
innermost life, written in solitude and for oneself, that one
gives to the public." It is removed as far as possible from journalism and "those drawing room essays, whittled down to suit a
particular circle and scarcely more than conversation in print
. . . the product of a quite superficial self, not of the innermost
self which one can only recover by putting aside the world and
the self that frequents the world . . ."

Les Lundis, he says, were not composed of immortal diamond
but of some very good paste. He gives them their due as literary
journalism; they are genuinely entertaining and at times really
delightful. Some people, according to Proust (though we gather
that these are not on the highest level of discernment) might say
of Sainte-Beuve himself what he said of Horace: "Among modern
nations, and particularly in France, Horace has become a breviary
of good taste, poetry, and practical worldly wisdom." But journalism even at its best for Proust aims at the effect it can produce
on a mob ("Even though it may be a highly select mob") and
this "effect is always slightly vulgar." (112) It is not, as genuine
creative writing always ought to be, the disinterested expression
of a personality for its own sake and without regard to its effect.

After Stendhal, Proust studies the relations between Sainte-
Beuve and Baudelaire. Here the objection of Proust seems to be
not that the critic did not appreciate the poet at all but that he
did so inadequately. Had Sainte-Beuve reacted to Baudelaire with
extreme revulsion (which was true of many of his nineteenth
century contemporaries, like the critic Edmond Schérer) it is
possible that Proust should not have blamed him at all. What he
finds fault with is Sainte-Beuve's lukewarmness, his restraint and
"moderation" with regard to a man whom he had better opportunities than most others for judging correctly. That was
because Baudelaire was not only a personal friend and correspond-
ent of his but in some ways functioned on the same poetic wave-
length with Sainte-Beuve and, though he went infinitely further,
styled himself a disciple who had schooled himself on the verses
of the critic. To Proust, Baudelaire is without a doubt "the
greatest poet of the nineteenth century." (120)

He points out that, though *Les Lundis* are quite frequently concerned with such men as Comte Daru and d'Alton Shée (whose names we must look up in the Encyclopaedia in order to identify them), there is not even one full-length article among them devoted to Baudelaire, and this despite the poet's repeated and pathetic entreaties for the favor of such an article (which should have repeated in public the assurances of the critic in private). When *Les Fleurs du Mal,* like *Madame Bovary,* became the occasion of a public trial, Sainte-Beuve did help the defence by drawing up an anonymous plan to conduct it. He wrote, too, a letter to Baudelaire later included in the *Causeries du Lundi,* a letter which Proust analyzes in the finest, most patient detail and with a novelist's emotional insight to demonstrate precisely how stingy the critic was with the few crumbs of praise he dropped to the poet. (pp. 121–122)

He quotes Sainte-Beuve's famous description of *Les Fleurs du Mal* as "this little lodge, which the poet has built himself on the tip of the Kamschatka of literature, I call it 'the Baudelaire Folly' "—a description which was widely quoted and became fashionable and which Proust makes fun of with merciless irony. The story of Baudelaire's candidature for the French Academy and of Sainte-Beuve's ambiguous role in relation to it is analyzed by Proust with skill (pp. 123–125). How pitiful, he makes us feel, is Baudelaire's unfailing subservience to the man he called Uncle Beuve: "As for what you call my Kamschatka, if such rousing encouragements often come my way, I believe I shall feel equal to enlarging it into a whole Siberia, etc. When I see how energetic you are, how fertile, I am thoroughly ashamed."

This imaginative demonstration by Proust dovetails neatly into his argument that there are two selves in every writer—one, a social self which may be very inferior, the other "a man of genius . . . who shares his skin . . . (but) has very little in common with the other inmate." The cringing figure which the writer as social climber sometimes presents to the eyes of the world (we feel that Proust may here be speaking not only of Baudelaire but also of himself) is contemptible indeed in our eyes if we forget the man of genius and pitiable if we remember him. But Proust comes to the curious conclusion that the ignorance of the genius concerning his own true status as a "king among men" (p. 127) is perhaps providential so far as his work is concerned: "He sees himself as a poor man who would be highly gratified if a duke asked him to dinner or the Académie gave him an award. And if this humility is a condition to his sincerity, and to the sincerity of his work, let it be called blessed." (p. 127) Yet he strongly communicates to us a feeling of sadness at the spectacle of first-rate artists like Baudelaire, Stendhal, and Flaubert abasing themselves and currying favor with second-raters such as Sainte-Beuve, Mérimée, and George Sand. The whole last part of Proust's chapter on Baudelaire (129–143) is devoted to an ardent appreciation of his poetry such as he never received from Sainte-Beuve or other influential critics of his time.

Gérard de Nerval, the subject of the tenth chapter of Proust, was "consigned" (p. 144) by Sainte-Beuve to an obscurity even more profound than that which surrounds the name and work of Baudelaire in *Les Lundis*. Proust, in this case, leaves Sainte-Beuve behind at the very beginning of the chapter and writes an enthusiastic appreciation of Nerval's *Sylvie* (the narrative technique of which he was later on to compare with his own in *Remembrance*). The relevance of the chapter in general to his argument is that Sainte-Beuve, by remaining oblivious to so valuable (albeit strange) a talent among his contemporaries was in reality condemning his own criticism to ultimate oblivion.

The last critical case-history (Chapter 11) to be examined by Proust is Sainte-Beuve's relationship to the work of Balzac. Here, of course, there was no dearth of attention or voluminousness in the criticism. Balzac was too successful, too popular to be ignored or patronized. But Proust is blunt in expressing his judgment that "one of the writers of his day that Sainte-Beuve was wrong about is Balzac." (p. 157) Perhaps the most striking observation of Proust on the criticism of Sainte-Beuve is the one in which he points out that the critic failed completely to appreciate "Balzac's masterly invention of retaining the same characters throughout his novels." (p. 182) In a passage, which carries us forward in thought to the method of construction used in *Remembrance*, Proust writes: "Sainte-Beuve completely failed to understand this business of retaining names and characters: 'This affectation finally led him to take up a theory that could scarcely have been falser or more thwarting to what makes a book interesting; I mean the way he continually introduces his characters from one novel to another like actors with walking-on parts. Nothing is more damaging to the piquancy which depends on novelty nor to the charm of the unexpected which gives a novel its appeal. Wherever one turns one encounters the same faces.' It is Balzac's stroke of genius that Sainte-Beuve here fails to understand." (p. 182) He goes on to point out that Balzac did not hit on this means of unifying his work at once, but neither did Wagner realize the desirability of certain felicitous connections (he composed the Good Friday music before writing *Parsifal*) until afterwards. The new relations which Balzac perceived between separate parts of his work after they were written, was one of his "finest creative intuitions" and well, says Proust, may he have been ecstatically happy (as his sister described him to be) the day when the idea first occurred to him. We feel, in reading these passages, that Proust was preparing himself to use this belated discovery of Balzac and the leitmotif method of Wagner as the idea for beginning his own masterpiece.

The basic objection of Proust to the method of Sainte-Beuve is not so very different from what which was being stated around the same time (1912) by Babbitt in his *Masters of Modern French Criticism:* "Criticism in Sainte-Beuve is plainly moving away from its own center towards something else; it is ceasing to be literary and becoming historical and biographical and scientific . . . We are scarcely conscious of any change when Sainte-Beuve passes, as he does, especially in the later volumes of the *Nouveaux Lundis,* from writers to generals or statesmen."

In other words, Sainte-Beuve paid the price for reducing literature from its high prophetic and poetic estate to a datum useful in a scientific approach to society. His failures of sensibility which are ruthlessly exposed by Proust, are the consequences of that initial mistaken assumption. Proust, on the other hand, always insists upon the special nature of the literary experience. The reduction of the Bible to literature by various critics and poets of the eighteenth and nineteenth centuries is accompanied, on the part of other literary men in the nineteenth and twentieth centuries, by the elevation of literature to the status of a bible. Proust is in full-fledged reaction against the conception of the "relationship between literature and society upon which the nineteenth century was to insist more than any previous century." Sainte-Beuve, on the other hand, was in complete consonance with the major current of his time; he gave his age an additional push in the direction in which it was already going.

Again, it is Irving Babbitt (carrying on where Matthew Arnold and Emerson had left off and preparing the way for his pupil, T. S. Eliot) who adequately sums up the objections which Proust raises against Sainte-Beuve and his whole school: "Yet history and biography and science are at best preparations for literary criticism, preparations that are always relevant to be sure, but likely to be less relevant in direct ratio to the distinction of the man who is being criticized. The greater the man, for example, the more baffling he is likely to be to students of heredity. The higher forms of human excellence, says Dante, are rarely subject to heredity; and this God wills in order that we may know that they come from Him alone. The truth Dante thus puts theologically is, I believe, a matter of observation so far as the past is concerned . . . The genius of Keats is precisely that part of him that cannot be explained by the fact that he was the son of the keeper of a London livery stable. In this sense we may say with Emerson that 'great geniuses have the shortest biographies.' 'Can any biography,' he says, 'shed light on the localities into which the *Midsummer Night's Dream* admits me? Did Shakespeare confide to any notary or parish recorder, sacristan, or surrogate, in Stratford, the genesis of that delicate creation? . . . The Genius draws up the ladder after him, when the creative age goes up to heaven, and gives way to a new age, which sees the works and asks in vain for a history.' "

How near in spirit Emerson's words are (and Proust who loved Emerson and drew epigraphs from his work for some of the stories in *Les plaisirs et les jours* may have read them) to a passage in the chapter on *The Method of Sainte-Beuve:* "It is taking things too easily to suppose that one fine morning the truth will arrive by post in the form of an unpublished letter submitted to us by a friend's librarian or that we shall gather it from the lips of someone who saw a great deal of the author."

Now, having attended to the central argument of *Contre Sainte-Beuve*, let us go back to the beginning—those introductory chapters which are not essential to the argument but foreshadow the themes of *Remembrance*. From one point of view— perhaps that of Sainte-Beuve himself rather than of Proust—these chapters may appear to be mere gingerbread, unessential to the serious intellectual aim of the author. But Proust, as I have already said, informed us in his first sentence that "every day I set less store on intellect," and this oblique circumlocutory approach to his thesis may be his way of showing contempt for the geometrical, straightforward approach of logic.

In his Prologue to *Contre Sainte-Beuve* he treats the theme of memory and brings in the cup of tea that is to play such an important role in *Remembrance;* the madeleine of the later work is replaced by some slices of dry toast in this one. Some of the most striking images in *Remembrance* are developments of images here. The effect of the taste of toast and tea in reawakening impressions of an earlier time is compared by Proust to "those Japanese flowers which do not re-open as flowers until one drops them into water." What is involved here is a phenomenon of the *involuntary memory:* "intellect can lend us no hand in these resurrections." Much of the other material of the opening sections of *Remembrance* is here, too—the feeling of uncertainty, for example, of the sleeper just awakened as to exactly where he is in the world, in which of the many rooms he has occupied in the course of his existence. The only thing that is changed is the *order* in which this material is presented. It is not that what we have in *Contre Sainte-Beuve* is disorder—far from it—but it is not yet *the most effective order* that is discovered.

The past, Proust tells us in this *Prologue,* is nothing less than the "private essence of ourselves." He is more than ever fixed upon this great central idea of all his work. What he is desperately in quest of are those "jewels of feeling which only here and there show through . . . a net of intellect." This should not be an unusual view for the successful, popular writers of the time to take. What is so engaging and paradoxical is to find an intellectual, using intellectual means, to defend a non-intellectual position. It is this surprise and unexpectedness that accounts for a good deal of Proust's power.

Chapter 1, after the Prologue, contains many of the sentences, paragraphs, passages which are lifted verbatim later into *Remembrance:* "Often I fell asleep almost as soon as I had put out the light, so quickly that I was growing drowsy; so that half an hour later, awakened by the thought that it was time to go to sleep, I would try to throw away the newspaper which I supposed I was still holding." (p. 27)

Chapter 2 continues to ramble among recollections of bedrooms in various houses and localities that the author has known. We recognize Combray and Balbec and Tansonville of the later book. And sometimes a whole sentence leaps from its context, almost or completely identical with a sentence in *Remembrance* that had imprinted itself in our minds once and for all with the finality of initials carved in newly-laid cement. Here is a perfectly Proustian insight which could have occurred to no one else: "I sometimes wonder if the immovableness of things around us is not wished on them by our conviction that they are what they are and no other. The fact remains that whenever I woke up without knowing where I was, all—things and years and places— swirled round me in the darkness." (p. 33)

Chapters 3 and 4 meander pleasantly among recollections, the most important of which is that of the Countess, who is recognizable as a first sketch of the very important Duchesse de Guermantes in *Remembrance*. With Chapter 5, we reach the most purposeful (albeit still indirect) introduction of a theme connected with Sainte-Beuve, who is to make his entrance three chapters later. Proust had proposed, we should recall (in outlining his plans for this work to a friend), to "begin with an account of a morning, Mamma would come to my bedside and I would tell her about the article on Sainte-Beuve I want to write and enlarge (on) it to her." (p. 10) Actually, as we have seen, he had begun his exposition even further back than that, with purely personal impressions of the process of going to sleep, dreams, waking, memory, a picturesque character he had known, etc.

But at last in this chapter he comes to his originally planned point of departure for a criticism of Sainte-Beuve. It is an account (to be repeated in substance towards the very end of *Remembrance*) of a morning when his mother unexpectedly brings to his bedside a copy of the newspaper *Le Figaro* in which an article by the young Marcel appears on the front page. She says nothing about the article to him, merely leaves it beside his bed, "like an anarchist who had put down a bomb." (p. 59) The author at the time is evidently a beginner in the field of letters—this is one of his first published articles, and it has been kept so long by the editor that he has despaired of seeing it in print at all. The purpose of introducing this story of a journalistic tyro appears to be that Proust wishes to describe the psychology of a writer of articles for the newspapers. One may say that there is a tremendous difference between Marcel Proust at this stage of his career and Sainte-Beuve at the time when he was the cynosure of sophisticated attention with his weekly articles in the Parisian press. Proust recognizes the difference, but he insists, too, upon a certain similarity. The beginner reflects (p. 64) that "I would like to think that my marvellous ideas are even now running in every head . . ." And what of the experienced and much older man of the world and famous critic? "On a Monday morning, at that hour when in winter only a wan daylight shows above the drawn window-curtains, he opened his *Constitutionnel,* and felt that at that same moment, in rooms all over Paris, the words he had enlisted were proclaiming the brilliant ideas he had hit on . . ." (p. 109) Just as the beginner pictures his readers in his imagination opening the paper and reading his words, so even the writer who had become invested with the dignity of an institution must have "pictured Mme. de Boigne in her tall four-poster opening *Le Constitutionnel;* he told himself how at two o'clock that afternoon the Chancellor would pay his call and discuss it with her, how during the evening he would have a note from Mme. Allart or Mme. d'Arbouville telling him what people had thought of it." (111)

For no matter how lofty or humble its station, all journalism may be described as "a sort of arc . . . plunging its further end into the minds and admiration of . . . readers, where it completed its curve and took on its final coloring." (111) "The beauty of a piece of journalistic writing does not lie wholly in the article; cut off from the minds where it finishes its course, the article is but an armless Venus." (111–112) Real literature, wholly sincere writing, is a very different matter, however. There, the search is not for a rhetorical effect upon the susceptibilities of a certain audience. The artist is trying to give satisfactory expression to some pressing inner truth, and he has no particular audience in mind at all. Art is essentially a solitary activity for Proust; it becomes a *social* fact only afterwards and by the merest accident. Between the artist and the impresario who exploits his art (even when this happens to be the artist himself in an uninspired phase) there is the deepest gulf. But social purpose and consciousness of this purpose is of the very essence of journalism. It is timely by intention and grows "immortal" only by accident;

whereas all true literature is immortal in intention (even when it fails) and timely only by accident.

After considering the lengthy introduction to the central section of the work, let us now consider the not inconsiderable conclusion of it. What is the purpose of those chapters, beginning with Chapter 12 on *Monsieur de Guermantes' Balzac?* The primary purpose of this particular chapter seems to be to contrast the view of a simple reader of Balzac, who reads him not out of duty or because he has to instruct his audience but because of the immediate enjoyment he derives from his stories with the sophisticated and professional critic. We have already seen how wrong Sainte-Beuve was about Balzac, according to Proust. Well, M. de Guermantes does not look upon himself as a critic; he is not intellectual at all, but the few remarks he makes about Balzac are guided by the right feeling of appreciation. This is another of Proust's ways of underlining his conviction as to the nugatory importance of the intellect in the understanding of art. Even while noting the satirical elements in the portrait of this Count of Guermantes (the *Duke* of the same name is one of the coarsest characters in the pages of *Remembrance*), how poverty stricken his vocabulary is for terms of approbation (he keeps repeating: "It's capital . . . capital, isn't it?"), how he confuses works by Balzac with those of Roger de Beauvoir and Céleste de Chabrillon simply because all these authors have the same sort of bindings in his inherited library, we should also be aware that his genuine, unaffected enthusiasm as a reader serves to redeem him in Proust's eyes and that Proust identifies himself with the silly Count against much more highly cultivated critics: "There are times when I wonder whether even today my way of reading is not more like M. de Guermantes's than contemporary critics'. To me a book is still a living entity, which I begin to know from the first line, which I listen to with deference, and which, while we remain together, I unreservedly and undemurringly agree with. When I find M. Faguet saying in his *Critical Essays* that the first volume of *Le Capitaine Fracasse* is splendid and the second volume tame, or that in *Le Père Goriot* everything to do with Goriot is first-rate and everything to do with Rastignac shoddy, I am quite as surprised as if I heard someone saying that the country round Combray is ugly on the Méséglise side, but on the Guermantes side, beautiful. When M. Faguet goes on to say that lovers of Gautier do not read beyond the first volume of *Le Capitaine Fracasse*, I, who took so much pleasure in the second, can only feel sorry for the lovers of Gautier, but when he adds that the first volume was written for the lovers and the second for schoolboys, my pity for the lovers turns to scorn of myself, since I realize how schoolboyish I still am. Finally, when he declares that Gautier wrote the second volume in a state of intense boredom, I am amazed that what was so boring to write should later on become so entertaining to read." (p. 202)

The irony here at the expense of the critic Faguet is of course equally applicable to Sainte-Beuve, as Proust makes clear at the beginning of the next paragraph: "So, too, with Balzac, where Sainte-Beuve and Faguet pick and choose and analyze, and think that the beginning is wonderful and the end worthless." (p. 203) At this point, Proust has a footnote worth quoting, which makes a satiric thrust at the contradictions into which an excess of intellectual analysis leads us: "What is rather odd and rather comforting is that Sainte-Beuve said: 'Who has ever drawn the duchesses of the Restoration better than (Balzac)?' M. Faguet laughs uproariously at the duchesses and invokes M. Feuillet. Finally, M. Blum, who likes making distinctions, admires his duchesses, but not in so far as they claim to represent duchesses of the Restoration." One is reminded by this last observation of M. Homais's criticism of Racine's *Athalie* in *Madame Bovary*: "He could make distinctions. . . . In this tragedy, for example, he found fault with the ideas, but admired the style; he detested the conception, but applauded all the details, and loathed the characters while he grew enthusiastic over their dialogue. . . . And in this confusion of sentiments he would have liked at once to crown Racine with both hands and argue with him for a good quarter of an hour." Flaubert evidently suffered the imbecilities and analytical affectations of criticism no more gladly than Proust did.

Chapter 13 of *Contre Sainte-Beuve* introduces the most notable advance over *Jean Santeuil* and towards *Remembrance* with a discussion of homosexuals and homosexuality, large segments of which are repeated verbatim, though in a somewhat different order, in the volumes of *Cities of the Plain*. In the Marquis de

Quercy in this book, we recognize the first tentative sketch of what is, by common consent, perhaps the most impressive of Proust's character creations, the Baron de Charlus. All of the eloquence, all of the anguish, and all of the insight, which Proust was to bring to bear on the subject of homosexuality later on are potentially present here—even that strange, unexpected, yet striking analogy between the situation of the Jew in society and that of the homosexual: "If in the depth of almost every Jew there is an anti-Semite whom we best flatter when we attribute every kind of fault to him but treat him as a Christian, so in the depth of every homosexual there is an anti-homosexual to whom we cannot offer a greater insult than by acknowledging that he has talents, virtues, intellect, heart, and in sum, like all human characters, the right to love in the form that nature allows us to conceive of it, though respect for truth meanwhile compels us to confess that this form of love is strange and that these men are not like other men." (222)

Chapter 16, the last one of *Contre Sainte-Beuve*, recapitulates the central thesis of the book, namely that real "books are the work of solitude and the children of silence." (272) He accuses Sainte-Beuve here of producing "a materialistic criticism, sayings that roll off the tongue, and gratify pursed lips, raised eyebrows, shrugging shoulders, and whose adverse current daunts the mind from exploring further." (273–274)

The concluding paragraph of the book (276) is both a prophecy of things to come and a fulfillment in itself: "The fine things we shall write if we have talent enough, are within us, dimly, like the remembrance of a tune which charms us though we cannot recall its outline, or hum it, nor even sketch its metrical form, say if there are pauses in it, or runs of rapid notes. Those who are haunted by this confused remembrance of truths they have never known are the men who are gifted; but if they never go beyond saying that they can hear a ravishing tune, they convey nothing to others, they are without talent. Talent is like a kind of memory which in the end enables them to call back this confused music, to hear it distinctly, to write it down, to reproduce it, to sing it. There comes a time in life when talent, like memory, fails, and the muscle in the mind which brings inward memories before one like memories of the outer world, loses its power. Sometimes, from lack of exercise or because of a too ready self-approval, this time of life extends over a whole lifetime; and no one, not your own self even, will ever know the tune that beset you with its intangible delightful rhythm."

What is to be said of *Contre Sainte-Beuve* as a whole? Insofar as it is a legitimate ancestor of *Remembrance of Things Past*, it goes to prove that there is no such thing as creation *ex nihilo*. As Lear so truly says to Cordelia, "Nothing will come of nothing." The materials of art, the evidence of distinguished sensibility must be there before they can be transmuted into the final form that is responsible for the wonder which art arouses in its beholder. Chaos is identified in the Book of Genesis with darkness, and the saving words of God: "Let there be light!" presumably dispels both darkness and chaos.

All the elements in Proust are present and prepared for the creator's hand long before he is able to use them adequately, before he is able to preside over them and say: "Let there be form, unity, and the order given by planning!" Here, as in *Jean Santeuil*, he is still struggling largely in the dark; he feels the potential value of the materials he is handling but he is as yet incapable of those "architectural labors" (as Proust himself called them) which will incorporate them eventually into a unified construction. In few other writers is the drama of producing a viable work of art as long drawn out as it is in Proust.

12. Conclusion

A FEW YEARS AGO IN HIS BOOK CALLED *A Lifetime Reading Plan,*
CLIFTON FADIMAN INCLUDED PROUST BUT WARNED HIS AUDIENCE
that three distinct attitudes had been taken towards *Remembrance*
by readers in the past. First, there were the cultists for whom
it was self-evidently the greatest novel ever written. Then there
were those for whom it was altogether unreadable. Finally, he
quoted a critic with whom he did not agree who had called
Proust's masterwork "mammoth but minor." Still a fourth attitude is possible, and it is the one which is closest to my own,
namely to regard *Remembrance* as both mammoth and major.
It is not for me the greatest novel ever written (the choice I
think should be between Dostoyevsky's *Brothers Karamazov* and
Tolstoy's *War and Peace*), but it is definitely not a minor work
in any sense which might be given this description. The description "mammoth but minor" might apply, in my own estimation,
to a work like Jules Romains' *Men of Good Will* which is even
more *monumental* in extent than *Remembrance* but never rises
to its level of sensitivity on the individual page or to its symmetry
of form and larger philosophical significance when considered as
a whole.

The English academician F. R. Leavis says somewhere that
he should consider the prospect of re-reading Samuel Richardson's multi-volumed *Clarissa* with a good deal more pleasure
than that of re-reading Proust's *Remembrance*. Such a judgment
seems unintelligible to me for whom any reading of Richardson
even once is an intolerable penance. Richardson I think of sometimes as "the wicked uncle" of the English novel, and I find him
as insufferable as Henry Fielding, the true father of the novel,
once did. If Leavis meant his comment to be serious and something more than ostentatious literary provincialism ("Anything
English and old is preferable to these new-fangled foreign
fripperies which tasteless people are importing nowadays!"), I

regard it as a confession relevant to his personal history, interesting to the literary impressionist but without any objective critical meaning whatever.

Proust's work seems to me mammoth and major not only in comparison to other work of the twentieth century but also in comparison to the much more impressive examples of the art of prose fiction in the nineteenth and eighteenth centuries. In our twentieth century, the denigrating remark once made to me by Louis-Ferdinand Céline about his own work: "Among the blind, the one-eyed men are kings!" is only too widely applicable, and many of our contemporary idols will prove to have feet of clay. But Proust I am confident will not be one of these. He is a genuine *seer*, and not simply like some of his countrymen fashionable at this moment a *voyeur*. Unlike Céline himself, he strikes me as belonging with the great two-eyed men of literature, those who contain within themselves elements of normality, balance, self-criticism—which are qualities that works aspiring to set a standard of excellence for ages must have to survive.

Proust himself satirizes the fads and unstable fashions of taste in *Swann's Way*. At Madame de Saint-Euverte's party, one of the more obscure guests is the elderly provincial noblewoman, Madame de Cambremer, whose son has recently married the daughter of the climber Legrandin. This daughter-in-law of the Cambremers, as snobbish intellectually as her father is socially and "having got as far as Harmony and the Greek alphabet," feels qualified to act as taste-maker for her new family. She is a self-appointed member of the avant-garde and (as might be expected in the particular decade of the nineteenth century when the story takes place) a fervent Wagnerian enthusiast who claims that she cannot abide the outmoded music of Chopin and actually "fell quite ill when she heard him played." (S.W. 430) Her aristocratic mother-in-law, who knows Chopin's music well and has learned to play it beautifully on the piano, is nevertheless so timid in her taste as to allow herself to be browbeaten by her daughter-in-law. Only when the old Mme. de Cambremer is conscious of not being scrutinized by the younger one can she surrender herself to the pleasure of listening to the pianist's performance of the Polish master at the party "with a tender smile, full of intimate reminiscence, as well as of satisfaction (that of a competent judge) . . . She had been taught in her girlhood to fondle and cherish those long-necked, sinuous creatures, the phrases of Chopin, so free, so flexible, so tactile, which begin by seeking their ultimate resting place somewhere beyond and far wide of the direction in which they started, the point which one might have expected them to reach, phrases which divert themselves in those fantastic bypaths only to return more deliberately—with a more premeditated reaction, with more precision, as on a crystal bowl which, if you strike it, will ring and throb until you cry aloud in anguish—to clutch at one's heart." (S.W. 429)

The sensitivity and loving *exactness* of this description of the effect of Chopin's music (I use the word *exactness* in the sense which Middleton Murry must have had in mind when he said: "Try to be exact, and you are bound to be metaphorical") indicates the narrator's own attitude towards this music which is certainly much nearer to that of the old-fashioned Marquise de Cambremer than to that of her fashionable and snobbish young daughter-in-law. There is nothing wrong per se with the youthful avant-garde's cult of Wagner (Marcel himself evidently shares their enthusiasm for the German composer and in the volume *The Captive* writes some of the most appreciative pages on his music that have ever been written); it is only when the cult becomes so exclusive that it refuses to recognize the excellence of an older school of composition and rejects the genius of Chopin which is as real as that of Wagner (and not so distant from him, by the way, in the quality of its chromaticism) that it becomes manifestly silly. In a subsequent volume, Marcel meets young Madame de Cambremer in the presence of her mother-in-law and has the pleasure of telling her that Debussy, the latest rage of the avant-garde, delights in the music of Chopin and plays it all the time. He feels certain that this unexpected news will have its intended effect of transforming the snob's confident opinion that Chopin is old-hat. Unlike her mother-in-law's informed judgment, her own is based not on knowledge, first-hand experience, or sincere taste, but is a matter of hear-say and the product of the same kind of gregarious conformity which causes a flock of sheep to follow the path of its bellwether. No one is more slavishly imitative than a group of such "independent" spirits as the younger Madame de

Cambremer—all of them loudly asserting their individuality and freedom while marching together in lock-step.

Fashions in art, as in dress, come and go, and occasionally they come back. Proust tells the story of a lady who, being asked where she got her very modish hats, answered: "I do not get my hats; I keep them!" Fashion, according to this view, is a merry-go-round which periodically returns to the points it has once passed. Of no subject in the world are the words of Ecclesiastes more true than they are of fashion: "The thing that hath been, it is that which shall be; and that which is done is that which shall be done; and there is no new thing under the sun."

F. Scott Fitzgerald, speaking from bitter personal experience, once said that the true test of the artistic validity of a work is its ability to return to public favor after the initial period of its vogue was over—to be succeeded by a reaction in which it is in a shadowy eclipse for a longer or shorter time. Love may be, as Marlowe thought, a matter of recognition at first sight, but lasting fame seems to be a phenomenon of second sight. Of the many who are called by the voice of fashion, only a few are chosen by that of fame, and sometimes those who have been missed altogether at first still manage to attain to permanent renown. The examples to support these generalizations are particularly numerous in American literature. Melville's *Moby Dick*, Whitman's *Leaves of Grass* and Emily Dickinson's lyrics all had careers which might be cited to support one or another of the statements I have made. The well-known histories of Rembrandt's *Night Watch* and of Bach's *Passions* are also cases in point from the other arts.

Fifty years after Proust's birth in 1871, if we are to believe Derrick Leon who has written a study of his life and work, he was the most famous novelist in the world. Even if we reduce this claim somewhat as the exaggeration of an enthusiast, it must be granted that it comes close to being the truth to say that in 1921 and the years following, according to the tastes and opinions of the most influential, the most knowledgeable, and (in the good sense of the word) the most worldly people in Europe, Proust should have been ranked with James Joyce and with Thomas Mann as one of the three leading masters of prose fiction in the twentieth century. A decade later, this fashionable opinion reached America as well; in 1931 Edmund Wilson's fifty page essay on Proust in *Axel's Castle* established, so far as intellectual circles on this side of the Atlantic were concerned, his unquestionable pre-eminence in the modern movement in literature.

Now, forty years later, the literary situation seems to me to have changed profoundly. Though some readers may still be found who would stand by the old triple-rating of the great writers of our time (Proust, Mann, Joyce), many more should be found to question it. The supremacy of the "Big Three" of the twenties would be contested today, so far as many readers are concerned, on behalf of Faulkner and Hemingway, Camus and perhaps Sartre, Kafka and even Herman Hesse. Each of the separate nations, cultures, languages has withdrawn more than was formerly the case behind its own barriers. The position of Joyce in English, Mann in German, and Proust in French is perhaps as secure today as it was a generation ago, but something has happened to the cosmopolitan frame of mind for which the three of them existed almost on the same plane. The terrible events of the last twenty-five years have depleted the number of intellectual citizens of the world. World War I resulted in people, at least on the level of the mind, coming closer together, but World War II has resulted in their being driven further apart.

If Proust were to return to earth today, he might find that he had not outlived either his name or reputation but that it is much more difficult than it was twenty-five or thirty years ago to find general readers who enjoyed an extensive acquaintance with his work. The tides of literary opinion run inexplicably deep, and for the moment they are certainly not running in favor of Proust. Eventually, however, I am convinced that they are bound to turn to a more equitable estimate of his significance and a more active curiosity about his accomplishment. It remains as true as when Homer said it three thousand years ago that the world craves novelty for its own sake and that the new song is the one that always sounds sweetest to its ear. This does not mean naturally that for a certain number of sounder, less fickle, more curious minds, Homer himself or Catullus or even Proust will ever seem completely out of date.

The Baron Ernest de Seillière, con-gener of modern Humanism along with Irving Babbitt and Paul Elmer More, has written a thoughtful book, unfortunately never translated into English, on Proust and his work. He sees the initial impetus to the current of fashion which once brought him to the top of contemporary literature in the sexual perversity which supplies much of his subject, and which Proust himself thought would be his own greatest handicap in finding a tolerant audience. "I have often indicated," writes Seillière (I translate freely) "how naturalistic mysticism—that is to say, the affirmation of a beneficent nature, which is the real religion of our time—has for its principal ramification (along with the mysticism of the demagogue) the sort of mysticism which makes of the passions the voice of God in the human heart—a voice which it is necessary to obey piously even though it should speak out loudly against all of our social regulations, whose purpose it is to guarantee as much as possible the existence of order and peace in the midst of human groups. For a long time, the axiomatic assumption was limited to the encouragement of normal love-affairs which, however, were forbidden by the social code and by public opinion; I have in mind adultery mainly (though sometimes incest was included as well) and such was the role of George Sand as an apologist in the course of her tumultuous youth. Recently, however, the basic idea has become emboldened in direct proportion to the extent to which the religion of nature has extended its conquests. Impulses which were called until then unnatural because they showed themselves only rarely among men and seemed alien to nature, have been assimilated to the natural order nevertheless and have been given their places among the other quasi-sanctified passions. Tradition being what it is in the context of Christian civilization which is much stricter in its prohibition on these matters than on adultery or even on incest, a much more audacious approach was required to make such re-evaluations and rationalizations possible for contemporary naturalism.

"Marcel Proust, more frankly than anyone before him, approached these forbidden regions, even if he is less clean-cut in his conclusions than some of his successors. It has been remarked before that the undeniable charm of his childhood reminiscences (in the first half of *Swann's Way*) did not suffice to bring him any large public recognition; it was only when a set-piece from one of the succeeding volumes appeared in advance in the pages of an influential review that he attracted the attention of a larger audience. This extract from his writings took homosexuality as its subject. One is told, too, that he considered giving the title *Sodom and Gomorrah* to the whole of his autobiographical narrative instead of merely to the three central volumes (in the French edition) of the work. Such a decision, rejected by him finally, should not have greatly surprised readers of his monumental publication.

"He did not launch himself without hesitation upon this scabrous terrain. M. Pierre-Quint tells us that the author wrote to a friend after completing the first draft of his work . . . 'There are some strongly indecent pages in it . . . You will see the whole world turning its back on me, and especially the English. I will be treated like a mangy sheep.' He reckoned, however, without the rapid progress of naturalistic morality, on the other side of the Channel and elsewhere. He therefore witnessed the realization of the very inverse of his prediction, and instead of the anticipated brickbats it was incense to which he was treated, so that he no longer hesitated to develop in detail as he continued with the publication of his work this aspect of his psychological delineation of the passions . . . Zola himself in the preceding generation . . . had always recoiled, on principle, from the subject of homosexuality. . . ."

It is an interesting question (but one that unfortunately cannot be answered) whether the reaction against Proust in recent years is not in part at least a belated vindication of his own initial prognostication, and whether the advantage which his novel subject matter may have reaped for him a generation ago is not working against him at this moment. There are imponderables in the literary situation about which one cannot speak with any certainty. I notice, for example, that a prominent dramatist who has lately said in print that Proust is without doubt one of the two or three greatest writers that the world has produced in our century is himself generally known to be homosexual in his tastes, and I wonder if his declared preference is not discounted by readers as being an obvious plea *pro domo,* on behalf of his own known peculiarity. The general silence settling around Proust's name in the fashionable literary quarterlies seems to be much more significant of current literary taste than the exceptional voice which is raised on his behalf. It is this silence which needs to be broken more often if we are to decide whether he possesses that power to return to public favor (after the inevitable reaction following his day of fashion) which Fitzgerald recognized as the criterion of literary workmanship that is more than ephemeral in quality.

Appendix

PAGES 417–456 OF *Swann's Way* DEPICT A MUSICAL SOIRÉE AT THE
HOUSE OF THE MARQUISE DE SAINT-EUVERTE. SWANN, WHOSE TRAGIC
involvement with Odette has for a long time had the effect of
causing him to absent himself from his usual haunts in the Faubourg Saint-Germain, attends this great party as an exception.
In the development of the story of his affair, this section of
the narrative, as I have said in the analysis of *Swann In Love*,
is a digression. In itself, however, it is one of the most brilliant
examples of Proust's art and repays the most minute and attentive observation. Its place in the general scheme is that, by re-
moving him for a while from the society of Odette, it enables
Swann to see himself objectively and to realize how hopeless
his quest for a reciprocal love has become. As a prelude to the
evening at the Saint-Euvertes, Swann asks his friend the Baron
de Charlus to pay a visit to Odette and to use his good influence
upon her in Swann's favor (417) Swann, who is so fearfully
jealous of all other males, knows that he has little to fear from
the Baron so far as the female sex is concerned.

The emphasis in the opening pages describing Swann's entry
into the Saint-Euverte mansion and his greeting by the various
servitors of the Marquise is upon his *detachment* from the worldly
life he has hitherto cultivated, as a result of his exclusive passion for Odette, so that he is able to observe the scene for the
first time as it is in itself, objectively, without the accompani-
ment of that social anxiety which had prevented him once from
seeing it: "In the cloak-room, into which, in the old days, when
he was still a man of fashion, he would have gone in his over-
coat, to emerge from it in evening dress, but without any impression of what had occurred there, his mind having been,

during the minute or two that he had spent in it, either still at the party which he had just left, or already at the party into which he was just about to be ushered, he now noticed, for the first time, roused by the unexpected arrival of so belated a guest, the scattered pack of splendid effortless animals, the enormous footmen who were drowsing here and there upon benches and chests, until, pointing their noble greyhound profiles, they towered upon their feet and gathered in a circle round about him." (419)

Now that he is no longer a creature of will in relation to society but is divorced from it and able to contemplate it purely as "idea," fashionable life appears to him to possess a certain charm which he had never fully realized before. It presents to his view "a series of pictures" upon which he comments silently in his own mind with genial amusement. One of the footmen who takes his hat, for example, gives him "a steely glare (that) was compensated by the softness of his cotton gloves" and seems to Swann to exhibit "an utter contempt for his person and the most tender regard for his hat." (419) He compares these servants mentally (419–422), in his usual fashion, to various works of art by Mantegna, Durer, Goya, and Benvenuto Cellini.

At last, he enters the concert room where "he speedily recovered his sense of the general ugliness of the human male, when, on the other side of the tapestry curtain, the spectacle of the servants gave place to that of the guests." (422) Yet, as had been the case earlier, even in these generally ugly faces the detached aesthetic gaze of Swann detects "something new and uncanny, now that their features—instead of being to him symbols of practical utility in the identification of this or that man, who until then had represented merely so many pleasures to be sought-after, boredoms to be avoided, or courtesies to be acknowledged—were at rest, measurable by aesthetic co-ordinates alone, in the autonomy of their curves and angles." (422) This whole section seems to be impregnated with the spirit and vocabulary of the philosopher Schopenhauer's discussions of the nature of art.

There follow two pages (423–424) which might be entitled "Monocles" because at least half a dozen of the guests are wittily characterized by Swann in terms of the most striking artificial item in their visual appearance. There is the stodgy General de Froberville's monocle "stuck like a shell-splinter in his common, scarred, victorious, overbearing face, in the middle of a forehead which it left half-blinded, like the single-eyed flashing front of the Cyclops" and seeming to the sensitive Swann like "a monstrous wound which it might have been glorious to receive but which it was certainly not decent to expose." (423) We almost hear the stifled laughter of Swann as he hits upon this striking simile. The monocle of the smart M. de Bréauté seems in Swann's eyes "a festive badge, with his pearl-grey gloves, his crush hat and white tie, substituting it for the familiar pair of glasses (as Swann himself did) when he went out to places." In this case, what impresses the observer is the quality of the look of the eye behind the monocle, "glued to its other side, like a specimen prepared on a slide for the microscope, an infinitesimal gaze that swarmed with friendly feeling and never ceased to twinkle at the loftiness of ceilings, the delightfulness of parties, the interestingness of programmes and the excellence of refreshments." (422) Next, we have a "society novelist", whose monocle "fitted into the angle of eyebrow and cheek . . . (is) . . . the sole instrument that he used in his psychological investigations and remorseless analyses of character." The monocles of the Marquis de Forestelle, of M. de Saint-Candé, and of M. de Palancy are variously compared to a figure in a painting by Giotto, to "Saturn, with an enormous ring," etc. (424) The paragraph describing these three is a rare instance of Proustian virtuosity in characterization and description which has to be read in its entirety if its wit and flavor are to be completely savored.

After the "chapter on monocles" there begins, in the paragraph at the bottom of page 424 a series of closely interwoven sketches which mimic to perfection the affectations and attitudes of "music-lovers" and snobs. The first two ladies to be drawn are the Marquise de Cambremer and the Vicomtesse de Franquetot "who, because they were cousins, used to spend their time at parties in wandering through the rooms, each clutching her bag and followed by her daughter, hunting for one another like people at a railway station, and could never be at rest until they had reserved, by marking them with their fans or handkerchiefs, two adjacent chairs." (424–425) Mme.

de Cambremer knows almost no one in Paris, since she belongs to the provincial nobility, while her cousin, Madame de Franquetot, is extremely popular but delights in showing her fine friends that she prefers the company of her obscure country cousin with whom she played together when she was a child. The piece that is now being played is Liszt's "Saint Francis preaching to the birds" (earlier an aria from *Orfeo* had been rendered on the flute); we are not allowed to lose sight of the larger transactions of the party—to which reference is later to be made in the dialogue that ensues—while keeping our eyes focused with the narrator's on the delightful and droll minutiae of individual behavior. Swann "with ironical melancholy" watches the two women who "followed the virtuoso in his dizzy flight; Mme. de Franquetot anxiously, her eyes starting from her head, as though the keys over which his fingers skipped with such agility were a series of trapezes, from any one of which he might come crashing, a hundred feet, to the ground, stealing now and then a glance of astonishment and unbelief at her companion, as who should say: 'It isn't possible, I would never have believed that a human being could do all that!'" (425) Here is a music-lover obviously who has not risen above the rudimentary stage of responding to what may be called the circus-element of art. There are many like her at Mme. de Saint-Euverte's. She belongs to the general type represented in its perfection by the Comtesse de Monteriender "famed for her imbecilities" (456) who, at the very end of this episode some thirty pages later after Swann had had his unforgettable experience of listening to the Vinteuil Sonata, leans over to him and, dazzled by the virtuosity of the performers, confides: "It's astonishing! I have never seen anything to beat it . . ." and adds the reservation, inspired by a scrupulous regard for accuracy: "anything to beat it . . . since the table turning!" (456) Such is the guffaw with which Proust punctuates the ending of the Saint-Euverte party. But to return to Madame de Franquetot and her humble companion. Madame de Cambremer is much the more sincere and sophisticated of the two in her appreciation of music. She is "a woman who had received a sound musical education" (425); nevertheless, she, too, is a little ridiculous "beating time with her head—transformed for the nonce into the pendulum of a metronome, the sweep and rapidity of whose movements from one shoulder to the other (performed with that look of wild abandonment in her eye which a sufferer shows who is no longer able to analyze his pain, nor anxious to master it, and says merely 'I can't help it') so increased that at every moment her diamond earrings caught in the trimming of her bodice, and she was obliged to put straight the bunch of black grapes which she had in her hair, though without any interruption of her constantly accelerated motion." (425)

Seated to one side of these "music-lovers" is the snob, the Marquise de Gallardon, and the sketch of her (426–428), unimportant as she is in the general scheme of the novel, is one of the most exquisite and amusing things in this section.

The music that is being performed holds neither her interest nor even attention, since she is absorbed in her favorite meditation —namely, her relationship to the great aristocratic house of Guermantes. About this relationship she has mixed feelings: on the one hand, she is proud of it because it constitutes her only claim to fame, yet on the other hand she is deeply ashamed of it because the most brilliant representatives of that house treat her coolly "perhaps because she was just a tiresome old woman, or because she was a scandalous old woman, or because she came from an inferior branch of the family, or very possibly for no reason at all." (426) These hesitations as to human motivations, the leaps between various possibilities, and the reflections upon the irrationality of things which such thoughts inspire are characteristically witty and Proustian. Madame de Gallardon feels particularly frustrated at this moment because she is seated next to Mme. de Franquetot, who does not know who she is, and she wishes "that her own consciousness of her Guermantes connection could . . . be made externally manifest in visible characters, like those which, in the mosaics in Byzantine churches, placed one beneath another, inscribe in a vertical column by the side of some Sacred Personage the words which he is supposed to be uttering." (426) The *art-simile*, which if not an invention of Proust's is used by him with greater frequency than by any other author I know, appears to very good advantage in this passage.

Madame de Gallardon is bitter at the fact that she has not yet received an invitation from her young cousin, the Princesse des Laumes (later, after the death of her father-in-law, to become the Duchesse de Guermantes), in the six years since the latter's marriage. She says to herself: "After all, it isn't for me to take the first step; I am at least twenty years older than she is." This silent resolution restores her self-confidence so effectively that "she flung her shoulders proudly back until they seemed to part company with her bust." (427) Proust's *x-ray vision* detects evidences of character even in trivial details of posture where few writers would think of looking for it—as when he says of the Marquise that "successive mortifications had given her a backward tilt, such as one may observe in trees which have taken root at the very edge of a precipice and are forced to grow backward to preserve their balance . . . and had given her a sort of 'bearing' which was accepted by the plebeian as a sign of breeding, and even kindled, at times, a momentary spark in the jaded eyes of old gentlemen in clubs." (427) Note how these figures reinforce the indefinite suggestion at the very beginning of the sketch that she may have been "a scandalous old woman."

Proust next subjects the speech of the Marquise to semantic analysis and discovers that no expression, not even the commonest forms of speech, occurs in it as frequently as "at my cousins the Guermantes," "at my aunt Guermantes's" "Elzear de Guermantes's health," "my cousin Guermantes's box." Upon hearing some famous name, she would say coldly that, though not personally acquainted with him, she had seen him "hundreds of times at her aunt Guermantes's" leaving the impression that her lack of personal acquaintance with the celebrity was due only to "the ineradicable principles against which her arching shoulders were stretched back to rest, as on one of those ladders on which gymnastic instructors make us 'extend' so as to develop the expansion of our chests." (427–428)

Such is the preparation by description of this lively character, who remains so vividly imprinted upon the careful reader's imagination that after a lapse of several volumes when she makes her appearance once more at the close of the great party at the Princesse de Guermantes's in *Cities of the Plain,* she seems perfectly familiar to us and completely unchanged, for snobs of such intensity have a heedless tenacity about them which makes it possible for them to be killed but not to be changed in any way. In the Proustian scheme, however, this preparation precedes putting the character into action and, above all, making her talk, since Proust is convinced that nothing gives character away so much as the words that come out of one's mouth, and fortunately he is as accomplished a mimic of speech as Dickens. While Madame de Gallardon has been ruminating her dark thoughts, her cousin, the Princesse des Laumes, is actually in the same room with her. The Princess has come to the Saint-Euvertes' as an act of condescension. She is sitting near Madame de Cambremer and is watching the antics of that impassioned music-lover with "cold interest" though the spirit of imitation in an alien environment impels her to imitate her neighbor's movements so that "she would beat time for a few bars with her fan, but, so as not to forfeit her independence, she would beat a different time from the pianist's." (429) The Princess is one of the most lovely women in Paris and is narcissistically conscious of the fact as she straightens "her shoulder-straps or feels in her golden hair for the little balls of coral or of pink enamel, frosted with tiny diamonds, which formed its simple but effective ornament." (429)

While the music is being played, Madame de Gallardon reaches a point in her thought where she regrets that she has had so few opportunities of meeting her cousin, the Princess, because she meant *to teach her a lesson by not acknowledging her bow.* This, at least, is what the Marquise's conscious mind tells her, but there are depths within depths of the human psyche, as Freud has taught us to recognize and as literary artists like Proust recognized a long time before, so that when "a movement of Mme. Franquetot's head disclosed the Princess . . . Mme. de Gallardon dashed towards her, upsetting all her neighbors." (431) Yet her snobbery is checked to some extent by the pride, which is her next most important trait, and in the ensuing conversation—which must be quoted entire to be fully appreciated—her contradictory impulses find the opportunity to express themselves in a kind of complex counterpoint.

> Although determined to preserve a distant and glacial manner . . . she felt bound to modify this air of dignity and reserve by some non-committal remark which would justify her overture and would force the Princess to engage in conversation, and so, when she reached her cousin, Mme. de Gallardon, with a stern countenance and one hand thrust out as though she were trying to 'force' a

card, began with: "How is your husband?" in the same anxious tone that she would have used if the Prince had been seriously ill. The Princess, breaking into a laugh which was one of her characteristics, and was intended at once to show the rest of an assembly that she was making fun of some one and also to enhance her own beauty by concentrating her features around her animated lips and sparkling eyes, answered: "Why, he's never been better in his life!" And she went on laughing. [The conversation consists of a successive number of feeble gambits by the Marquise, which the Princess from her highly superior position finds no difficulty in wittily repelling.]

Mme. de Gallardon then drew herself up and, chilling her expression still further, perhaps because she was still uneasy about the Prince's health, said to her cousin:

"Oriane," (at once Mme. des Laumes looked with amused astonishment towards an invisible third, whom she seemed to call to witness that she had never authorized Mme. de Gallardon to use her Christian name) "I should be so pleased if you would look in, just for a minute, tomorrow evening, to hear a quintet, with the clarinet by Mozart. I should like to have your opinion of it."

She seemed not so much to be issuing an invitation as to be asking a favor, and to want the Princess's opinion of the Mozart quintet just as though it had been a dish invented by a new cook, whose talent it was most important that an epicure should come to judge.

"But I know that quintet quite well. I can tell you now—that I adore it."

"You know, my husband isn't at all well; it's his liver. He would like so much to see you," Mme. de Gallardon resumed, making it now a corporal work of charity for the Princess to appear at her party. [The desperation of the dodges of Mme. de Gallardon are pathetic enough to evoke our sympathy, except for our realization, mainly through Proust's efforts, that snobbery is in essence masochistic and asks for its own punishment. At best, as he shows us, it is a foible; at worst, it is a vice.]

The Princess never liked to tell people that she would not go to their houses. Every day she would write to express her regret at having been kept away—by the sudden arrival of her husband's mother, by an invitation from his brother, by the Opera, by some excursion to the country—from some party to which she had never for a moment dreamed of going. In this way she gave many people the satisfaction of feeling that she was on intimate terms with them, that she would gladly have come to their houses, and that she had been prevented from doing so only by some princely occurrence which they were flattered to find competing with their own humble entertainment. And then, as she belonged to that witty 'Guermantes set'—in which there survived something of the mentality, stripped of all commonplace phrases and conventional sentiments, which dated from Mérimée, and found its final expression in the plays of Meilhac and Halévy—she adapted its formula so as to suit even her social engagements, transposed it into the courtesy which was always struggling to be positive and precise, to approximate itself to the plain truth. She would never develop at any length to a hostess the expression of her anxiety to be present at a party; she found it more pleasant to disclose to her all the various little incidents on which it would depend whether it was or was not possible for her to come.

"Listen, and I'll explain"; she began to Mme. de Gallardon. "Tomorrow evening I must go to a friend of mine, who has been pestering me to fix a day for ages. If she takes us to the theater afterwards, then I can't possibly come to you, much as I should love to; but if we just stay in the house, I know there won't be anyone else there, so I can slip away."

"Tell me, have you seen your friend M. Swann?" [Here, at last, Mme. de Gallardon is inspired to open a promising subject, although with her spleen and contrary impulses she soon succeeds in ruining her own chances.]

"No! my precious Charles! I never knew he was here. Where is he? I must catch his eye."

"It's a funny thing that he should come to old Saint-Euverte's," Mme. de Gallardon went on. "Oh, I know he's very clever," meaning by that "very cunning," "but that makes no difference; fancy a Jew here, and she the sister and sister-in-law of two Archbishops."

"I am ashamed to confess that I am not in the least shocked," said the Princesse des Laumes. [This is the time still before the Dreyfus Case; the effect of the Case later on, as I have elsewhere indicated, is to give the social kaleidoscope a violent shake so that "rich Jewesses" if not Swann himself fall out of the pattern altogether, while the venom of frustrated Madame de Gallardons enters the tone of social intercourse and is not rebuked as it is here.]

"I know he's a converted Jew, and all that, and his parents and grandparents before him. But they do say that the converted ones are worse about their religion than the practising ones, that it's all just a pretence; is that true, d'you think?"

"I can throw no light at all on the matter."

The pianist, who was 'down' to play two pieces by Chopin, after finishing the Prelude had at once attacked a Polonaise. But once Mme. de Gallardon had informed her cousin that Swann was in the room, Chopin himself might have risen from the grave and played all his works in turn without Mme. des Laumes's paying him the slightest attention. She belonged to that one of the two divisions of the human race in which the untiring curiosity which the other half feels about the people whom it does not know is replaced by an unfailing interest in the people whom it does. [The aptness with which such a thought is expressed has caused critics like F. L. Lucas to class Proust with the type of the *penseur* of whom France

has supplied more brilliant examples than of any other country.]
As with many women of the Faubourg Saint-Germain, the presence, in any room in which she might find herself, of another member of her set, even although she had nothing in particular to say to him, would occupy her mind to the exclusion of every other consideration. From that moment, in the hope that Swann would catch sight of her, the Princess could do nothing but (like a tame white mouse when a lump of sugar is put down before its nose and then taken away) turn her face, in which were crowded a thousand signs of intimate connivance, none of them with the least relevance to the sentiment underlying Chopin's music, in the direction where Swann was, and, if he moved, divert accordingly the course of her magnetic smile.

"Oriane, don't be angry with me," resumed Mme. de Gallardon, who could never restrain herself from sacrificing her highest social ambitions, and the hope that she might one day emerge into a light that would dazzle the world, to the immediate and secret satisfaction of saying something disagreeable, "people do say about your M. Swann that he's the sort of man one can't have in the house; is that true?"

"Why, you, of all people, ought to know that it's true," replied the Princesse des Laumes, "for you must have asked him a hundred times, and he's never been to your house once."

And leaving her cousin mortified afresh, she broke out again into a laugh which scandalized everyone who was trying to listen to the music, but attracted the attention of Mme. de Saint-Euverte, who had stayed, out of politeness, near the piano, and caught sight of the Princess now for the first time. [One must appreciate the smoothness, the adroitness with which the critical turns of the narrative are negotiated and the punctuation of wit which signalizes the end of one movement and the beginning of another.] Mme. de Saint-Euverte was all the more delighted to see Mme. des Laumes, as she imagined her to be still at Guermantes, looking after her father-in-law, who was ill.

"My dear Princess, you here?"

"Yes, I tucked myself away in a corner, and I've been hearing such lovely things."

"What, you've been in the room quite a time?"

"Oh, yes, quite a long time, which seemed very short; it was only long because I couldn't see you." [The hypocrisy of this sentiment is exposed very soon, but hypocrisy is the rule rather than the exception in this social scene as in the others painted by Proust.]

Madame de Saint-Euverte offered her own chair to the Princess, who declined it with:

"Oh, please, no! Why should you? It doesn't matter in the least where I sit." And deliberately picking out, so as the better to display the simplicity of a really great lady, a low seat without a back: "There now, that hassock, that's all I want. It will make me keep my back straight. Oh! Good heavens, I'm making a noise again; they'll be telling you to have me 'chucked out'."

Meanwhile, the pianist having doubled his speed, [such rubato treatment of the tempo is not very musical but it is an easy way of securing an effect and it may be expressive, too, of the pianist's desire to be done with the piece] the emotion of the music-lovers was reaching its climax, a servant was handing refreshments about on a salver, and was making the spoons rattle, and, as on every other 'party-night', Mme. de Saint-Euverte was making signs to him, which he never saw, to leave the room. A recent bride, who had been told that a young woman ought never to appear bored, was smiling vigorously, trying to catch her hostess's eye so as to flash a token of her gratitude for the other's having 'thought of her' in connection with so delightful an entertainment. And yet, although she remained more calm than Mme. de Franquetot, it was not without some uneasiness that she followed the flying fingers; what alarmed her being not the pianist's fate but the piano's, on which a lighted candle, jumping at each *fortissimo*, threatened, if not to set its shade on fire, at least to spill wax upon the ebony. At last she could contain herself no longer, and running up the two steps of the platform on which the piano stood, flung herself on the candle to adjust its sconce. But scarcely had her hand come within reach of it when, on a final chord, the piece finished, and the pianist rose to his feet. Nevertheless the bold initiative shown by this young woman and the moment of blushing confusion between her and the pianist which resulted from it, produced an impression that was favorable on the whole.

"Did you see what that girl did just now, Princess?" asked General de Froberville, who had come up to Mme. des Laumes as her hostess left her for a moment. "Odd, wasn't it? Is she one of the performers?"

"No, she's a little Mme. de Cambremer," [the younger one, of course; thus does the terrifying Wagnerian daughter-in-law erupt upon the scene.] replied the Princess carelessly, and then, with more animation: "I am only repeating what I heard just now, myself; I haven't the faintest notion who said it, it was some one behind me who said that they were neighbors of Mme. de Saint-Euverte in the country, but I don't believe anyone knows them really. They must be 'country cousins'! By the way, I don't know whether you're particularly 'well-up' in the brilliant society which you see before us, because I've no idea who all these astonishing people can be. What do you suppose they do with themselves when they're not at Mme. de Saint-Euverte's parties? She must have ordered them in with the musicians and the chairs and the food. 'Universal providers,' you know. You must admit, they're rather splendid, General. But can she really have the courage to hire the same 'supers' every week? It isn't possible!"

"Oh, but Cambremer is quite a good name; old, too," protested the general [A sense of humor is not precisely the strong point of the general, who plays the role of 'straight man' against whom all the Princess's irony, wit, and barbed shafts bounce harmlessly off. As for her, she will do anything to raise a laugh, even suggest that her dear hostess, to whose face she has just been so polite, is so unpopular that she must have special caterers to supply guests to fill out her parties.]

"I see no objection to its being old," the Princess answered dryly, "but whatever else it is, it's not euphonious," she went on, isolating the word euphonious as though between inverted commas, a little affectation to which the Guermantes set were addicted. [That is to say, Swann and the rest of her circle all talk like the later Henry James, for whom the language that serves everyone else is too commonplace and must be grasped with the pincers of quotation marks and sterilized by irony.]

"You think not, eh! She's a regular little peach, though," said the general, whose eyes never strayed from Mme. de Cambremer. "Don't you agree with me, Princess?"

"She thrusts herself forward too much; I think, in so young a woman, that's not very nice—for I don't suppose she's my generation," replied Mme. des Laumes. . . . And then seeing that M. de Froberville was still gazing at Mme de Cambremer, she added, half out of malice towards the lady, half wishing to oblige the General. "Not very nice . . . for her husband! I am sorry that I do not know her, since she seems to attract you so much; I might have introduced you to her," said the Princess, who, if she had known the young woman, would most probably have done nothing of the sort. "And now I must say good night, because one of my friends is having a birthday party, and I must go and wish her many happy returns," she explained, modestly and with truth, reducing the fashionable gathering to which she was going to the simple proportions of a ceremony which would be boring in the extreme, but at which she was obliged to be present, and there would be something touching about her appearance. "Besides, I must pick up Basin. While I've been here, he's gone to see those friends of his— you know them, too, I'm sure,—who are called after a bridge—of, yes, the Iénas." [The irony is wasted on the general who in reply reads the Princess a history lesson!]

"It was a battle before it was a bridge, Princess; it was a victory!" said the general. "I mean to say, to an old soldier like me," he went on, wiping his monocle and replacing it, as though he were laying a fresh dressing on the raw wound underneath, while the Princess instinctively looked away, "that Empire nobility, well, of course, it's not the same thing, but, after all, taking it as it is, it's very fine of its kind; they were people who really did fight like heroes."

"But I have the deepest respect for heroes," the Princess assented, though with a faint trace of irony. "If I don't go with Basin to see this Princesse d'Iéna it isn't for that, at all, it's simply because I don't know them. Basin knows them; he worships them. Oh, no, it's not what you think; he's not in love with her. I've nothing to set my face against! Besides, what good has it ever done when I have set my face against them?" she queried sadly, for the whole world knew that, ever since the day upon which the Prince des Laumes had married his fascinating cousin, he had been consistently unfaithful to her. "Anyhow, it isn't that at all. They're people he has known for ever so long, they do him very well, and that suits me down to the ground. But I must tell you what he's told me about their house; it's quite enough. Can you imagine it, all their furniture is 'Empire'!"

"But, my dear Princess, that's only natural; it belonged to their grandparents."

"I don't quite say it didn't [the cutting edge of the tone here is against the illegitimacy of the Bonapartist upstarts] but that doesn't make it any less ugly. I quite understand that people can't always have nice things, but at least they needn't have things that are merely grotesque. What do you say? I can think of nothing more devastating, more utterly smug than that hideous style—cabinets covered all over with swans' heads, like bath-taps!"

"But I believe, all the same, that they've got some lovely things; why, they must have that famous mosaic table on which the Treaty of . . ."

"Oh, I don't deny, they may have things that are interesting enough from the historic point of view. But things like that can't ever be beautiful . . . because they're simply horrible! I've got things like that myself, that came to Basin from the Montesquious. Only, they're up in the attic at Guermantes, where nobody ever sees them. But, after all, that's not the point. I would fly to see them, with Basin; I would even go to see them among all their sphinxes and brasses, if I knew them, but—I don't know them! D'you know, I was always taught, when I was a little girl, that it was not polite to call on people one didn't know." She assumed a tone of childish gravity. "And so I am doing just what I was taught to do. Can't you see those good people, with a totally strange woman bursting into their house? Why I might get a most hostile reception."

And she coquettishly enhanced the charm of the smile which the idea had brought to her lips, by giving to her blue eyes, which were fixed on the General, a gentle, dreamy expression.

"My dear Princess, you know that they'ld be simply wild with joy."

"No, why?" she inquired, with the utmost vivacity, either so as to seem unaware that it would be because she was one of the first ladies in France, or so as to have the pleasure of hearing the General tell her so. "Why? How can you tell? Perhaps they would think it the most unpleasant thing that could possibly happen. I know nothing about them, but if they're anything like me, I find it quite boring enough to see the people I do know; I'm sure if I had to see people I didn't know as well, even if they had 'fought like heroes,' I should go stark mad. Besides, except when it's an old friend like you, whom one knows quite apart from that, I'm not sure that 'heroism' takes one very far in society. It's often quite boring enough to have to give a dinner party, but if one had to offer one's arm to Spartacus, to let him take one down . . . ! Really, no; it would never be Vercingetorix I should send for to make a fourteenth. I feel sure, I should keep him for really big 'crushes.' And as I never give any . . ." [The reference to the Helvetian chieftain in Caesar's *Gallic Wars*, recalling the General's Latin classes, finally awakens him to the sparkle of the Princess's conversational style, which made Clive Bell remark once that if all the hostesses of Mayfair spoke as well as she did it might make one more resigned to endure the fashionable life.]

"Ah! Princess, it's easy to see you're not a Guermantes for nothing. You have your share of it, all right, the 'wit of the Guermantes'!"

"But people always talk about the wit of *the* Guermantes; I never could make out why. Do you really know any *others* who have it?" she rallied him, with a rippling flow of laughter, her features concentrated, yoked to the service of her animation, her eyes sparkling, blazing with a radiant sunshine of gaiety which could be kindled only by such speeches—even if the Princess had to make them herself—as were in praise of her wit or of her beauty. "Look, there's Swann talking to your Cambremer woman; over there, beside old Saint-Euverte, don't you see him? Ask him to introduce you. But hurry up, he seems to be just going!"

"Did you notice how dreadfully ill he's looking?" asked the General.

"My precious Charles! Ah, he's coming at last; I was beginning to think he didn't want to see me!" [This second transition of the conversation, whereby the Princess will become the partner of Swann—who is most worthy of her mettle—as she has just been the partner of the General and before that of the Marquise de Gallardon, is manipulated very smoothly once more. Proust gives us the impression that these people move through their social paces as if they were the steps of a graceful eighteenth century minuet.]

Swann was extremely fond of the Princesse des Laumes, and the sight of her recalled to him Guermantes, a property close to Combray, and all that country which he so dearly loved and had ceased to visit, so as not to be separated from Odette. Slipping into the manner, half artistic, half-amorous—with which he could always manage to amuse the Princess—a manner which came to him quite naturally whenever he dipped for a moment into the old social atmosphere, and wishing also to express in words, for his own satisfaction, the longing that he felt for the country:

"Ah!" he exclaimed, or rather intoned, in such a way as to be audible at once to Mme. de Saint-Euverte, to whom he spoke, and to Mme. des Laumes, for whom he was speaking. "Behold our charming Princess! See, she has come up on purpose to hear Saint Francis preach to the birds [the allusion is to the piece by Liszt played earlier by the pianist] and has only just had time, like a dear little titmouse, to go and pick a few hips and haws and put them in her hair; there are even some drops of dew upon them still, a little of the hoar-frost which must be making the Duchess down there shiver. It is very pretty indeed, my dear Princess."

"What! The Princess came up on purpose from Guermantes? But that's too wonderful! I never knew; I'm bewildered," Mme. de Saint-Euverte protested with quaint simplicity, being but little accustomed to Swann's way of speaking. And then, examining the Princess's head-dress, "Why, you're quite right; it is copied from . . . what shall I say, not chestnuts, no,—oh, it's a delightful idea, but how can the Princess have known what was going to be on my programme? The musicians didn't tell me even." [The intelligence of Mme. de Saint-Euverte and her sense of humor are on a par with those of General de Froberville!]

Swann, who was accustomed, when he was with a woman whom he had kept up the habit of addressing in terms of gallantry, to pay her delicate compliments which most other people would not and need not understand, did not condescend to explain to Mme. de Saint-Euverte that he had been speaking metaphorically. As for the Princess, she was in fits of laughter, both because Swann's wit was highly appreciated by her set, and because she could never hear a compliment addressed to herself without finding it exquisitely subtle and irresistibly amusing.

"Indeed! I'm delighted, Charles, if my little hips and haws meet with your approval. But tell me, why did you bow to that Cambremer person, are you also her neighbor in the country?"

Mme. de Saint-Euverte, seeing that the Princess seemed quite happy talking to Swann, had drifted away.

"But you are, yourself, Princess!"

"I! Why, they must have 'countries' everywhere, these creatures! Don't I wish I had!"

"No, not the Cambremers; her own people. She was a Legrandin, and used to come to Combray. I don't know whether you are aware that you are Comtesse de Combray, and that the Chapter owes you a due."

"I don't know what the Chapter owes me, but I do know that I'm 'touched' for a hundred francs, every year, by the Curé, which is a due that I could very well do without. But surely these Cambremers have a rather startling name. It ends just in time, but it ends badly!" she said with a laugh. [The Princess's indecent play on the word *merde* cannot come through the English translation, of course, which those who do not like scatological humor might think is just as well.]

"It begins no better," Swann took the point.

"Yes; that double abbreviation!"

"Some one very angry and very proper who didn't dare to finish the first word."

"But since he couldn't stop himself beginning the second, he'ld have done better to finish the first and be done with it. We are indulging in the most refined form of humor, my dear Charles, in the very best of taste [Fortunately, the Princess is able to be ironic at her own expense as well as at that of others] but how tiresome it is that I never see you now," she went on in a coaxing tone; "I do so love talking to you. Just imagine, I could not make that idiot Froberville see that there was anything funny about the name Cambremer. Do agree that life is a dreadful business. It's only when I see you that I stop feeling bored."

Which was probably not true. But Swann and the Princess had the same way of looking at the little things of life—the effect, if not the cause of which was a close analogy between their modes of expression and even of pronunciation. This similarity was not striking because no two things could have been more unlike than their voices. But if one took the trouble to imagine Swann's utterances divested of the sonority that enwrapped them, of the moustache from under which they emerged, one found that they were the same phrases, the same inflexions, that they had the 'tone' of the Guermantes set. On important matters, Swann and the Princess had not an idea in common. But since Swann had become so melancholy, and was always in that trembling condition which precedes a flood of tears, he had the same need to speak about his grief that a murderer has to tell some one about his crime. And when he heard the Princess say that life was a dreadful business, he felt as much comforted as if she had just spoken to him of Odette.

"Yes, life is a dreadful business! We must meet more often, my dear friend. What is so nice about you is that you are not cheerful. We could spend a most pleasant evening together."

"I'm sure we could; why not come down to Guermantes? My mother-in-law would be wild with joy. It's supposed to be very ugly down there, but I must say, I find the neighborhood not at all unattractive; I have a horror of 'picturesque spots'."

"I know it well, it's delightful!" replied Swann. "It's almost too beautiful, too much alive for me just at present; it's a country to be happy in. It's perhaps because I have lived there, but things there speak to me so. As soon as a breath of wind gets up, and the cornfields begin to stir, I feel that some one is going to appear suddenly, that I am going to hear some news; and those little houses by the water's edge . . . I should be quite wretched!"

"Oh! my dearest Charles, do take care; there's that appalling Rampillon woman; she's seen me; hide me somewhere, do tell me again quickly, what it was that happened to her; I get so mixed up; she's just married off her daughter, or her lover. (I never can

remember)—perhaps both—to each other! Oh, no, I remember
now, she's been dropped by her Prince . . . Pretend to be talking,
so that the poor old Berenice shan't come and invite me to dinner.
I'm going. Listen, my dearest Charles, now that I have seen you,
once in a blue moon, won't you let me carry you off and take you
to the Princesse de Parme's, who would be so pleased to see you
(you know), and Basin too, for that matter; he's meeting me there.
If one didn't get news of you sometimes from Mémé . . . Remember,
I never see you at all now!"

Swann declined. Having told M. de Charlus that, on leaving Mme.
de Saint-Euverte's, he would go straight home, he did not care to
run the risk, by going on now to the Princesse de Parme's, of missing a message which he had all the time been hoping to see brought
to him by one of the footmen, during the party, and which he was
perhaps going to find left with his own porter, at home. (431–444).

This is not the end of the Saint-Euverte party. In fact, the
main business of the narrative (so far as it ties into the Swann-
Odette affair is concerned) is yet to come. For Swann, after
conversing with General de Froberville (444–445) and introducing him to the young Madame de Cambremer whom he had
wanted to meet (445–446), finds that he cannot leave the room,
as he had intended in order to go home, because the concert
has begun once more. And this time, the piece that the musicians are playing is not by Gluck or Liszt or Chopin but by
his own favorite Vinteuil, the composer of that Sonata which
had become the "national anthem" of his love for Odette. And
what an experience with music this unexpectedly turns out to
be! It brings back the past, the early springtime of his affair
with her as nothing else had ever done before. It summons that
past into living existence again as imperiously, as magically as
the madeleine soaked in lime-flower tea had summoned up Combray in the mind of the narrator Marcel. The music heard at
this particular juncture of the life of Swann is instinct with
nostalgia for him as it had never been before, as Proust tells
us in one of his endlessly unwinding, serpentine sentences: "In
place of the abstract expressions 'the time when I was happy,'
'the time when I was loved,' which he had often used till then,
and without much suffering, for his intelligence had not embodied in them anything in the past save fictitious extracts
which preserved one of the reality, he now recovered everything that had fixed unalterably the peculiar, volatile essence of

that lost happiness; he could see it all: the snowy, curled petals of the chrysanthemum which she had tossed after him into his carriage, which he had kept pressed to his lips—the address 'Maison Dorée,' embossed on the note-paper on which he had read 'My hand trembles so as I write to you,' the frowning contraction of her eyebrows when she said pleadingly: 'You won't let it be very long before you send for me?'; he could smell the heated iron of the barber whom he used to have in to singe his hair while Loredan went to fetch the little working girl; could feel the torrents of rain which fell so often that spring, the ice-cold homeward drive in his victoria, by moonlight; all the network of mental habits, of seasonable impressions, of sensory reactions, which had extended over a series of weeks its uniform meshes, by which his body now found itself inextricably held." (447) [This is a single sentence in the French text as well, and Scott Moncrieff has attempted to capture all its twists and turns in his translation.]

"He remembered the gas-jets that were being extinguished along the Boulevard des Italiens when he had met her, when all hope was gone, among the errant shades upon that night which had seemed to him almost supernatural and which now (the night of a period when he had not even to ask himself whether he would be annoying her by looking for her and by finding her, so certain was he that she knew no greater happiness than to see him and to let him take her home) belonged indeed to a mysterious world to which one never may return again once its doors are closed. And Swann could distinguish, standing, motionless, before that scene of happiness in which it lived again, a wretched figure which filled him with such pity, because he did not at first recognize who it was, that he must lower his head, lest anyone should observe that his eyes were filled with tears. It was himself." (448–449)

But Swann is not simply swimming in a sea of nostalgia and free associations; he is also listening to the music attentively and apprehends the physical contours of its phrases so accurately, so sensitively that the Proustian description of what he hears reminds me of a talk I once had with a well-known modern composer who said that Proust alone among writers who attempt to recapture the effect of music upon their sensibilities can be read by the musician without any sense of embarrassment. Instead of concentrating exclusively on himself, Swann's sympathies are directed towards Vinteuil himself who has managed to create so much beauty out of his own anguish (the cause of much of which is that daughter whom the narrator Marcel surprised in the midst of a vicious sensual scene with her Lesbian friend after her father's death—insulting his photograph for the perverse thrill it gave them): "And Swann's thoughts were borne for the first time on a wave of pity and tenderness towards that Vinteuil, towards that unknown, exalted brother who also must have suffered so greatly; what could his life have been? From the depths of what well of sorrow could he have drawn that god-like strength, that unlimited power of creation." (450–451)

This musical experience, as powerful as any experience in the life of Swann, involves every aspect of his being—intellectual and emotional—even what may be called the Platonism of his philosophy: "Swann had regarded musical *motifs* as actual ideas, of another world, of another order, ideas veiled in shadows, unknown, impenetrable by the human mind, which none the less were perfectly distinct one from another, unequal among themselves in value and in significance. When, after that first evening at the Verdurins', he had had the little phrase played over to him again, and had sought to disentangle from his confused impressions how it was that, like a perfume or a caress, it swept over and enveloped him, he had observed that it was to the closeness of the intervals between the five notes which composed it and to the constant repetition of two of them that was due that impression of a frigid, a contracted sweetness. . . ." (452)

Music for Swann redeems human life from seeming to be a meaningless mockery. Such sonatas as Vinteuil's show us "what richness, what variety lies hidden, unknown to us, in that great black impenetrable night, discouraging exploration, of our soul, which we have been content to regard as valueless and waste and void." (452) It even promises immortality to us, since to conceive of the evanescence or destruction of such beauty is nearly impossible: "Perhaps it is not-being that is the true state, and all our dream of life is without existence; but, if so, we feel that it must be that these phrases of music, these conceptions which exist in relation to our dream, are nothing either.

We shall perish, but we have for our hostages these divine captives who shall follow and share our fate. And death in their company is something less bitter, less inglorious, perhaps even less certain." (453) For an aesthete of such intensity it is impossible to become a complete nihilist.

When he describes the music Swann hears directly rather than indirectly in terms of its effects on his thoughts and sensibilities, Proust is no less felicitous in finding inventions which are neither sentimental nor banal: "The suppression of human speech, so far from letting fancy reign there undisturbed (as one might have thought), had eliminated it altogether. Never was spoken language of such inflexible necessity, never had it known questions so pertinent, such obvious replies. At first the piano complained alone, like a bird deserted by its mate; the violin heard and answered it, as from a neighboring tree. It was as at the first beginning of the world, as if there were not yet but these twain upon the earth, or rather in this world closed against all the rest, so fashioned by the logic of its creator that in it there should never be any but themselves; the world of this sonata." (455)

Even the least sensitive people in that audience appear to be transfixed by what they hear in that violin and piano sonata: "Swann dared not move, and would have liked to compel all the people in the room to remain still also, as if the slightest movement might embarrass the magic presence, supernatural, delicious, frail, that would so easily vanish. But no one, as it happened, dreamed of speaking. The ineffable utterance of one solitary man, absent, perhaps dead (Swann did not know whether Vinteuil were still alive), breathed out above the rites of those two hierophants, sufficed to arrest the attention of three hundred minds, and made of that stage on which a soul was thus called into being one of the noblest altars on which a supernatural ceremony could be performed." (456)

The Saint-Euverte episode considered as a whole has a tripartite division. The introduction is descriptive of Swann's impressions of the servants, the "enormous staircase," porter's lodge, hat-check room which he has to pass before he enters the drawing room where the concert is being given. The middle section consists almost entirely of a series of conversations, though some necessary description is interspersed among these. And finally, as a conclusion there is the description of the effect of the great Vinteuil Sonata upon Swann. The conversations in the middle section are the following: 1.) The Princesse des Laumes and her cousin, the Marquise de Gallardon. 2.) The Princesse and her hostess, the Marquise de Saint-Euverte. 3.) The Princesse des Laumes and General de Froberville. 4.) The Princesse des Laumes and Swann. 5.) Swann and General de Froberville. 6.) Swann's introduction of the General to young Madame de Cambremer and the beginnings of the conversation between them, broken off by the beginning of the Vinteuil Sonata. The perfection of the dramatic rhythm with which each of these subdivisions of the episode follows every other is as remarkable as the minute sensitivity and finish with which every detail, every word of every conversation is rendered. I have quoted enough of these for the reader to be able to judge for himself if I am exaggerating the consummate artistry which Proust exhibits in every phase of narration. This "corner" of his vast canvas is as successful as anything he ever did and represents him worthily in the anthologies, though Proust like Whitman is not an anthology writer because of the massive and spacious way he goes about securing his effects. Still, if there are people who are in too much of a hurry to read him long and slowly as he should be read, such a section as this of thirty-nine pages (417–456) may fairly be chosen to represent his power, his finesse, the patience and perfection of his workmanship at its best.

For a full appreciation of what he is doing, we must not lose sight of the place which this episode has in the scheme of *Swann In Love* as a whole. This place is indicated by the post-script to the Saint-Euverte party at the top of page 457: "From that evening, Swann understood that the feeling which Odette had once had for him would never revive, that his hopes of happiness would not be realized now." In other words, his "heavenly" experience with the music of Vinteuil has succeeded in bringing Swann down to earth, in giving him perspective upon his subjective situation, in making him more realistic about his own predicament, in discouraging him from deceiving himself and taking his wish-fulfillments for sober, objective fact. To put it another way, in this Platonic vision beauty is closely united with truth. We are not only delighted by art; we are improved by it and our appreciation makes us better and more sincere people. If this message sounds a trifle old-fashioned and stodgy to the ear of our contemporaries, we must not forget that Proust was a great admirer of Ruskin and should not have been that if he had not to some extent shared the Victorian master's feeling about the relationship between art and morality.

The bibliography that is primarily important to an understanding of Proust is that which is listed in my Prefatory Note—the various works, major and minor, of Proust himself. The three best biographies so far, in my own order of preference, are: *Marcel Proust* by Richard Barker (New York, 1958), *Proust: The Portrait of A Genius* by André Maurois (Harper and Brothers: New York, 1950), and *Proust: The Early Years* by George Painter (Little Brown: Boston, 1959). Among the most stimulating criticisms of Proust are those by Edmond Wilson in *Axel's Castle* (Scribner, New York, 1931), Samuel Beckett's *Proust* (published originally in 1931 and recently reissued by Grove Press), and Ernest de Seillière's *Marcel Proust* (Paris, 193—). Guides to Proust appear in *A Reader's Handbook to Proust* by P. A. Spalding (London, 1952), *Introduction to Proust* by Derrick Leon (London, 1940), *Introduction a la Lecture de Proust* by Léon Guichard (Paris, 1956), and *Nostalgia: A Psychoanalytic Study of Proust* by Milton Miller (Boston, 1956). Appreciations of Proust (and occasionally sharp criticisms) from various hands appear in Gladys Lindner's *Marcel Proust: Reviews and Estimates* (Stanford University Press—) and *Marcel Proust: An English Tribute* (London, 1923). Letters of Proust have been published in many individual collections in both French and English and a more general collection in translation has been made by Mina Curtiss and published by Random House. An additional extensive bibliography for the interested reader can be found in my own *The Proustian Vision* (The Columbia University Press, New York, 1954). Among the various volumes of Proust's letters that have been published, I should single out for mention especially George Painter's translation of Proust's *Letters To His Mother*, published by Citadel Press, New York, 1957, from which I have quoted brief passages in my introductory chapter.

Index